Counseling
For Effective
Decision Making

Counseling For Effective Decision Making

A Cognitive-Behavioral Perspective

John J. Horan
Pennsylvania State University

DUXBURY PRESS
North Scituate, Massachusetts

Duxbury Press
A Division of Wadsworth Publishing Company, Inc.

Counseling for Effective Decision Making: A Cognitive-Behavioral Perspective was edited and prepared for composition by Sylvia Stein. Interior design was provided by Elizabeth Spear. The cover was designed by Oliver Kline.

Library of Congress Cataloging in Publication Data

Horan, John J., 1945-
  Counseling for effective decision making.

  Bibliography: p.
  Includes index.
  1. Counseling. 2. Behavior modification.
3. Cognitive therapy. 4. Decision making.
I. Title.
BF637.C6H65   158   78-15071
ISBN 0-87872-195-9

Printed in the United States of America
1 2 3 4 5 6 7 8 9 — 83 82 81 80 79

To my wife, Susan
and to my children, Erin and Ryan.

Contents

Part 2 COUNSELING THEORY AND DECISION MAKING

10 Pertinent Problem-Solving Literature 137

Part 3 SYNTHESIS

11 Toward Synthesis: The Components of Counseling, Problem Solving, and Decision Making 153

12 Assessment in Decision-Making Counseling 187

13 Intervention in Decision-Making Counseling 201

14 Evaluation in Decision-Making Counseling 217

Foreword

The value of a book is often gauged by the needs it is intended to satisfy. On this criterion alone *Counseling for Effective Decision Making* is a valuable contribution to the literature. After surveying a sprawling literature, John Horan has produced a timely and integrative work that should be of interest to clinical and counseling psychologists alike. He goes well beyond a valuable review of existing theories and offers a conceptual synthesis that is commanding and heuristic. Likewise, he places his commentary in historical perspective and offers one of the first applications of recent cognitive-behavioral theory to counseling practice. The book has a well-balanced focus on both theoretical and applied issues and I was particularly impressed with its inclusion of ethical concerns in counseling. It is a scholarly, provocative, and well-written volume that should prove stimulating and useful to both student and practitioner. In *Counseling for Effective Decision Making* it is clear that useful knowledge can be conveyed in a readable—and often entertaining—style, and I hope that this is a sign of our developing appreciation of the scholar who can communicate in an entertaining fashion.

I am not only an admirer of John Horan's work; I have also had the privilege of working and socializing with him. When I first learned he was writing a book on decision making, my interest was immediately aroused. Given my professional interests, it is not surprising that I became extremely eager to see the manuscript when I learned he was integrating recent cognitive-behavioral developments into an innovative model for counseling. As soon as I had read the finished manuscript, I asked for the honor of writing its foreword. I learned much by reading the manuscript and I thoroughly enjoyed John's talent for weaving humorous anecdotes into technical discussions. He manages to educate painlessly in a style that balances erudition and relevance. Although I won't argue for a genetic explanation, there is a certain welcome ring of Irish levity that is unmistakably present in this volume. I think you will enjoy the liveliness of his writing style and the breadth of his thinking. This book is an important contribution to the field.

Michael J. Mahoney

Preface

I have often observed that one's academic pursuits seem fueled by one's personal pathology. This book is no exception. Over the past two and a half years I have given it a week here and a month there and still remain indecisive as to whether my timing is appropriate, five years too early, or ten years too late.

The 1960s witnessed a barrage of studies showing the impact of a few behavioral counseling strategies on even fewer vocational decision-making skills. Then interest waned. More glamorous and easily quantifiable client problems captured the behavioral counseling researcher's attention. The prevailing attitude seemed to be "Sure, modeling can get kids to visit a career library, but I want to research a cure for their test anxiety, find a method to help them lose weight, and develop a program to improve their terribly deficient social skills." Actually, decision making is a far more complex and crucial issue than such an attitude would suggest. Information seeking is only one of about a dozen decision-making skills that behavioral counseling strategies can foster, and career choice is only one of an infinite array of personal concerns that decision-making counseling can address.

During the 1970s many behavioral counseling researchers grew weary of their exclusive relationship with motor behavior and entered into a polygamous marriage with humanistic philosophy, cognitive psychology, and rational psychotherapy. The cognitive-behaviorist was born of this tempestuous union. Though it is hard to trace exact lines of parentage, expressed attitudes may provide a clue. Those who believe that all cognitive-behavioral endeavors can be explained in terms of traditional learning theory show a preponderance of behavioral stock. Others seem less interested in this issue and prefer to define the cognitive-behavioral discipline in terms of methodology, that is, replicable counseling procedures and precise quantification of client problems. The latter offspring shows only the faintest residuals of behavioral lineage.

In any event, as we stand on the threshold of the 1980s I suspect we shall soon see hundreds of studies on the efficacy of cognitive-behavioral interventions. I hope many will focus on improving decision-making skills. The most frequent and perhaps the most important client concerns are problems of choice, and decision making is one of the most sorely neglected counseling technologies.

A number of individuals have assisted me in writing this book. Many of my colleagues read various chapter drafts or provided me with resource materials. I am especially greatful to Stan Baker, Linda Craighead, Art Dell Orto, Peter Fishburn, Barbara Green, Gail Hackett, Ed Herr, George Hudson, Ken Hylbert, Ken LaFleur, Norm Stewart, Chris Stone, and Paul Zumoff for serving as checks on my periodic autism. Also, our highly proficient secretarial staff made quick and clean copy out of my illegible scrawl. I greatly appreciate Betty Blazer's help in coordinating the meticulous work of Suzy Lutz, Ginny Henning, Karen Homan, Margie Luckovich, Dottie Oliver, Kay Royer, Linda Schreffler, and Audrey Snyder.

Special thanks are due to the Duxbury staff: Steve Keeble, who recruited me; Ed Murphy, who had faith in my ability to get the job done; Virginia Lakehomer, who guided the manuscript through the production process; and Sylvia Stein, who taught me how to spell and when to use "that" instead of "which." Sylvia also deserves credit for drafting the chapter summaries.

Finally, I would like to express my gratitude to Mike Mahoney, for his kind words expressed in the foreword of this book. In sifting through the soil surrounding my Irish roots I came upon an excerpt from a letter by the English author Samuel Johnson to the Bishop of Killaloe. "The Irish are a fair people," Johnson wrote, "they never speak well of themselves." Most readers are aware that fellow Irishman Mahoney is the Padraic Pearse of the cognitive-behavioral rebellion. His own *Cognition and Behavior Modification* is one of the most important books of the decade. Thus I awaited his commentary on my own work with a certain degree of apprehension. I am pleased to observe that Johnson's cultural stereotype can be laid to rest.

JJH

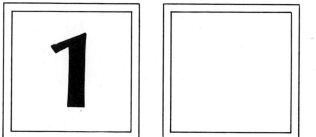

FOUNDATIONS

Decision Making in the Context of Behavioral Counseling

Over two hundred years ago Benjamin Franklin provided the British scientist Joseph Priestley with the rudiments of a technology for making personal decisions. Franklin's letter to Priestley, dated September 19, 1772, read in part:

To get over this (indecision), my way is to divide half a sheet of paper by a line into two columns; writing over the one Pro, and over the other Con. Then, during three or four days consideration, I put down under the different heads short hints of the different motives, that at different times occur to me, for or against the measure. When I have thus got them all together in one view, I endeavor to estimate their respective weights; and where I find two, one on each side, that seem equal, I strike them both out. If I find a reason pro equal to some two reasons con, I strike out the three. If I judge some two reasons con, equal to some three reasons pro, I strike out the five; and thus proceeding I find at length where the balance lies; and if, after a day or two of further consideration nothing new that is of importance occurs on either side, I come to a determination accordingly. (cited by MacCrimmon, 1973, p. 27)

Franklin labeled his method for making decisions "moral algebra." Primitive as it may seem, Franklin's perspective included many landmark concepts in decision theory, such as the need to avoid making an impulsive response and the selection of an alternative that maximizes subjec-

1

tive value. Also apparent is the key assumption that we ourselves can engage in specific activities that may improve the quality of our decisions. This assumption placed Franklin a quantum leap ahead of many contemporaries, who felt that reliance on the advice of "authoritative" books or individuals was the appropriate way to select a course of action.

The literature on personal decision making has grown in sophistication over the past two centuries. Franklin's method was largely introspective; current thinking stresses the need for seeking external sources of data. There are strategies available, for example, that facilitate the generation of alternatives and the determination of potential consequences by encouraging the individual to go beyond solitary thought. Effective decision making calls for a variety of preparatory behaviors prior to choosing.

Since Franklin's time history has recorded the emergence of a new helping profession, counseling, which along with law and medicine exists to provide specialized services to those in need. A number of prominent individuals in the counseling profession (for example, Gelatt, 1962; Herr, 1970; Tyler, 1969) have suggested that the primary responsibility of counselors is rendering assistance to clients with decision-making concerns. Unfortunately, there has not been strong consensus in the counseling profession as to how this service ought to be provided. All major counseling theories either ignore the topic of decision making or address it imperfectly. Moreover, the counseling literature has paid scant attention to theory construction and research on decision making that has occurred in other fields. Much of this work has strong implications for the practice of decision-making counseling.

There are several reasons for my selecting behavioral counseling as a foundation on which to construct a model for helping clients resolve problems of choice. In the first place, the languages of behaviorism and classical decision theory are conceptually similar. Hence, in comparison to other schools of thought, behavioral theory offers the greatest promise for a technology of decision-making counseling.

Second, I am personally pleased by the eager acquiescence of behavioral counseling to accountability pressures from within and outside the counseling profession. In my opinion the only thing more discomforting than not having a positive impact on my clients' lives would be not knowing if I had an impact. At least under the former circumstance I am allowed the option of selecting another potentially effective intervention.

Third, I am convinced that the empirical orientation of behavioral counseling enhances rather than diminishes its relevance to the solution of human problems in living. Although behaviorism is frequently attacked as being antihumanistic, such charges are usually based on a fundamental misunderstanding of both behaviorism and humanism. Contrary to uninformed opinion, behavioral counseling is compatible with humanism; in fact one might argue that it has the distinction of being effective humanism (Horan, 1973a; Hosford, 1974). Unfortunately, the stigma of the antihumanist indictment is a heavy yoke to bear. Many behaviorists thus carry the lighter banner of cognitive-behaviorism as a public affirmation that thinking behaviors are pertinent to understanding human misery and joy.

In this chapter we shall see that behavioral research and practice have traditionally focused on strategies for accelerating or decelerating particular kinds of behaviors to the neglect of building a technology for helping clients resolve problems of choice. This has left a significant gap in the services behavioral counselors ought to be able to provide. We shall also explore the benefits of accountability in counseling and the compatibility of behavioral counseling with the humanist point of view.

The Traditional Focus of Behavioral Counseling

Behavioral research has supplied the counselor with many strategies for dealing with client problems. Most of these strategies can be neatly fitted into either of two categories: promoting adaptive behavior and eliminating maladaptive behavior.

Maladaptive behaviors are self-defeating yet self-perpetuating (Mowrer, 1948). They cause distress or in some way place the individual in jeopardy, despite even deliberate attempts by the individual to remedy the situation. For example, some people have overwhelming fears of heights. Simply looking out of a second story window might bring about heart palpitations, profuse sweating, and a feeling of dizziness. Smoking and overeating are other maladaptive behaviors that ultimately bring on cardiovascular impairment but that nonetheless may persist despite the individual's attempts to bring such activity under control.

Adaptive behaviors, on the other hand, are beneficial to both the individual and society. For students wanting higher grades and a job, the acquisition of better study habits and interviewing skills could be judged as adaptive. A married couple might likewise wish to improve the quality of their communication or their sex life. All parents attempt to foster adaptive behavior in their children when they teach them to speak, to dress, and to use the toilet properly.

When behavioral counselors attempt to promote adaptive behavior, they are essentially fulfilling the traditional stimulus or developmental counseling role. Elimination of maladaptive behavior, in contrast, connotes a remedial or treatment function. One could make a case for distinguishing counseling and psychotherapy along these lines: Counselors focus on promoting adaptive behavior; psychotherapists concentrate on eliminating maladaptive behavior. Unfortunately, such a distinction would be of academic value only. In practice the boundaries of counseling and psychotherapy become blurred and the differences break down. For example, raising the grade point average of a student wanting admission to graduate school would be considered in the promoting adaptive study behavior category. Similar activities with a failing student would have to be labeled eliminating maladaptive study behavior. Furthermore, by job description or preference, many counselors find themselves working extensively in a treatment capacity.

In addition to a good deal of overlap, both of these counselor roles have something else in common: *The goals of the counseling process are obviously desirable and their attainment is easily assessed.* A loss of weight or an increase in assertiveness, a reduction in test anxiety or an improvement in grade point average, a decrease in smoking or an increase of positive self-referent statements are all examples of behavioral counseling goals. Regardless of whether a behavior is to be accelerated or decelerated, the need for change is clear to both client and counselor and the effects of counseling can be readily determined.

When the Goal Is a Choice

Unfortunately, not all client problems are easily resolvable via existing strands of behavioral research; at least this is so in the initial stages of counseling. Let us consider for the moment a dilemma faced by a counselor working with a male homosexual client. Should the client wish to change his sexual orientation, there are a number of strategies the counselor might adopt, depending, of course, on a more exact description of the client's problem. For example, if he is afraid of criticism from women, systematic desensitization would be appropriate; or if he is simply not attracted to women, orgasmic reconditioning might be in order (see Adams & Sturgis, 1977; Marquis, 1972).

On the other hand, the client might wish to remain homosexual and essentially need help in coping with problems he confronts in the course of his gay life-style. For example, if his family is harassing him about being homosexual, assertion training (Alberti & Emmons, 1970) would be a viable counseling strategy. Along similar lines Serber developed a social skills training program for homosexuals faced with the problem of loneliness (cited by Liberman, 1974).

Although behavioral research has provided the counselor a number of strategies for helping the homosexual client reach a particular goal, the question of which goal—a functioning heterosexual or homosexual life-style—remains unresolved. Obviously, an initial goal of counseling here is to arrive at a decision. But what decision? Behavioral research has thus far ignored the problem of building a technology for helping clients arrive at satisfactory decisions. The homosexual client must receive help in making a choice before counseling can proceed in a goal-directed manner.

Some Common Decision-Making Concerns

Problems of choice are legion. Perhaps the most common—at least those counselors most frequently encounter—relate to the matter of careers. Clients may wonder, for example: What courses should I take? Should I stay in school or drop out? Which college? Should I go to work instead? What kind of career do I want? Should I change majors? Schools? Jobs?

Career choice problems often lead to other decision-making concerns: Do I want a career outside of the home or am I content with the role of houseperson? Do I ever want to get married? If so, to this person? What about kids—any? How many? Now?

And the list goes on: What kinds of premarital or extramarital sexual activity are appropriate for me? What should I do about this problem pregnancy? Would I be better off divorced? Should I change my religious practices, or my social group, or both? Do I want to go through with this elective surgery? Should I lose weight? Stop smoking? Cut down my drinking? Become a vegetarian? What goals are important for me to achieve?

The most common concerns presented to counselors are undoubtedly problems of choice. Considering the significance of many client decisions and the frequency with which counselors are called upon for assistance, it is somewhat of a mystery why decision making has received so little attention in the behavioral literature.

Making a Decision

Some individuals choose among existing alternatives by a random process such as flipping a coin. Others are more systematic. Before deciding, they carefully solicit information pertaining to the potential consequences of many possible courses of action. There is a good deal of variability among all of us as to how much a priori deliberation we invest in a given decision. Consider for a moment the purchase of a mattress. Do we decide how we are going to spend eight hours a day (one-third of our lives!) on the paid testimony of a scantily clad starlet? Or would we make such a purchase only after thoroughly examining all the available consumer literature?

Interestingly enough, careful deliberation before making a decision does not ensure a favorable outcome; neither does random choice guarantee an unfavorable outcome. Let us look, for example, at the vocational choices of Al and Roger. Al avoided all contact with his high school guidance counselor. He dropped out of school and let his friend talk him into going to work at the local foundry. Today he is a foreman and quite content with his previous vocational decisions. Roger, on the other hand, eagerly participated in his school's career education program. Interest and aptitude testing, along with readings, talks with professionals, and job-simulation exercises, all supported his tentative plans for a career in architecture. Today, upon graduation, he finds himself among the 40 percent unemployed architects and bitterly regrets his career choice. Thus what we commonly refer to as a "good" decision (that is, a decision with a favorable outcome) may or may not have anything to do with whether the decision was made in a random or systematic manner.

Fortunately for those who value systematic decisions, "lady luck" is capricious. Though many people make choices without deliberation that eventually prove quite advantageous, the fact remains that consistently good random decisions are highly improbable. The purpose of decision-making counseling, then, is basically to increase the probability that the client will make a good decision. Decision-making counseling cannot guarantee that the alternative selected will result in a favorable outcome; at most it can only increase the likelihood that such will occur.

This leads us to a new conceptualization. From a behavioral counseling perspective the effectiveness or "adaptiveness" of a particular decision depends on the client behaviors that preceded the decision rather than on the events that follow it. Paradoxically, then, an adaptive decision may result in an unfavorable outcome and a maladaptive decision may prove to be quite favorable! But such occurrences are not to be expected. The effects of behavioral decision-making counseling have yet to be closely examined from an empirical standpoint, but in theory adaptive decisions will in all likelihood prove to be good decisions.

In subsequent chapters we will closely examine the preparatory behaviors needed to make an adaptive decision and the behavioral counseling strategies designed to foster their display. We shall see that many concepts in the decision-making literature can be assimilated into the practice of behavioral counseling. A behavioral counseling approach to decision making is viable, but considerable research and development remains to be done. Let us now turn to the topic of accountability, which behavioral counseling so eagerly embraces.

Accountability in the Counseling Profession

Student counselors often express concern about "how to counsel." They seem to be seeking a map, or at least a series of guidelines, that will tell them where to go in their counseling sessions and how to get there. More advanced counselor trainees, having fumbled or flown through a series of initial interviews, frequently wonder, "How do I know when I'm doing a good job?" (Herr & Horan, 1973; Horan, Herr & Warner, 1973; Horan, Shute, Swisher, & Westcott, 1973).

Far too often counselor educators and supervisors sidestep legitimate inquiries of this sort with evasion ploys such as, "You seem concerned about your adequacy as a counselor" or "What is it about your performance that is causing you to doubt your ability?" Although discussion of such trainee concerns is a highly appropriate supervisory function, mere reflection is not sufficient. Simply tossing the problem back to the trainee serves only to free supervisors from committing themselves to concrete answers for which they may later be held accountable. Such reluctance has historical precedence. Counseling has long been described as a vague process applied to undefined problems without clear solutions (Raimy, 1950).

But today there is no excuse for such supervisory behavior. Counselors can, in fact, be accountable (Burck, Cottingham, & Reardon, 1973; Horan, 1972a; Krumboltz, 1974). Experimental methodologies through which counselors can demonstrate effectiveness (or lack thereof) with their own caseloads have been developed and are being subjected to continuing refinement (Campbell & Stanley, 1967; Hersen & Barlow, 1976; Kazdin, 1973c, Sidman, 1960; Thoresen, 1972a). Various factorial research designs, for example, allow the counselor to determine if drug or career education programs are registering any changes in student behaviors (Horan, 1973b, 1974a; Horan & Williams, 1975). And single-subject research designs let counselors know if their efforts with diverse, idiosyncratic client problems are at all successful. The ultimate criterion of counselor competence has come to be recognized as the ability to effect adaptive changes in the cognitive, affective, motor, and somatic behaviors of clients (Horan, 1972a). In the words of Winborn, Hinds, and Stewart (1971 p. 137), "Performance . . . is the counselor's 'raison d' etre'."

Along with advances in evaluation methodology, counselors are finding that they no longer need rely on the "grand old men" of human development for treatment programming. To be sure, the influence of powerful historical figures like Allport, Erikson, Havighurst, and Maslow is still felt. However, there has been a recent explosion in the technology of human behavior. Procedures derived from armchair speculation *followed by* careful laboratory experimentation have enabled many clients to define and obtain their personal goals (for example, Krumboltz & Thoresen, 1969, 1976; Ullman & Krasner, 1965).

Some of these techniques are fairly simple and straightforward. Systematic desensitization and its variations, for example, has proved relatively successful in freeing anxious individuals of their environmental fears. A number of human problems are fairly circumscribed and are easily resolvable through the application of a single behavioral counseling procedure. Other problems are complex and require multifaceted or comprehensive treatment approaches (Horan, 1973c). Impressive behavioral technologies have been built and successfully applied to a wide variety of such concerns that heretofore have met with therapeutic failure. Lovaas's (1967) work with autistic children and the obesity research of Stuart and Davis (1972) and the Mahoneys (Mahoney, 1973; Mahoney & Mahoney, 1976) are classic examples. Similar success may be realized from evolving comprehensive programs for the control of cigarette smoking (Hackett & Horan, 1977; Horan & Hackett, 1978) and the reduction of pain (Horan, 1976; Horan, Hackett, Buchanan, Stone, & Demchik-Stone, 1977). Behavioral decision-making counseling also lends itself to experimental scrutiny. For example, it would be quite possible to determine if a particular package of counseling interventions has any impact on client behaviors that have been shown to be essential for adaptive decision making.

In any event, accountability pressures in the counseling profession have produced a beneficial side effect for the counseling student and practitioner. Adequate research and evaluation procedures demand that the structure and content of each counseling program be clearly specified so that other investigators can replicate the program as an independent check on its effects. These program descriptions provide convenient guidelines for counseling students and practitioners (for example, Horan, Stone, & Herold, 1976). They unambiguously detail where to go in counseling and how to get there, thus dispelling much of the counseling mystique. Provision of such a road map for counselors confronted with clients who need help in making a decision is a major goal of this book.

Behaviorism versus Humanism?

The emphasis on accountability in behavioral counseling has certainly not resulted in any lessened concern for humanity. The true humanist would settle for nothing less than concrete evidence that his or her work with humans produced positive changes. Such has been the humanist tradition since occidental scholars shifted their preoccupation with the theism of the Dark Ages to the scientific study of themselves.

In any event, the so-called distinction between humanism and behaviorism has been examined and found wanting (Horan, 1973a; Hosford, 1974; Thoresen, 1972b, c). Many of the differences result from crude stereotypes rather than from actual counseling practice. Typical behavioral counselors do not function like computers dispensing jelly beans (though some do), nor were their nonbehavioral counterparts given oatmeal instead of cerebrums (though some seem so deprived). Rather, what we find is tremendous variability *within* each school of counseling and a good deal of overlap *between* them.

Both behavioral and nonbehavioral counselors are beginning to talk the same language (though admittedly with varying degrees of precision). Their primary concerns seem compatible, if not identical. Thoresen (1972c), for example, has identified a number of humanistic ideals, translated them into behavioral goals, and suggested that behavioral technologies be employed in order to help clients attain them. On another front, several studies have demonstrated that traditional humanistic concepts like self-concept and creativity can be enhanced through behavioral programming (Krop, Calhoon & Verrier, 1971; Krop, Perez, & Beaudoin, 1973; Meichenbaum, 1975).

Furthermore, in recent years behavioral counseling researchers have shown an increasing preoccupation with cognitive behaviors, a rather radical departure from a subject matter almost exclusively "external" or animal in orientation. Only the naive would respond "no" to London's (1967) question, "Do men leap from cliffs for reasons other than those for which dogs salivate to bells?" Homme (1965) has suggested that these "internal" behaviors (thoughts, images, feelings, reflections, and the like) follow the same laws of learning as their "external" counterparts. Indeed, Cautela (1972, 1973) and his associates have committed a decade of their lives to the design and evaluation of technologies for modifying covert behavior. Some evidence, however, suggests that present formulations or explanations of covert counseling techniques are inadequate; that is, they may work, but not for the reasons specified (Foreyt & Hagen, 1973). Mahoney (1974), in a remarkably prescient and readable review of cognition and behavior modification, has underscored the theoretical decay in both areas and suggested new directions for thinking and research. Nevertheless, the incursion by behaviorists into a traditionally nonbehavioral subject matter has increased the relevance of behaviorism to the practicing counselor and diminished the so-called distinction between the behavioral and humanistic points of view.

Finally, most behaviorists consider themselves humanists and are accepted as such by other humanists. In fact, the most eminent behaviorist of the twentieth century, B. F. Skinner, was named "Humanist of the Year" by the American Humanist Association.

Summary

The literature on personal decision making has grown in sophistication over the past two centuries. Today a number of prominent individuals in the counseling profession have suggested that the primary responsibility of counselors is rendering assistance to clients with decision-making concerns. But there has not been strong consensus in the profession as to how to provide this service.

Behavioral research has supplied the counselor with a number of strategies for promoting adaptive behavior and eliminating maladaptive behavior but has had little to say about decision making—perhaps the most common client concern. Nevertheless the behavioral perspective is that the effectiveness or "adaptiveness" of a client's decision depends on the behaviors preceding the decision rather than on the events following it. Behavioral counselors attempt to promote these behaviors in order to increase the likelihood that their clients will experience a favorable outcome.

Pressures for accountability in the counseling profession have produced a beneficial side effect for the counseling practitioner, namely, clear descriptions of where to go in counseling and how to get there. Provision of such a road map for decision-making counseling is a major goal of this book.

The popularized distinction between behaviorism and humanism is not valid. Moreover, the increasing preoccupation of behaviorists with cognitive behaviors and with traditional humanistic goals may foretell a reconciliation between behavioral and nonbehavioral points of view. Behavioral counseling, with its emphasis on accountability and its compatibility with humanism, offers the possibility of a technology for helping clients resolve problems of choice.

This book is divided into three sections. Part I, "Foundations," includes five more chapters, which deal with the basic languages of behaviorism and decision theory, current topics in each area, and the pervasive issue of ethics. Part II, "Counseling Theory and Decision Making," contains three chapters that explore the place of decision making in psychodynamic, rational, and behavioral approaches to counseling and a fourth chapter that focuses on pertinent problem-solving literature. Part III, "Synthesis," consists of four chapters. The first attempts to integrate counseling with previous theories of problem solving and decision making. The final three chapters are devoted to an explication of assessment, intervention, and evaluation procedures in a cognitive-behavioral perspective of decision-making counseling.

2

The Language of Behavioral Counseling

A scientific theory is neither good nor bad; nor is it true or false. Rather, a theory may or may not be "useful." A theory is useful only to the extent that it can help a scientist explain, predict, and control a phenomenon. To illustrate this utility criterion let us consider for a moment the science of chemistry. The seventeenth-century chemist believed that when a metal was heated it released an invisible vapor called phlogiston into the air. Phlogiston was assumed to have "negative weight," which explained why the heated metal became heavier. Today we have a more useful theory that adds prediction and control to the explaining dimension of the phlogiston theory. We now believe (perhaps delusionally) that the heated metal combines with the oxygen in the air, forming oxides, which explains why the new metallic compound weighs more than the pure metal did before it was heated. We can predict how much the new compound will weigh by measuring the amount of heat, metal, or oxygen we started with; and we can control the phenomenon, for example, by heating the metal in an oxygen-free atmosphere, thus not permitting any reaction to take place.

The social sciences, education, and counseling have long suffered from a plethora of theories that purport to explain a phenomenon but are of little help in predicting or controlling it. Everyone has a theory, for example, on criminal behavior and how it ought to be prevented or controlled; yet the recidivism rate from our correctional programming suggests we have a long way to go to eliminate this crippling social problem. In many such areas we are no more advanced in our thinking than the seventeenth-century chemist. Interestingly enough, the physical sciences sometimes construct theories that seem to defy explanation but serve very well in a predicting and controlling capacity. The wave-particle theory of light is a classic example. In some experiments light behaved like a wave; in other experiments it behaved like a particle. Scientists "explained" away the problem with the enigmatic concept wave-particle!

Without the requirement of offering prediction and control, theories of behavior can very quickly assume bizarre proportions. In attempting to explain overeating, for example, one author went so far as to claim, "the enlarged body may represent a fortress-like defense against a hostile world, a symbol of independence, importance and prowess, an intimidation to enemies, a symbol for a wished-for pregnancy or a socially acceptable justification for underactivity that permits the person to take fewer risks and thus helps keep anxiety low" (Brosin, 1953, p. 975). Not only is it impossible to distinguish the obese from the nonobese on these so-called psychological factors, but formulations of this sort have proved to be quite impotent insofar as the generation of effective treatment programming for the obese is concerned (Stunkard, 1958, 1959).

Essentially, then, the behavioral counselor believes that a science of human behavior can be formulated. The scientist's task is to discover and refine certain "laws" or behavior principles and then apply them to upgrading the human condition. Behavioral counseling, like other sciences, has its own peculiar language. This chapter contains a brief review of the behavioral vocabulary. Because many of these concepts have been fully described in many other introductory texts, the reader familiar with the basics of behavioral counseling may now wish to skip ahead to chapter 3.

Kinds of Behavior

There are a number of ways of classifying behavior, one of which is the operant-respondent dichotomy. Operants are behaviors we can engage in voluntarily. They act or "operate" on the environment. Rats pull levers; human beings push doorbells or pencils. Respondents, on the other hand, occur whether or not we want them to. The smell of food may cause us to salivate or the screech of tires may send shivers up and down our spine.

Usually the term operant refers to a physical activity observable by anyone. Bouncing a ball, picking up a cue stick, or raising our hand in class are operant behaviors visible to all. Each of us has an "internal world," however, observable only to ourselves. Operants occurring in this world-beneath-our-skin are sometimes called "coverants," a term coined by Homme (1965) from "covert operants" (thoughts, images, reflections, feelings, and the like).

In the past operants and respondents were seen as very different kinds of behavior. Recent research and speculation, however, now leads us to believe that the voluntary versus nonvoluntary distinction may no longer be valid. For example, people can learn to lower their heart rates or raise their skin temperature. There is a new and rapidly burgeoning branch of contemporary behavioral technology called "biofeedback" that promises to provide a nonchemical means of helping people lower their blood pressure, eliminate migraine headaches, and ward off epileptic seizures (Fuller, 1978; Stern & Ray, 1975). Even male birth control is under investigation. Knowing that sperm cannot survive relatively small temperature increases, some men take hot baths before intercourse in the hopes of rendering themselves temporarily infertile. Although no one suggests relying on this method, teaching men how to raise their scrotal temperature through biofeedback may someday accomplish the same goal. (Women readers are cautioned to be wary of males claiming to have developed this skill!) The biofeedback branch of contemporary behavior technology is still in its infancy, however; more research is needed to support its claims and fulfill its promises.

In addition to the operant-respondent dichotomy there is another classification method. We can speak of cognitive, affective, motor, and somatic behaviors. *Cognitive* behaviors are thinking behaviors such as ideas, images, fantasies, reflections, and so forth. *Affective* behaviors are feelings or mood states. Examples include relaxation, rage, affection, fear, and anxiety. *Motor* behaviors encompass all forms of physical activity; *somatic* behaviors are physiological responses like heart rate and salivation.

These categories are somewhat arbitrary and certainly not mutually exclusive. All four can occur simultaneously. For example, the thought of an unfair high school teacher (or the image of the teacher's face) is a cognitive behavior that might be accompanied by affective behaviors such as anger or resentment. Also occurring at the same time might be motor behaviors like frowning and fist clenching as well as somatic behaviors such as increased heart rate and stomach contractions.

We can view behaviors in still another manner, that is, in regard to the potential benefit or harm that such behavior is bringing (or might ultimately bring) the individual or society. The behavioral counselor uses the dichotomy "adaptive versus maladaptive" in this regard. As was seen in chapter 1, *maladaptive* behaviors are self-defeating yet self-perpet-uating. They cause distress or in some way place the individual in jeop-ardy, despite his or her attempts to remedy the situation. *Adaptive* behaviors, on the other hand, are beneficial to both the individual and society. Mental health professionals sometimes use terms like sick, unhealthy, inappropriate, or neurotic to describe maladaptive behavior. We should be very careful about using such words casually because they very often connote unwarranted value judgments. (Female enjoyment of sex used to be considered "unhealthy" [see Robinson, 1959].) Behavioral counselors prefer the adaptive-maladaptive dichotomy because it is less subject to misapplication.

Behavior, then, broadly defined, is the subject matter of behavioral counseling. Behavioral theory is concerned with explaining, predicting, and controlling behavioral increases and decreases. To this end a number of principles have been formulated. Like the phlogiston theory of seven-teenth-century chemistry, however, these principles are already showing signs of decay and inadequacy (Mahoney, 1974). Nevertheless, an under-standing of their meaning is prerequisite to the remainder of this book.

Acquisition, Maintenance, and Acceleration of Behavior

There are a number of principles that explain how we acquire a particu-lar behavior and how the behavior develops into a habit of a given fre-quency. Both adaptive and maladaptive behaviors are subject to these principles. If we shirk our responsibility to promote adaptive behavior, Mother Nature will manage our lives. A cursory inspection of our mental hospitals, prisons, and sundry pockets of poverty and depravity, how-ever, suggests she is a less than compassionate matron. The principles to be discussed are respondent conditioning, positive reinforcement, nega-tive reinforcement, and modeling.

Respondent Conditioning

Back in the early 1900s a Russian physiologist named Pavlov was study-ing salivation in dogs. He observed that whenever the aroma of food was presented to the dogs, their salivation increased. One day, as the story goes, Pavlov noticed that even though no food aroma was present, the dogs began to salivate when he walked into the experimental chamber. Pavlov later found that other stimuli such as bells and lights when repeatedly presented to the dogs in conjunction with the aroma of food would also evoke salivation even in the absence of food. This process has come to be called respondent or classical conditioning (Rachlin, 1970).

Another form of respondent conditioning may be relevant to the learning of human fears. Several decades ago Watson and Reyner (1920) found that a young boy who was frightened by a loud noise in the presence of a white mouse learned to fear the mouse. His fear generalized to include other furry animals, certain articles of clothing, and even a Santa Claus mask. We all have a variety of irrational fears (such as of spiders, heights, closed places, and so forth), the origins of which we cannot explain. Perhaps they were learned in a similar manner.

Both forms of conditioning just described can be stated more formally. Unconditional stimuli (food odors or loud noises) evoke unconditional responses (salivation or fear). If a conditional stimulus (a lighted bulb or a white mouse) is repeatedly presented at the same time as or immediately before the unconditional stimulus, it will eventually evoke by itself the same response, which is now termed a conditional response (see figure 2.1). Switching our examples around a bit, people can learn to salivate at the sight of white mice and dogs can learn to fear a turned on light bulb.

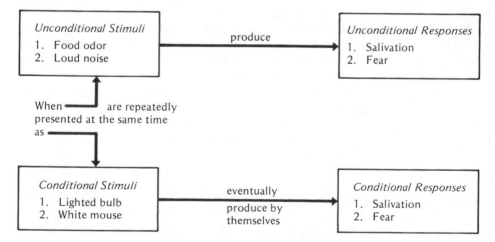

FIGURE 2.1.   Schematic diagram for repondent or classical conditioning

All of the foregoing is called first-order conditioning. Higher-order conditioning involves introducing a new conditional stimulus into a previously established reaction. For example, having already learned to fear white mice, our young boy encountering such a creature in a dimly lit hallway might thus learn to fear the dark. Perhaps fortunately for the human condition, higher-order conditioning is much less powerful than first-order conditioning. One trivial fear might otherwise produce an endless chain reaction.

Most therapeutic applications of respondent conditioning such as aversion therapy are designed to reduce problem behavior rather than promote desirable ones (see Rachman & Teasdale, 1969; Weitzel, Horan, & Addis, 1977). In contrast to this trend, Barlow and Agras (1973) described an interesting procedure for promoting the capacity for heterosexual arousal in homosexuals who have decided to change their sexual orientation. They use slide projectors to present gradually increasing heterosexual stimuli and gradually decreasing homosexual stimuli during periods of homosexual arousal until heterosexual stimuli, alone, are sufficient to produce sexual arousal.

Positive Reinforcement

In the operant conditioning literature, positive reinforcement is perhaps the most widely researched principle for accelerating behavior. Its definition is simply any thing or event that increases the frequency of a preceding response. The "circularity" criticism of this definition leveled by Chomsky (1959) is vitiated by the fact that reinforcers so identified can accelerate other behaviors in other situations (see also MacCorquodale, 1970, and Premack, 1965). Positive reinforcement is often confused with the concept of reward. Although there are connotative similarities, it is important to note that what is reinforcing to us may not be so to others and vice versa. To quote a popular song by Sly and the Family Stone, "Different strokes for different folks!" Several aspects of reinforcement deserve further comment: kinds, schedules, stimulus control, and shaping (see also figure 2.2).

Kinds of Reinforcers

Primary reinforcers are stimuli required for survival, such as food and water. Secondary reinforcers obtain their power through association with primary reinforcers. For example, in token economies institutionalized populations can earn tokens for displaying adaptive behavior and later cash them in for privileges or primary reinforcers (Kazdin & Bootzin, 1972). Social reinforcement is another form of secondary reinforcement

Antecedent ⟶ Target Behavior ⟶ Consequence			Effect on Target Behavior
Delta stimulus: playground	Studying	No positive reinforcement	Studying not likely on playground
Discriminative stimulus: classroom	Studying	Positive reinforcement in form of teacher, parent, and self-praise	Studying likely in classroom
Discriminative stimulus: classroom	Studying	Continuous positive reinforcement	Weak study habit quickly acquired
Discriminative stimulus: classroom	Studying	Intermittant positive reinforcement	Strong study habit slowly acquired

Since studying is complex it might need to be shaped. Successive approximations include reading skills improvement, coming to class, looking at the book, and so forth.

FIGURE 2.2. **Schematic diagram for concepts related to positive reinforcement**

highly relevant to human learning. One of the strongest social reinforcers is simple attention. We cannot reinforce people without also paying attention to them; consequently attention alone is extremely powerful.

Reinforcement Schedules

Delivery of reinforcement after every occurrence of a behavior is called continuous reinforcement; occasional delivery of reinforcement is called partial or intermittent reinforcement. The regularity with which reinforcement follows behavior is called the reinforcement schedule. Ferster and Skinner (1957) have chronicled the effects of various intermittent schedules, which need not be explored in this book. Suffice it to say that continuous reinforcement will produce a weak habit very quickly; intermittent reinforcement will produce a strong habit relatively slowly. Hence the following generalization: To get a behavior going, use continuous reinforcement; to keep it going, gradually change to an intermittent schedule.

Stimulus Control

Reinforcement rarely occurs in a vacuum; there are usually a variety of other stimuli (antecedent conditions) that precede the behavior and the delivery of reinforcement. A discriminative stimulus (S_D) signals that reinforcement will be presented pending display of a particular behavior. A delta stimulus (S_Δ), on the other hand, indicates that no reinforcement will be forthcoming. Two clowning school children signal reinforcement to each other, hence the teacher who seats them on opposite sides of the room is exercising stimulus control. So likewise are counselors who suggest to overspending clients that they destroy their credit cards and carry only limited amounts of cash when shopping.

Shaping

Much human behavior is extremely complex and cannot be accounted for in terms of simple positive reinforcement. Shaping refers to the process of positively reinforcing successive approximations to a terminal behavior. The learning of language, for example, requires the shaping of sounds into syllables, into words, into sentences, and so forth. Decision making, as we shall see, is also a complex behavior the development of which to some extent resembles a shaping paradigm.

Therapeutic applications of positive reinforcement are legion. Reinforcement-based programs have contributed to the socialization of psychotic, retarded, and delinquent children and adults and have enhanced the academic and personal development of normal individuals. Any volume of the following journals will provide dozens of such examples: *Behaviour Research and Therapy, Behavior Therapy, Journal of Applied Behavioral Analysis,* and *Journal of Behavior Therapy and Experimental Psychiatry.* Further reviews and illustrations can be found in Bandura (1969), Krumboltz and Thoresen (1969), O'Leary and Wilson (1975), and Ullman and Krasner (1965). Traux (1966) has shown that even Carl Rogers uses social positive reinforcement to accelerate certain kinds of cognitive and affective behaviors that are valued in client-centered theory.

Negative Reinforcement

Because negative reinforcement generally involves uncomfortable or noxious events, it is sometimes confused with punishment. Actually, negative reinforcement is intended to increase a behavior, not suppress it; and thus it has something in common with positive reinforcement. But positive reinforcers reinforce by their appearance; negative reinforcers reinforce by their disappearance. Technically, negative reinforcement occurs when there is an increase in a behavior due to the removal of a particular stimulus. Speaking loosely for a moment, positive reinforcers might be thought of as pleasant consequences of a behavior. Negative reinforcers are unpleasant and they precede the behavior. If a donkey pulls a cart because a carrot is dangled in front of its nose, cart-pulling behavior is positively reinforced. If the same donkey pulls the cart to escape the sting of a whip, cart-pulling behavior is negatively reinforced. The room-cleaning behavior of adolescents can be positively reinforced through an allowance or negatively reinforced by nagging. Both positive and negative reinforcers serve to *increase* or *strengthen* a behavior.

Two common learning paradigms employ negative reinforcement. In *escape* learning the negative reinforcer is actually presented and terminated only by the display of the target behavior. For instance, the boot camp instructor does not stop screaming until he is content with the recruit's performance. In *avoidance* learning a discriminative stimulus signals that negative reinforcement will be forthcoming unless a particular behavior is exhibited. The sight of a police car, for example, may increase our safe driving behavior.

Negative reinforcement has very little, if any, therapeutic potential. To the contrary, it shares many of the disadvantages of punishment, which will be discussed later.

Modeling

Not all human behavior can be accounted for by respondent and operant conditioning procedures. Much of what we learn is learned vicariously, that is, from watching others. Fortunately we do not learn to fly airplanes or to perform surgery by trial and error but rather by careful observation of skilled models. Bandura (1971) has posited four major subprocesses in his theory of observational learning: attentional, retentional, motoric reproduction, and reinforcement-motivational. These processes account for the effects of modeling.

Attentional Processes

Before a behavior can be learned, it must be attended to or observed. Several variables, such as the power and interpersonal attractiveness of the model or the perceptual set of the observer, can influence whether the model is ignored.

Retentional Processes

Once observed, the behavior must be stored in some symbolic form if it is to be reproduced without the model's continued presence. Two representational systems, the imaginal and the verbal, are involved. The imaginal system is exemplified by the fact that whenever reference is made to a familiar person, place, or thing, a vivid image inevitably follows. The word Paris, for example, might call to mind a picture of the Eiffel Tower. More important, however, is the verbal representational system. The route traversed by a model might be learned more efficiently if the observer verbally codes it into a series of right and left turns (RRLRR) rather than relying on a visual image of the itinerary. Retention can then be strengthened by practice (overt rehearsal). Covert rehearsal is also effective when practice is not possible.

Motoric Reproduction Processes

Motoric reproduction processes involve using the retained symbolic representations of the modeled behavior to guide the observer's performance in a later time period. They are affected by factors such as physical ability and accuracy feedback.

Reinforcement and Motivational Processes

We may acquire and retain the capability of exhibiting a modeled behavior but never do so if we are likely to be punished. Television, for example, has provided us with numerous murdering models, yet most of us refrain from duplicating such violent behavior. Positive reinforcement, on the other hand, can promptly transform observational learning into action. Reinforcement variables may also influence our attention to the original modeled behavior. For example, we pay more attention to a lottery winner than we do to a loser.

Effects of Modeling

Bandura (1971) has further argued that models can produce three distinctly different effects. Such effects occur "naturally" in the real world or may be deliberately fostered in the context of behavioral counseling. In the first place, observers can acquire new or novel behavior by watching the performance of others. Counselors can teach job interviewing skills, for example, by accurately defining them and showing a filmed model engaged in their correct display.

Second, models can strengthen or weaken previously learned behavior. *Inhibitory* effects occur when observers show decrements in a behavior as a result of seeing models punished for such behavior. *Disinhibitory* effects are apparent when observers show increases in previously inhibited behaviors after witnessing models engage in those behaviors without adverse consequences. Fear of snakes, for example, might be overcome by watching a bold model confidently approach and pick up the harmless reptile. Meichenbaum's (1971, 1973) research suggests that nonconfident models who talk themselves out of their fear and into the activity are even more effective—perhaps because of their increased similarity to the observer.

Finally, models can also serve as cues or discriminative stimuli to facilitate the performance of existing responses. When others applaud, we also clap; when others look up, we do likewise, and so forth.

Both live and symbolic models may influence behavior. Examples of symbolic models include audiotapes, films, and even instructional manuals. Counselors themselves can serve as models for the kinds of behavioral skills their clients would like to acquire. Basically, behavioral counselors believe that showing a client how to do something is far more effective and efficient than waiting for the skill to pop out like a piece of toast after a warm relationship.

Deceleration and Elimination of Behavior

Just as there are principles that describe how behavior is acquired, maintained, and accelerated, there are principles that explain how behavior can be weakened. The laws of learning are impartial to the value our culture places on certain kinds of behavior. The lonely third-grade boy who spends most of his time gazing out the window and rarely ever completes his assignments has learned to behave in this manner. The behavior of his outgoing, highly achieving classmate is also a product of learning. The principles underlying the development of each behavior pattern might be the same in spite of the obvious behavioral differences. Let us now turn to those principles that account for how any behavior might be decelerated or eliminated.

Extinction

Both operant and respondent behavior can be extinguished. In respondent conditioning extinction will eventually occur if the conditional stimulus is repeatedly presented apart from the unconditional stimulus. Pavlov's dog would eventually stop salivating to the sight of Pavlov if his presence was never again accompanied by the aroma of food. *In vivo* desensitization is a behavioral counseling strategy based on extinction. Clients are helped to overcome their fears of various objects by gradually approaching the objects. As each successive step proves to be free of aversive concomitants, the fear becomes extinguished (Wolpe & Lazarus, 1966).

In operant conditioning extinction refers to withholding the reinforcement for a particular behavior. Many parents know, for example, that meeting a child's whining behavior with undue attention and concern will only serve to reinforce it. To be rid of the annoyance, such behavior should be consistently ignored.

Oftentimes children with behavior problems are referred to a counselor. Being aware that the act of referral may be reinforcing in itself, the behavioral counselor determines exactly what the problem behavior is and carefully notes what usually occurs immediately before and after it is exhibited. In other words, are there alterable discriminative stimuli or positive consequences that now seem to trigger and maintain the undesirable activity? In those instances where the referring adult can control the reinforcement for a child's problem behavior, the wise counselor counsels the adult rather than the child, thus teaching the laws of learning to the person most able to put them into effect.

Though extinction is an effective way to eliminate problem behaviors, its use is handicapped by at least three phenomena: In the first place there is the problem of the "extinction burst." When reinforcement is withheld, there may be a short period of rapid responding; temper tantrums, for example, may initially grow louder before subsiding. Second, behavior that has been intermittently reinforced is very difficult to extinguish. Gambling, for example, has occasional payoffs and is thus a very durable habit that might be expected to outlast all but permanent extinction periods. Finally, use of extinction implies control over the sources of reinforcement for a given activity. Nature is not necessarily so constructed. Parents, for example, cannot change the fact that marijuana smoking by their offspring is physiologically reinforced by the resulting euphoria and socially reinforced by the peer group (Horan, 1973e).

Punishment

Technically, punishment is the presentation of an aversive stimulus or event after the occurrence of a particular behavior by someone who is interested in suppressing that behavior. Unlike negative reinforcement, punishment is intended to reduce a behavior. In some instances where the sources of reinforcement for a problem behavior cannot be controlled, we might be tempted to employ punishment. Whether it works or not, punishment is oftentimes positively reinforcing to punishers because they may observe a temporary decrease in the troublesome response.

Contrary to popular opinion and impressions fostered by grossly distorted films like A Clock-Work Orange, behaviorists did not invent punishment. They have only sought to describe it and for the most part are loath to use it. Punishment as a means of suppressing behavior has severe limitations and disadvantages.

The literature on punishment is inconclusive. Severe punishment in some instances can produce permanent cessation of a given behavior. Solomon (1964) reported on research that cats and dogs subjected to excruciating pain after eating later starved themselves to death. Mild punishment, on the other hand, can actually increase the frequency and severity of the problem behavior because the positively reinforcing effects of attention may override the slight consequences. Moderate punishment (the "severest" option permissible with U.S. citizens under the Bill of Rights) can cause a temporary suppression of a particular activity but only if certain conditions are met. For example, the punishment must be delivered immediately after the target behavior, and it must be delivered after every instance of that behavior. When we consider that only a small percentage of criminals are ever apprehended and even if they are brought to trial, it is only after a long period of time has elapsed, it should be no surprise if an exclusively punishment-oriented correctional system does not significantly lower our crime rate. Azrin and Holz (1966) have thoroughly discussed numerous other essential conditions that must be provided if punishment is to be effective.

Even if we are successful in using punishment to suppress a particular behavior, we must be aware of a plethora of disadvantages. In the first place, the effects of punishment are generally temporary. The problem behavior usually reverts to its prepunished level—and oftentimes higher—after the punishing contingency is removed (Estes, 1944). Second, people tend to avoid the punishing agent rather than to cease emitting the punished response. Hence we may lose the opportunity to control behavior; it will still occur but now "behind the barn." Third, punishment breeds elicited and operant aggression as well as a host of other negative emotional responses. Operant aggression might be exemplified by the individual who learns that acting aggressively reduces the possibility of further punishment. The melodramatic cliché of a fired employee who subsequently upbraids the spouse, who in turn takes it out on the kids, who then begin to fight among themselves provides an illustration of elicited aggression and its perpetual effects. Skinner (1971) neatly summed up the disadvantages of punishment with his comment that aversive control sows the seeds of its own destruction.

Because of punishment's inherent disadvantages, its therapeutic applications are limited. Azrin and Fox (1974) suggest punishing "models" rather than the child as a small part of a rather comprehensive and generally positive approach to toilet training. Response cost and time out are punishment-related procedures that are both humane and relatively effective. For example, the "cost" of using foul and abusive language to a delinquent youth living in a token economy might be the loss of a prespecified number of tokens used to buy privileges. A retarded child who behaves in a physically assaultive manner might be sent alone to a "time out room" for a short while, away from sources of positive reinforcement (see Azrin & Holz, 1966). Finally, punishment is probably warranted when extinction alone would produce injury. For example, upon removal from restraints, an autistic girl might be slapped or shocked on the leg after each self-inflicted punch to her head. Once her self-destructive behavior is brought under control, punishment is terminated and positive reinforcement of desirable behavior becomes the major therapeutic activity.

Positive Approaches to Reducing Behavior

There are several other principles that account for how behavior might be weakened or eliminated. They are generally positive in orientation and unlike extinction and punishment produce few if any unpleasant side effects. The four discussed below are counterconditioning, differential reinforcement procedures, satiation, and modeling.

Counterconditioning

Counterconditioning involves the joint presentation of a negative and positive stimulus such that the former becomes neutral or slightly positive and the latter becomes neutral or slightly negative. In Jones's (1924) classic study a young boy's fear of various furry objects, particularly rabbits, was counterconditioned by feeding him in the presence of a caged rabbit. Initially, the rabbit was placed at a non-fear-arousing distance while the boy consumed a favorite food. During subsequent daily feeding sessions, the rabbit was gradually brought closer to the boy and eventually released from the cage. In the final stage of treatment, the boy not only spontaneously verbalized a fondness for the previously terrifying animal but also showed a marked reduction in related fears. Presumably, the positive food stimuli counterconditioned the generalized fear.

Differential Reinforcement Procedures

There are at least three methods of reducing problem behavior through differential reinforcement. The first and most important procedure, known as the "differential reinforcement of incompatible alternative behavior" (Alt R) attempts to accelerate incompatible operant behavior. Just as two objects cannot occupy the same point in time and space, neither can an individual concurrently exhibit two or more incompatible behaviors. An incompatible behavior is any behavior that when emitted precludes the possibility of another behavior.

Let us assume, for example, that a fourth-grade girl continually gazes out the window and rarely attends to the work on her desk. The teacher has unwittingly reinforced the problem behavior by repeatedly attending to it for the past several weeks. The counselor-consultant suggests the following procedure: The teacher is to ignore the child during window gazing episodes and reinforce desk work by attention, praise, and pats on the back. (The effectiveness of this procedure might be enhanced by a stimulus control technique, that is, seating the child on the windowless side of the room, thus eliminating a troublesome S_D).

Closely related to the reinforcement of incompatible behavior is another procedure known as "differential reinforcement of other behavior" (DRO). This strategy, also known as omission training, refers to a procedure in which a reinforcer follows any performance the individual emits except an undesirable one (Ferster & Perrott, 1968). The music teacher who smiles at the violin student every ten seconds except if a wrong note is being played at the moment would be using a DRO procedure, as would the parent who delivers frequent reinforcement except when the child happens to be biting his or her nails.

Still another variation has been labeled the "differential reinforcement of low rates" (DRL). This procedure is desirable when a reduction rather than elimination of a particular behavior would be appropriate. For example, occasional clowning around might be fun, but too much interferes with the work at hand. In group career counseling, participation—not domination—by any individual is desirable. The DRL procedure involves delivery of reinforcement if the particular behavior has decreased in a specified preceding time interval.

Satiation

The repeated provision of large amounts of immediate reinforcement for a particular behavior can actually cause a behavioral decline. Ayllon (1963) found that "rewarding" the towel-hoarding behavior of a psychotic woman with still more towels eventually eliminated the hoarding. Similarly, a teacher's repeated encouragement of class laughter and applause following an elementary student's episode of deliberate burping or hiccuping will inevitably diminish the problem. Unfortunately, the effects of satiation are not permanent; and because we may have to put up with temporarily increased levels, satiation should be used only with mildly unpleasant target behaviors.

Modeling

There are many ways that modeling can reduce problem behavior. Modeling offers an efficient alternative to counterconditioning strategies. Instead of desensitization, for example, clients can be helped to overcome fears by observing models approach and confront the feared objects (Bandura, 1971). Assertion training (Alberti & Emmons, 1970; Holmes & Horan, 1976; Kwiterovich & Horan, 1977) is another popular behavioral counseling strategy for reducing excessive timidity by therapist modeling of how to confront situations in which one's rights are being violated.

Modeling is also apropos for teaching new skills that are incompatible with or at least compete with various problem behaviors. Sarason and Ganzer (1969), for example, have developed model scripts for teaching juvenile delinquents how to engage in appropriate conversation with themselves, with police, and with potential employers. Various modeling strategies to help clients overcome fears are well known (Bandura, 1971). Other research suggests that modeling is a potentially useful strategy for reducing academic failure (Horan, DeGirolomo, Hill, & Shute, 1974) and for providing alternatives to drug use (Horan, 1973e; Horan, D'Amico, & Williams, 1975; Warner, Swisher, & Horan, 1973).

Summary

Scientific theories are always evaluated in terms of their usefulness, that is, their ability to explain, predict, and control a phenomenon. Thus, counseling theories should not only explain and predict the development of human problems in living but should also offer the opportunity for control, namely, improvement in the quality of our clients' lives.

Behaviors may be classified in several ways: as operant or respondent; as cognitive, affective, motor, or somatic; and as adaptive or maladaptive.

Several principles account for how behavior is acquired, maintained, and accelerated: respondent conditioning, positive reinforcement, negative reinforcement, and modeling. Other principles, extinction and punishment, refer to how behavior is decelerated and eliminated. More positive approaches to reducing behavior include counterconditioning, differential reinforcement, satiation, and modeling. Behavioral counseling strategies are based on one or more of these principles, but some principles have more therapeutic potential than others.

We cannot judge the usefulness of behavioral counseling in an absolute sense. The question is not whether behavioral counseling works, but rather how well it works in comparison to alternative counseling theories when applied to particular client problems. Even a cursory look at the scientific literature suggests that behavioral counseling has done quite well. Tomorrow's counselor, however, must ask, "Can behavioral counseling improve upon itself?" The next chapter explores several current areas of inquiry.

3

Current Topics in Behavioral Counseling

Behavioral counseling as a professional discipline has had a noticeably rebellious youth. Its advocates have subjected the "wisdom" of their psychoanalytic fathers to a good deal of ridicule, not all of it undeserved. For example, Ayllon, Haughton, and Hughes (1965) reinforced a psychotic woman with cigarettes for holding onto a broom. A consulting psychoanalyst then unwittingly interpreted the broom-holding behavior as a love-giving child, a phallic symbol, and the scepter of an omnipotent queen, thus supporting the notion that all psychoanalytic interpreting may be "unreal." Behavioral counselors may have also behaved rather impetuously in dismissing the "fuzzy" goals of existentialism. Krumboltz's (1966) classic statement on counseling goals, for example, denigrates self-understanding and self-acceptance. In retrospect, close inspection followed by behavioral definition may have been the wiser course of action (Horan, 1972a; Thoresen, 1972c). On the other hand, behavioral counselors may have needed to be noisy in order to be known. In any event, as behavioral counseling passes from a rebellious childhood on through puberty, several signs of maturity are clearly visible. This chapter focuses on several current topics in behavioral counseling that may well foretell a reconciliation between behavioral and nonbehavioral points of view.

Self-Management

Nearly all human behavior is learned; our thoughts, feelings, and actions are all a function of our environment. But the relationship between environment and behavior is reciprocal in that our behavior can in turn modify our environment. In fact, deliberately structuring our environment to ensure that we behave the way we would like is one facet of self-management, an exciting new frontier in behavioral counseling research and practice (Mahoney & Thoresen, 1974; Thoresen & Mahoney, 1974; Watson & Tharp, 1972; Williams & Long, 1975). Nature does not care who manages the contingencies of behavior; the client is perfectly capable of serving as his or her own contingency manager (Homme & Tosti, 1965). Self-management, also known as self-control, is a generic name for three processes clients can adopt to improve the quality of their lives: self-monitoring, altering behavioral antecedents, and altering behavioral consequences.

Self-Monitoring

Self-monitoring consists essentially of observing and recording one's own behavior. Clients might be asked, for example, to keep track of the number of instances in which they smoked, overate, studied, or made positive comments to their spouses. Because self-monitoring can have a reactive effect on desirable and undesirable behaviors, we might expect decreases in smoking and calories consumed and increases in grade point averages and marital happiness (Hayes & Cavior, 1977). What causes self-monitoring to work (the active ingredient) is not clear (Kazdin, 1974a). It might be the simple act of observing, the process of recording, or the instructions and expectancies generated by the counselor. Furthermore, the reactive effects of self-monitoring have not been consistent; some people with some problems are helped some of the time. Self-monitoring might be construed as the behavioral equivalent of "insight," necessary but insufficient for the attainment of self-control (Horan, Hoffman, & Macri, 1974).

Altering Behavioral Antecedents

We can learn to control our behavior by manipulating the cues that precede it. For example, impulse buyers who chronically overspend their budgets might find that closing charge accounts and carrying limited amounts of cash will help keep them out of debt. Similarly, overweight individuals might learn to shop for groceries after dinner, because an empty stomach generally triggers more food-buying behavior.

Both of the above examples involve elimination of troublesome discriminative stimuli. We can also change our behavior by inserting desirable discriminative stimuli. Just as the alarm clock cues us to wake up on time, a piece of tape on our wrist watch might prime us to say something positive to a family member with whom we have a less than adequate relationship. Likewise, Mahoney (1971) used printed cards attached to a cigarette package to stimulate a depressed and self-deprecating client into thoughts reflecting self-esteem.

Finally, we can physically alter the environment so our behavioral problem cannot occur. One humorous example was reported by the reader of a newspaper column: "In trying to lose weight, I find it truly helps to leave my dentures in the bathroom while I am cleaning up and putting food away after dinner" (Shoemacher, 1976). On a more serious note, an advertising salesman with a drinking problem observed that his clients were continually filling his glass at business and social functions. He solved this delicate problem by carrying around a glass filled with tonic water, a beverage he disliked.

Altering Behavioral Consequences

We can increase the frequency of our adaptive behavior through self-administered reinforcement. For example, we might reward our own good eating, exercising, or studying habits by sunbathing, going to a movie, or buying ourselves a gift we would not otherwise have purchased. Essentially, we can facilitate the attainment of a long-range goal by providing self-administered payoffs along the way.

Similarly, we can decrease the frequency of our problem behavior through self-administered punishment. Chronic fingernail biters, for example, can be taught to snap a thick rubber band on the inside of their wrists each time they place their fingers in the mouth area. Because all forms of punishment may produce "treatment avoidance" rather than declines in the problem behavior, it is generally a good idea to embed self-punishment in a program that is rewarding in other ways (for example, Horan, Hoffman, & Macri, 1974).

Covert Behavioral Counseling

Most discussions on how behavior might be learned and unlearned rarely include covert behavior. The ancient history of behaviorism would have us believe that covert behaviors such as thoughts, images, and feelings were not proper objects of study, if indeed they existed at all. Later behaviorists (Dollard & Miller, 1950; Skinner, 1953) not only acknowledged their existence but also conceded that these "inner responses" or "private events" probably obey the same laws of learning as observable behaviors, an idea many recent behaviorists have accepted as fact. Such covert behaviors as thinking about sex and overt behaviors as engaging in sex are topographically similar; we are thus relatively secure in assuming that reinforcement and punishment, for example, will affect each in an identical manner. The practice of covert behavioral counseling is widespread today.

Covert behavioral counseling procedures roughly parallel the respondent, operant, and modeling techniques of more traditional behavioral counseling. Covert operant conditioning may involve not only covert target behaviors but also pleasant or aversive covert antecedents, consequences, or both. Similar complexities exist with covert respondent and modeling paradigms, hence the range of possible permutations of covert behavioral counseling approaches infinity. The four groupings that follow are certainly not exhaustive, but simply represent the major covert behavioral counseling modalities as currently practiced.

Covert Respondent Procedures

Orgasmic reconditioning is a rather straightforward application of covert respondent conditioning for developing the capacity for heterosexual arousal. In the latter phase of this procedure, homosexuals desirous of change engage in heterosexual imagery during a masturbation-induced orgasm (Marquis, 1970).

Many covert responding procedures are based on the principle of counterconditioning. Such techniques involve the "blocking" of anxiety through another covert behavior. Wolpe (1958) was the first to capitalize on this possibility in developing a counseling strategy known as systematic desensitization. Clients with various fears are trained in deep muscle relaxation and while relaxed are asked to imagine themselves gradually confronting the feared stimulus. Because one cannot be anxious and relaxed at the same time, the fear is presumably counterconditioned. There is little question that systematic desensitization works; but there is a controversy concerning why (Evans, 1973). Relaxation is not absolutely essential (Waters, McDonald, & Koresko, 1972), so an extinction process may in fact be occurring.

Cue-controlled relaxation (Lent & Russell, 1978; Russell & Sipich, 1974) promises to be a relatively efficient alternative to desensitization. Briefly, clients are trained to associate a state of relaxation with a self-spoken cue word such as "calm." Then upon encountering a tension-producing stimulus in real life, clients simply cue themselves to relax.

Emotive imagery (Lazarus & Abramovitz, 1962; Tasto & Chesney, 1977) is a derivative of desensitization. In lieu of relaxation, however, classes of images assumed to arouse positive feelings such as pride, affection, and mirth are used to block the anxiety arising from the feared scene. The technique is particularly appropriate for treating children's phobias.

In vivo emotive imagery is an effective means of coping with inescapable discomforting situations. Images that generate positive emotions have blocked the anxiety or pain arising from ice water immersion (Horan, & Dellinger, 1974; Stone, Demchik-Stone, & Horan, 1977; Westcott & Horan, 1977), childbirth (Horan, 1973d, 1976), dental discomfort (Horan, Layng, & Pursell, 1976), and turbulent airplane flights (Horan, 1976; Thoresen, 1972b).

Anger can also be used to block anxiety. In fact, because of anger's possible physiological incompatibility with anxiety (Gellhorn, 1967; Siminov, 1967), anger-induction techniques are potentially more powerful than those relying on positive imagery or relaxation. Such techniques have already increased pain tolerance (Westcott & Horan, 1977), reduced fears (Gershman & Stedman, 1971), and improved assertiveness (Goldstein, Serber, & Piaget, 1970; Holmes & Horan, 1976).

Flooding and implosion are theoretically grounded on extinction rather than counterconditioning. Unlike desensitization, which involves gradual confrontation with the feared situation "countered" by relaxation, flooding requires the client to entertain and hold a complete image of the feared event until extinction occurs. Implosion is similar to flooding except that psychoanalytic themes presumed to underlie or accompany the fear are also included in the image. Many behaviorists balk at the idea of implosion and the efficacy of both techniques has been a matter of debate (see Levis, 1974; Morganstern, 1973, 1974).

Covert Operant Procedures

Whereas the foregoing techniques are all based on the language of respondent conditioning, a number of covert operant procedures also exist. Covert reinforcement, extinction, and sensitization are rather direct adaptations of "overt" operant strategies to the realm of covert behavioral counseling.

Joseph Cautela and his students have been the primary developers of these techniques.

In covert positive reinforcement (Cautela, 1970a); clients are first asked to associate a very pleasant image with the word "reinforcement." The counselor then begins a narration that depicts the client progressively engaging in more adaptive behavior. At various intervals the counselor punctuates the imaginary scenario by uttering the word reinforcement. The positive image presumably reinforces imaginary client gains, for example, up a fear hierarchy. Success reportedly carries over into real life in a manner similar to desensitization.

In covert negative reinforcement (Cautela, 1970b) a noxious event is first identified, possibly by a fear survey schedule (Wolpe & Lazarus, 1966). Termination of this uncomfortable image is then followed by the client visualizing himself or herself engaging in adaptive behavior. Thus one "escapes" discomfort by making therapeutic progress.

In covert extinction (Cautela, 1971a) the client entertains an image of engaging in a maladaptive behavior (stuttering, for example). The event is followed by no consequence whatsoever. As in overt extinction, the problem behavior is expected to decrease upon removal of all forms of reinforcement.

In covert sensitization (Cautela, 1966; Little and Curran, 1978), a "relaxed" client imagines engaging in a compulsive maladaptive behavior such as overeating. This scene is followed immediately by an aversive imaginary experience such as vomiting and concomitant feelings of nausea, thus producing an expected decline in the compulsion to eat. Covert sensitization was originally intended to ape a respondent conditioning process, that is, the pairing of a problem behavior with an aversive stimulus. However, because the imaginary noxious event does not occur at the same time but rather follows the maladaptive behavior, covert sensitization more closely represents a covert punishment paradigm.

Mahoney (1974) has thoroughly reviewed the supporting evidence for covert operant conditioning paradigms. He reports that covert negative reinforcement and covert extinction have scarcely been researched. Furthermore, the data on covert positive reinforcement are equivocal. Finally, covert sensitization has had negligible effects on addictions, variable effects on obesity, and rather positive effects on sexual deviations.

Mixed Covert Operant Paradigms

Covert operant paradigms are often deployed in treatment packages involving several procedures. More recent applications of covert sensitization, for instance, blend covert positive and negative reinforcement components. For example, a pedophiliac would be asked to follow a child-molesting image with the likely but imaginary occurrence of a baseball bat assault by the child's father. Escape from this aversive image would lead to a scene involving age-appropriate sexual behavior, which in turn might be followed by a final positive image (Farr & Tucker, 1974).

One of the earliest covert behavioral counseling procedures was a multicomponent paradigm known as coverant control (Homme, 1965). In this treatment strategy an attempt is made to accelerate certain coverants or cognitive behaviors that are deemed incompatible with various problem behaviors such as overeating. Negative coverants focus on the aversive consequences of a behavioral disorder; positive coverants focus on the desirable aspects of overcoming the problem behavior. For example, an obese client might be asked to punish an urge to eat with a negative coverant such as an image of an early death. This act of self-punishment is then followed by a positive coverant such as the thought of looking good in (or out of) a bathing suit. The entire sequence is reinforced by having the client engage in a highly probable activity, for example, stroking a pet cat or sitting in a favorite chair (Horan & Johnson, 1971).

The coverant control paradigm is plagued with conceptual difficulties (Danaher, 1974; Mahoney, 1970). Furthermore, clients show an extreme reluctance to emit negative coverants; thus in practice the paradigm may break down or produce variable results (Horan, 1974b; Horan, Baker, Hoffman, & Shute, 1975; Horan, Smyers, Dorfman, & Jenkins, 1975). Elimination of the negative coverant component and reinforcement of positive coverants may prove to be an effective ancillary treatment procedure (Horan, Robb, & Hudson, 1975).

Thought stopping (Wolpe & Lazarus, 1966) is a covert behavioral counseling strategy designed to end obsessive ruminations (the sort of thinking that might precede the third checking of an alarm clock setting). Clients are first instructed to immerse themselves in their maladaptive thought patterns, which their counselors interrupt by shouting the word "stop." The startled clients are then told to notice the fact that they are no longer ruminating. After several practice sessions control gradually shifts to the clients, who eventually learn to end their ruminations with subvocal commands to stop. Mahoney (1974) recommends thought substitution as a more theoretically palatable version of thought stopping. Engaging in an incompatible alternative thought might be a more powerful means of ending maladaptive ruminations (see also Emmelkamp & Kwee, 1977).

Covert Modeling

Cautela (1971b) first described covert modeling but Kazdin (1973a, b, 1974b, 1976) has conducted much of the work on procedural refinement and empirical evaluation. Essentially, fearful or unassertive clients are asked to imagine themselves engaging in adaptive behavior. The effects of covert modeling seem to be enhanced by the same factors that enhance overt modeling (see Cautela, 1976). For example, models of the same age and sex are more effective than models of differing age and sex (Kazdin, 1974b). Furthermore, mastery models (those who confidently strive toward a feared stimulus) are less effective than coping models (those who talk themselves out of their initial reluctance) (Kazdin, 1973a). Finally, the use of multiple models and the delivery of realistic reinforcement to successful models adds to the effectiveness of the covert modeling procedure (Kazdin, 1973b 1976). Although Cautela, Flannery, and Hanley (1974) found no differences between covert and overt modeling procedures, Thase and Moss (1976) reported that overt modeling in which the model guides the subject's performance was substantially more effective than covert modeling.

An Expanding Cognitive Horizon

The covert behavioral counseling strategies just discussed have generated a good deal of controversy. One problem springs from the philosophy of science; namely, even if we accept the shaky hypothesis that a given covert behavioral counseling strategy has proved to be effective, we cannot then assume it works *because* of the underlying theory. For example, any changes produced by covert positive reinforcement may not be due to the fact that it resembles overt positive reinforcement. This potential logical error is highlighted by an amusing study of covert sensitization in which a control group conjured up pleasant rather than aversive scenes following their imagined eating behavior. In effect the control group received covert positive reinforcement for maladaptive eating; but instead of gaining weight, they lost an average 8.5 pounds in comparison to the covert sensitization group's loss of 4.1 pounds (Foreyt & Hagen, 1973). Covert behavioral counseling techniques may indeed work, but not necessarily because of the reasons offered.

This philosophical problem applies to all scientific endeavors, not just the field of covert behavioral counseling. A greater source of controversy stems from the fact that several covert procedures only remotely approximate the behavior change principles on which they are supposed to be based. For example, negative reinforcement demands that the escape response (an adaptive behavior) produce a cessation of the noxious stimulus. Yet in covert negative reinforcement the noxious stimulus (an unpleasant image) is terminated before the adaptive behavior is begun.

Furthermore, coverant control, which Homme (1965) developed from the earlier work of Premack (1965), rests on Homme's assumption that certain desirable cognitive behaviors can be accelerated by reinforcing them with a number of "highly probable" (that is, reinforcing) activities. Unfortunately, few of the potential reinforcers suggested by Homme meet the rather rigid laboratory stipulations set down by Premack (Danaher, 1974; Mahoney, 1970).

This lack of theoretical fidelity has not met with forgiveness in many behavioral quarters. Wolpe (1976, p. 1), for example, presents a rather forceful defense for defining behavior therapy in terms of "treatment methods derived from experimentally established principles and paradigms of learning" and dismisses as malcontents those who wander too far from the principles that offer empirical credibility to the mental health profession. Wolpe himself might be considered a "liberal" by some standards. Several behavioral interpretations of systematic desensitization, including his own, are theoretically deficient despite the fact that the technique may be useful in reducing client fear levels (Evans, 1973). Other behavioral books and journals do not even acknowledge cognitive-behavioral counseling as a legitimate area of scientific inquiry.

Cognitive behaviorists, on the other hand, are quick to point out that applications of many noncognitive behavior change strategies such as time out and response cost only rarely correspond to their laboratory definitions (see Azrin & Holz, 1966). Furthermore, no scientific field has ever advanced by tenacious clinging to "acceptable" dogmas. Although this "new school" may be experiencing disenchantment with the limitations inherent in the language of the traditional learning laboratory, they rigidly adhere to the traditional requirements of behavioral research methodology. Treatment strategies, for example, are still clearly defined in terms of the operations or behaviors in which the counselor must engage, and claims for efficacy must still be based on the outcomes of carefully controlled experimentation. Several cognitive-behavioral treatment modalities that seem to be receiving a good deal of attention are cognitive restructuring, cognitive modeling, stress inoculation, problem solving, and decision making. Ironically, much of this work is compatible with the traditional language of behaviorism; but proponents have simply not bothered to make the necessary translations.

Cognitive Restructuring

Most behavioral counselors would probably take issue with Ellis's (1962) contention that neurotic misery is always caused by irrational thinking. Nevertheless, many will concede that some highly prevalent, learned, illogical thoughts seem to precede a variety of maladaptive feelings and actions and that direct verbal confrontation is one of the most effective and efficient therapeutic strategies in such situations. Beck (1970) and Lazarus (1971) have added to Ellis's compendium of illogical thoughts that lead to problems in living. Cognitive restructuring is a generic name for strategies used to disperse these maladaptive thoughts and to substitute adaptive thoughts in their stead. Mahoney (1973, p. 6 & 7) coined the term "cognitive ecology," that is "cleaning up what you say to yourself" to refer to the same process. Self-defeating thoughts and excuses offered by his overweight clients such as "It'll never work," or "I blew it with that doughnut," are directly challenged.

Cognitive Modeling

Whereas covert modeling makes extensive use of visual imagery, cognitive modeling relies mostly on auditory imagery or display. A cognitive model "thinks out loud" in an attempt to foster a similar adaptive thought pattern in the observer (see Sarason, 1973). Cognitive modeling, per se, has not been as popular a research topic as covert modeling; the same factors that enhance the latter will undoubtedly be found to improve the efficacy of the former. Cognitive modeling, however, is a major component of a well-researched treatment package known as "self-instruction training," a behavioral counseling analog of Ellis's (1962) rational emotive therapy.

In self-instruction training clients are initially led to discover the self-defeating thinking that causes or contributes to their problems in living. The counselor then serves as a powerful cognitive model for more adaptive thoughts. Clients are then asked to rehearse these new self-statements. A recent study, however, suggests that such rehearsal may have a detracting influence (Thorpe, Amater, Blakely, & Burns, 1976). The clinical application of self-instruction training also involves covert or overt practice in the development of the target skill and self-reinforcement for progress made. Meichenbaum and his associates have used self-instruction training to decrease irrational verbal behavior in schizophrenics (Meichenbaum & Cameron, 1973), impulsivity in children (Meichenbaum & Goodman, 1971), and anxiety in adults (Meichenbaum, 1972). Self-instruction training can also be used to enhance positive goals, such as creativity (Meichenbaum, 1975).

Stress Inoculation Training

Meichenbaum has extended his work in cognitive modeling and self-instruction to the development of a broader paradigm for the cognitive-behavioral management of anxiety, anger, and pain (Meichenbaum & Turk, 1976). Stress inoculation provides clients with a set of skills to cope with future stressful situations. This training essentially consists of three phases. In phase one clients receive a conceptual framework for understanding the nature of stressful reactions. During phase two clients practice a number of cognitive and behavioral coping skills. Finally, in phase three the clients have the opportunity to practice these skills during exposure to a variety of stressors. The efficacy of stress inoculation has been demonstrated in aggression management (Novaco, 1975; Schlichter & Horan, 1978) and pain reduction (Hackett, Horan, Buchanan, & Zumoff, 1978; Horan, Hackett, Buchanan, Stone, & Demchik-Stone, 1977).

Other Cognitive Procedures

Behavioral counselors are paying increasing attention to the problem-solving and decision-making literatures, which often include the use of the cognitive-behavioral counseling strategies previously discussed. Both of these broad topics will be explored in subsequent chapters.

Comprehensive Behavioral Programming

Behavioral counselors, especially those in applied settings, are beginning to realize that many problems in living cannot be solved by simply applying a given behavioral technique. Coverant control, for example, might be expected to produce a "statistically significant" weight loss of about six pounds for the average person (Horan & Johnson, 1971), but this miniscule amount is of little practical benefit to a three hundred-pound client.

Fortunately, many complex client problems can be resolved through comprehensive behavioral programming. For example, after following a number of behavioral prescriptions to gain self-control over her eating habits, the *least* successful client in Stuart's (1967) classic study lost a total of twenty six pounds. Mahoney and Mahoney (1976) offer a potentially more powerful program, which includes not only much of the Stuart program but a number of cognitive-behavioral counseling procedures as well.

Cigarette smoking is another behavior problem that has proved to be highly resistant to change. An aversion conditioning procedure known as rapid smoking (which involves having cigarette addicts take a normal inhalation every six seconds as long as they can) has produced rather consistent and durable results either by itself (Lichtenstein, Harris, Birchler, Wahl, &

Schmahl, 1973; Schmahl, Lichtenstein, & Harris, 1972) or in conjunction with multicomponent treatment programs (Hackett & Horan, 1977; Hackett, Horan, Stone, Linberg, Nicholas, & Lukaski, 1977). Unfortunately, the safety of the rapid smoking procedure has been called into question (Horan, Hackett, Nicholas, Linberg, Stone, & Lukaski, 1977; Horan, Linberg, & Hackett, 1977), and alternative treatment strategies have been conspicuously unsuccessful. A review by McFall and Hammen (1971) suggests that any smoking treatment technique will produce a low to moderate success rate (26 percent), which inevitably decays to practical insignificance (13 percent) after six months.

Preliminary evaluation of an unequivocally safe alternative to the rapid smoking procedure, however, now indicates that 50 to 60 percent of all cigarette addicts exposed to a new comprehensive treatment program can expect to be fully abstinent from all forms of tobacco six months after treatment (Hackett & Horan, 1978). This comprehensive program attacks the smoking problem on a number of fronts: A week-long period of self-monitoring provides information on the severity of the habit, builds an awareness of the antecedents and consequences of smoking, and often produces a reduction in the habit in and of itself.

Following the self-monitoring phase, participants sign contracts with family members and friends to facilitate self-management. Briefly, the "significant others" are asked never to offer cigarettes to the participant and never to criticize the participant for smoking. Furthermore, they are requested to provide liberal positive reinforcement (praise, for example) for any progress made. Cue-controlled relaxation is also part of the comprehensive program because even though cigarettes are stimulants, some individuals report that they smoke in order to combat anxiety (Schachter, 1973).

Other treatment components include thought stopping to interrupt smoking urges and focused smoking, an aversion technique that pairs the act of smoking with vivid images of its immediate and potential consequences. Finally, cognitive restructuring is an integral part of the comprehensive treatment program. Maladaptive thoughts (that is, self-doubts and rationalizations) are actively challenged.

If comprehensive behavioral programming is appropriate for relatively circumscribed personal difficulties such as smoking and obesity, the need to develop similar programs for dealing with more complex problems in living should be readily apparent. Comprehensive programs for pervasive problems such as depression and marital discord are now being designed and evaluated (for example, Jacobson & Martin, 1976; Lazarus, 1976).

Summary

Many of the topics that dominate the counseling literature today foretell a reconciliation between behavioral and nonbehavioral points of view. One such topic is self-management or self-control, a term that consists of three processes clients can adopt to improve the quality of their lives: self-monitoring, altering behavioral antecedents, and altering behavioral consequences.

Recently developed covert behavioral counseling procedures generally parallel the respondent, operant, and modeling techniques of more traditional behavioral counseling. There is an almost infinite range of possible permutations of these procedures, all of which can be grouped into four categories: covert respondent procedures, covert operant procedures, mixed covert operant paradigms, and covert modeling.

One controversy the topic of covert behavioral counseling has generated concerns the fact that the strategies may work but not necessarily because of the underlying theory. Another controversy stems from the fact that some of the procedures only remotely approximate the behavior change principles on which they are based. While the debates among behaviorists continue, several cognitive-behavioral counseling modalities receiving attention include cognitive restructuring, cognitive modeling, and stress inoculation training.

Comprehensive behavioral programming is an approach to resolving complex client problems by attacking them on a number of fronts. It has been effectively applied to relatively circumscribed difficulties and its use with more pervasive problems is under investigation.

This chapter touched on a number of current topics in behavioral quarters. In the next two chapters we shall see that the basic language of decision theory and current topics in the field have much in common with behavioral theory and the emerging cognitive-behavioral point of view.

4

The Language of Classical Decision Theory

Decision theory belongs to no single academic discipline; it is inextricably entwined with statistics, economics, and psychology and many applied fields, including business, politics, gambling, and, of course, counseling. Certain areas of decision theory are intelligible only to those who breathe easily in the rarefied air of the upper stratospheres of mathematics. In this chapter I shall try to walk the fine line between the obvious and the esoteric, hopefully distilling from an oftentimes intimidating literature those concepts of classical decision theory that are relevant to the conduct of counseling.

One of the first decisions of our ancestors was to climb out of a primeval swamp and establish residence on dry land (or to bite the apple if the reader is biblically inclined). History has recorded at least a few other significant decisions; but the process of making decisions was not formally studied until perhaps the eighteenth century. Pascal and other mathematicians found themselves eagerly employed by gamblers in the French court who needed to learn to distinguish between fair and unfair bets. For example, a roll of a pair of dice might produce any of eleven possible sums (two through twelve). Any "generous" con man would offer a passing patsy six of the outcomes (two, three, four, ten, eleven, twelve) against his five outcomes (five, six, seven, eight, nine) on a fifty-fifty wager. He would do so gladly because, as Bross (1953) reports, on 111 rolls of the dice at a dollar a bet he could expect to win seventy-four dollars while losing only thirty-seven dollars, a profit so tidy he might even offer better odds as an additional inducement to play! Thus the origins of formal decision theory were prescriptive in nature. Professional decision theorists provided advice on what "ought" to be done. Today such decision theory models are often labeled "normative" (Becker & McClintock, 1967).

How we ought to behave, however, often differs from how we do, in fact, behave. Buying life insurance or lottery tickets can hardly be called making fair bets, yet many of us eagerly seek out their salespersons knowing full well that a substantial portion of our potential return must be used to pay their salaries. Since the days of Pascal, many decision theorists have swung away from prescribing to describing behavior. Luce (1967) has argued that these functions should belong to separate academic disciplines. What we "ought" to do is properly the bailiwick of statistics; how we actually decide is a matter for psychology, and the study of group or institutional decisions belongs to the domain of economics or sociology. Edwards and Tversky (1967, p. 8), on the other hand, prefer not to make such distinctions: "For one thing, when the stakes are high we try very hard to do what we should; in this sense models of what we should do have descriptive as well as prescriptive usefulness." Rapoport and Wallsten (1972) echo this view.

In any event the study of decisions has given rise to a new vocabulary, which we shall now explore. Decision theory rests on the cornerstone concepts of value and probability, both of which can be either objective or subjective in nature. Models of behavior built on the various permutations of these concepts, accompanied by an assortment of rules and assumptions, constitute the subject matter of classical decision theory.

Value

In decision theory the concept of value refers to the desirability of an object or an outcome. Value might be thought of as an economic translation of the behavioral concept of reinforcement. Whereas a behaviorist might loosely speak of the reinforcing properties of a particular alternative, the decision theorist would discuss the value resulting from that course of action. Values are generally, but not always, positive. Negative value means that a given object or event is undesirable. Its correspondence to the behavioral concept of punishment is obvious. For example, we can speak of the potential consequences of electing a political candidate as being the lesser of two evils, the lesser of two punishing alternatives, or the lesser of two negative values.

Values may be either objective or subjective. Objective values are numbers representing physical quantities such as dollars, units of time or length, and so forth. In decision theory objective value refers to a particular object or outcome's desirability apart from any given individual's perception. Market values are sometimes thought of as being objective in that the market value of a new car or a pound of coffee, for example, is an entity apart from one's belief that the price of either is too high or too low. In reality, however, market values are a sort of averaging out of all the individual "subjective" values of a given population (Bross, 1953). If there are objective values other than those in the science of physics, decision theorists have ignored them or at least not assigned numbers to them. Instead they have invested considerable cerebral energy in exploring the concept of subjective value.

Subjective value is commonly known as utility, the study of which can be traced back to the eighteenth century. Daniel Bernoulli wondered if a pauper would be foolish to sell a lottery ticket for nine thousand ducats if that ticket gave him an equal chance of winning either nothing or twenty thousand ducats (cited in Savage, 1954). For what price should a rich man sell it?

To introduce their discussion of utility, Chernoff and Moses (1959, p. 79) pose a number of interesting contemporary betting dilemmas. In the first choice problem you receive two dollars if a well-balanced coin falls heads and you pay one dollar if it falls tails. Most of us would eagerly accept that wager. Now let us change the amounts but not the odds. Your entire fortune has a cash value of ten million dollars. You receive another twenty million dollars if the coin falls heads and lose your fortune if it falls tails. Few of us would ever accept such a bet in spite of the favorable odds for increasing the objective value of our estates. Our rationale would be one of diminished utility, that is, twenty million dollars would buy very little extra happiness in comparison to the possible misery of losing our entire ten-million-dollar fortune.

Thus the objective value of money may differ from its subjective value or utility. Economists have suspected this phenomenon for a long time but the first experiment formally demonstrating it was conducted fairly recently (Mosteller & Nogee, 1951). It is interesting to note that Bernoulli believed the utility of money could be closely approximated by the logarithm of the objective amount. His eighteenth-century contemporaries posited similarly "hopeful" relationships: Buffon, the French naturalist, believed that utility was the reciprocal of monetary value and Cramer, the Swiss mathematician and philosopher, felt that square root was the appropriate relationship (cited by Miller & Starr, 1967). Such precision is of course delusional. Generally speaking, all that can be concluded is that as we begin to acquire more and more money, the gap between its objective value and its utility begins to widen. Money becomes less and less useful to us, but how much less is an individual matter.

Circumstances other than vastly increased sums of money may also alter its utility. Let us contrast two more examples from Chernoff and Moses (1959, p. 79): You have only five dollars and intend to spend it all on beer to drink this evening. Because five dollars will buy a good deal of beer, it is most unlikely that you would accept a double-or-nothing, flip-of-the-coin bet. Losing the wager would mean an unhappy evening; but were you to win, you would be unable to spend the extra five dollars on beer for yourself tonight, there being limits to human capacities for such beverages. On the other hand, if you were a gymnastics enthusiast and were five dollars shy of the ten dollars admission price to a gymnastic exhibition, you would probably accept such a wager gladly. Thus the utility of money varies not only with amounts but also with individuals and situations.

The fact that we are culturally conditioned to think in terms of objective "dollar" values of products, however, rather than of their respective utilities has been a continuing source of frustration in decision-making research (Edwards, 1954, 1961). Even if we already have three color televisions, for example, we are likely to pick a nonresellable fourth instead of a sorely needed electric razor should we be given the free choice of either. This is not necessarily a defect in human nature; it might even be adaptive. But it does pose problems for the researcher.

In any event a utility scale composed of utiles (as a thermometer is composed of degrees) would certainly facilitate the description, as well as the making, of decisions. For example, it would readily lend itself to the subjective measurement of both monetary and nonmonetary values. Although today's oil companies have placed a price tag on an altruistic image and have decided to pay advertising consultants accordingly, many individuals would balk at assigning dollar values to friendships, the state of being married, truth telling, human life, and so forth. To speak in terms of utility, while still a bit abrupt, is much less abrasive.

Although the concept of utility is intuitively meaningful, its measurement can be rather cumbersome. There has been a long running debate, for example, as to whether utility ought to be measured on an ordinal or interval scale (Edwards, 1954). Ordinal utility refers to ranked data: I prefer strawberries to apples to pears (but my preference for strawberries over apples is much greater than my fealty for apples in comparison to pears). Cardinal utility refers to utility measured on an interval scale. Such a scale has the desirable mathematical property of equal distances between points. Thus instead of a simple ranking of 1, 2, and 3, my preference for strawberries to apples to pears might be precisely defined as 8, 4, and 3 utilities respectively. Then, of course, there is some question as to how utilities ought to be combined. Given the choice of strawberries or an apple-pear fruit cocktail, should I add or multiply the latter utilities (see Fishburn, 1967, and Supes & Walsh, 1959)?

Early economic work on the qualification of utility focused on indifference points, curves, and maps. We would begin by asking our subjects whether they preferred an apple or a pear. If they picked the apple, we would offer them the choice of one apple or two pears, then one apple and three pears, and so forth. An indifference point would reflect that our subject received the same amount of utility from each option, say one apple and five pears. From two such indifference points we can easily construct an indifference curve; a whole family of such curves is called an indifference map. Unfortunately, indifference maps are at least awkward if not inapplicable to the making of individual personal decisions.

Similarly, VonNeumann and Morgenstern (1947) developed the "standard-gamble-method" for determining utilities. Their procedure involved asking subjects to choose between several outcomes of varying certainty. By hypothetically adjusting these probability levels and requesting further choices, they derived a measure of utility that could be represented on an interval scale. Though ingenious, the method suffers from assumption problems and cannot be applied in certain cases (see Miller & Starr, 1967).

More recent attempts to measure utility (of money and valuable objects) involve its "backward" estimation from decisions already made (Davidson, Supes, & Siegel, 1957). Regrettably, no one has yet developed an adequate technology for assigning numbers to the objective and subjective values that might accrue from the various alternatives in a decision-making problem.

Two of the foremost authorities on decision theory, Edwards and Fishburn, recommend the use of very simple scales to measure utility in resolving individual choice problems (Fishburn, personal communication). For example, clients might simply be asked to rate the utilities of various outcomes on a 1 to 10 scale. Though such measuring procedures often precipitate snickers, if not outright laughs, from more esoteric behavioral quarters, in point of fact many crucial behavioral counseling variables such as fear and relaxation have been frequently measured in this manner (Sherman & Cormier, 1972).

Essentially, then, we do not have a relevant objective value taxonomy to facilitate decision making. Subjective values, or utilities, differ widely among individuals and situations. Although measurement is either crude or cumbersome, utilities can nonetheless be assessed. Utilities in conjunction with probabilities dictate what decisions are—or ought to be—made.

Probability

The English language has several words akin to the concept of probability. For example, we can speak of a given event as being likely or unlikely. Similarly, we might argue that the odds or chances for such and such a happening are favorable or unfavorable. The major problem with using a verbal system to describe probability, however, is that language can be quite "slippery"; we can phrase things so our verbal predictions seem true regardless of the actual outcome. Sportscasters and weather announcers have developed this skill to a fine art: "Penn State is favored to win today, but Stanford could pull an upset." "It looks like it's going to be a bright, sunny day, but there is a chance of showers."

Even if we scrupulously avoid using this kind of double-talk, we will find that a verbal system for describing probability suffers from a lack of precision. For example, the odds of our drowning on a given day at the beach are much "higher" than the odds of our being attacked by a great white shark, yet both sets of odds are very "slight."

To avoid the ambiguities inherent in a verbal probability system, mathematicians have developed a numerical scale for describing probability. The scale is bounded by the points "0" and "1." A "0" indicates that an event is not at all likely; a "1," on the other hand, means that the event is completely certain. Points in between reflect varying degrees of probability. For example, the weather forecaster who reports a precipitation probability of .7 is in fact saying that under similar atmospheric conditions it has rained on 70 percent of the occasions and our best guess is that history will repeat itself.

Probability theorists have developed a symbolic language for the brief and clear communication of their ideas. For example, we would refer to the probability of striking oil in our backyard as p (0|I), where p ( ) is read as "the probability of," and the 0 stands for "striking oil in our backyard." The vertical line means "given," and the I refers to whatever geological "information" we have at hand.

Mathematicians have arranged these symbols in certain ways to form laws. For example, one facet of the addition law tells us that the probability of rolling a two or a three on a six-sided die is equal to the sum of their separate probabilities (1/6 + 1/6 = 1/3). There are numerous other laws and special cases of laws, all of which can be deduced from the axioms in table 4.1. The reader is invited to glance through the material in the table but should not worry or become intimidated by it if years have lapsed since he or she formally studied probability. To discuss these axioms fully would require a book-length digression; we need only a superficial knowledge of them for our purposes. Readers interested in boning up on probability theory in the context of decision theory might wish to peruse excellent introductory texts by Bross (1953) or Lindley (1971).

TABLE 4.1. Probability axioms

Symbolic notation	*Explication*
Scale specification axioms	
a) $P(y \text{ or not-}y) = 1$	The probability of y or not-y is equal to 1.
b) $P(y \text{ and not-}y) = 0$	The probability of y and not-y is equal to 0.
c) $P(y) \geq 0$	The probability of y is 0 or greater than 0.
Multiplication axiom $P(z \text{ and } y) = P(y) \times P(z|y)$	The probability of z *and* y is equal to the probability of y times the probability of z if y occurs.
Addition axiom $P(y \text{ or } z) = P(y) + P(z) - P(y \text{ and } z)$	The probability of y *or* z or both occurring is equal to the probability of y plus the probability of z minus the probability of both y and z.
Bayes's theorem $P(y/z) = \dfrac{P(z|y) \, P(y)}{P(z)}$	

Mathematicians agree completely on the validity of the probability axioms in table 4.1 and have relatively little difficulty assigning probabilities to simple, repeatable events. One might get the impression, then, that probability theory is a strictly "objective" academic discipline. In fact, however, just as value can be either objective or subjective, so can probability. Savage (1954) suggests that all probability is "personal" or subjective.

The reasons for the controversial distinction between objective and subjective probability are intriguing. No one doubts that objective probability exists in the world beyond our senses; the question is how do we get at it. The commonly used formula for estimating probability is

$$\text{Probability of an outcome} = \frac{\text{Frequency of that outcome}}{\text{Total number of cases}}$$

We are essentially looking at past experience and assuming that such will hold true in the future. For example, if we toss a coin in the air 50 times and notice that it lands "heads" on 26 occasions, we can use the above formula to calculate the probability of coming up with heads on our next toss as 26/50 or .52. This figure would be an estimate of "objective" probability.

But now let us use a different coin. Does our probability estimate remain the same or close to it? In simple problems such as a coin toss, it might be safe to assume so; the principle of insufficient reason tells us that we have no cause for doubting a probability of .5. Unfortunately, the principle of insufficient reason is a poor way to fix belief. Because we have no proof that the Loch Ness monster is a hoax does not mean that it in fact exists. Although the manipulation of probabilities (that is, their addition and multiplication) follows very rigorous rules, the initial assignment of probabilities can be largely speculative, hence subjective.

In the coin toss event, our subjective estimate of .5 will undoubtedly correspond quite well to the objective probability of the event. And because the coin toss event is easily repeatable, we can perform an experiment to confirm or disprove our subjective estimate. Similarly, life insurance companies can turn to large actuarial tables to determine the likelihood of various events in the population at large. But many of the events that concern us as individuals in everyday life are simply not repeatable. Thus to speak of the probability of a particular marriage partner being suitable for us may be stretching the concept of probability beyond its logical boundaries.

We generally attach probability statements to these sorts of events by culling our individual experiences. Because we have all had different experiences, however, we are likely to come up with differing estimates. The "subjectivity" of probability here is unavoidable. And even if we all had the same experiences, there is still the problem of determining which experiences ought to be fed into our formula. For example, suppose I am managing a baseball team in the world series. My team is behind two runs in the top of the ninth inning, so I want to send in a pinch hitter who has the greatest chance of getting a hit or at least arriving safely on base. Hitter A has a .275 batting average, hitter B, a .250 average. On the basis of this information, I might send in hitter A rather than hitter B because my subjective probabilities are that he has a greater chance than hitter B of arriving safely. Such a choice might be unwise for any of the following reasons:

1. Hitter B draws a good many more walks than hitter A.
2. Hitter A's batting average has been steadily declining over the past few months. Hitter B's has been improving.
3. Hitter A does not do as well against left-handed pitching, with this particular team, or in away games as hitter B.

All these factors (and many more) could be included in a newly calculated "recent-on-base-under-certain-conditions average," but my sample of similar events may be so small that it yields a very unreliable probability estimate. Furthermore, there is no objective way of including my subjective estimate that in a world series game this particular rookie, hitter A, is more likely to get flustered and perform poorly in comparison to hitter B, a seasoned professional.

Essentially, then, there is no difficulty in assigning probabilities to simple repeatable events such as the flipping of coins and the rolling of dice. But for the more complex or nonrepeatable events of life our probability estimates must be considered subjective.

The notion of subjective probability literally opens a Pandora's box of problems. For example, objective probability is bounded by a scale of 0 to 1. One of the axioms tells us that the probability of an event and the probability of its nonoccurrence must sum to 1. Yet working backward from decisions already made, it is clear that the betting behavior of many individuals is not constrained by such logical conventions. For example, human beings are apt to estimate their chances of winning and losing as each being greater than .5 (Edwards, 1954, 1961).

If it is possible for us to gather new information, Bayes's theorem provides us with a partial way out of this dilemma. Bayes was an eighteenth-century English clergyman whose controversial theorem can be proved or derived using the axioms in table 4.1. Bayes's theorem suggests that the more information we have about objective probability, the greater the likelihood of agreement between that objective probability estimate and our own subjective probability estimate. Two individuals flipping bent coins, for example, and differing widely in their preflip estimates of the probability of heads will after several flips be in relatively close agreement—with themselves as well as with objective probability.

Permutations of Value and Probability

Value and probability are the basic components of classical decision theory. All models of how we make or ought to make decisions rest on the interplay between one of the following four possible permutations of objective and subjective value and probability.

Objective Value and Objective Probability

Since the days of Bernoulli and Pascal no one has seriously argued that people do in fact make decisions on the basis of objective value and objective probability. We know of very few objective values, and the instances where we can properly speak of objective probability are equally restrictive. This does not mean we should not act on the basis of such information but rather that we do not usually have it and even when we do it does not account for our behavior very well.

Objective Value and Subjective Probability

Although this value-probability permutation is conceptually possible, it is insignificant in a practical sense. The study of objective value gave way to utility long before the notion of subjective probability was formally explicated. I mention this model here only for the sake of completeness.

Subjective Value (Utility) and Objective Probability

The combination of utility and objective probability has been termed the "expected utility maximization model." In their classic text on game theory, VonNeumann and Morgenstern (1947) defended this model and popularized it. However, as statisticians became less confident about the existence of objective probability (for example, Savage, 1954) and as data that did not fit this model began to accumulate, attention shifted to another permutation.

Subjective Value (Utility) and Subjective Probability

Edwards (1954, 1961) has asserted that people make decisions on the basis of utility and subjective probability. He has labeled this permutation "the subjectively expected utility maximization model" (abbreviated as the SEU model). Most current work in formal decision theory and research occurs within the context of this model.

Decision-Making Rules

In Riskless Decisions

A decision maker is by definition someone who is faced with the task of choosing between several alternatives. Each alternative will result in the realization of various objective or subjective values. When a decision maker knows in advance which values will occur, he or she is confronted with what is known as a "riskless decision." "Riskless" is defined not as lack of danger but rather as certainty of outcome. In riskless decisions the probabilities attached to each value all equal 1, hence the mathematics and number of decision-making rules are greatly simplified.

Assume it is raining outside. Our choice is to go outside and certainly get wet or to stay inside and remain absolutely dry. If the state of being dry has more utility than the state of being wet, our choice is obvious: *We act in order to maximize utility;* we stay inside. Utility, however, is a fickle concept that changes with circumstances. We might be young and in love and the prospect of going outside with our steady and catching raindrops on our tongues has more utility than the option of staying inside under the not-disinterested eyes of our parents. Our choice is obvious here, too, unless our parents are certain to raise such a fuss that the total utility of going outside is now less than the total utility of staying inside. Although the utilities will vary with individuals and situations, the basic rule in riskless decision making is to act in such a way as to maximize utility.

Maximization of utility is equivalent to minimization of negative utility, a perhaps more accurate description of some choice situations. We might dislike going outside and getting wet but would do so in a hurry if our house were on fire. Being wet has less negative utility than being burned.

The foregoing examples involved the concept of utility or subjective value. An alternate rule in riskless decision making might be to act in such a way as to maximize objective value. But because there are remarkably few, if any, objective values, this rule must remain on the shelf for the time being.

In Risky Decisions

Although many counseling problems involve riskless decisions, the bulk of decision theory concerns decisions made at risk. Risky decisions are those in which the values realized by the selection of a particular alternative are not certain, that is, their probabilities are less than 1. Maximization of *expected* utility is the primary rule in risky decisions.

To illustrate, assume that Debbie and Gail are roommates and confidantes. Fred would like to ask either one out on a date. Although Fred is more interested in Gail than Debbie, he believes that Debbie is more likely to accept his invitation. Past experience has proved to Fred that he cannot ask both. If he is rejected by the first, he will undoubtedly be rejected by the second. Should the first accept, the second will inevitably decline. Fred must make a risky decision, so he adopts the maximization of expected utility rule.

First he assigns utilities to Gail and Debbie. On a 1 to 10 scale Gail has the edge at 8; Debbie checks in at 7. Based on the vibrations Fred gets in casual conversations with both girls, Fred then estimates the probabilities for each girl accepting his offer. Gail seems a bit aloof; Debbie appears neutral. So Fred estimates his chances for success as .4 and .5 respectively. Expected utilities are calculated by multiplying the utilities by the subjective probabilities. Gail's expected utility is .32; Debbie's is .35. The maximization of expected utility rule demands that Fred extend an invitation to Debbie.

Suboptimization

Maximization of utility or expected utility are sometimes referred to as "optimizing" strategies. At first blush strategies that do not imply optimization might appear to be irrational. In some instances, however, it has been argued that optimization is neither possible nor desirable. Before making the first move in chess, for example, one would have to identify and evaluate the outcomes of 10^{120} move combinations (Eastman, 1972). Optimizing strategies that require the processing of large amounts of information can easily overload our psychological circuitry, causing our cognitive computers to blow a fuse. Miller (1956) points out that the human capacity for processing information is 7 ± 2 relevant categories. "Information inundation can be quite as debilitating as information scarcity" (Miller & Starr, 1967, p. 62).

Simon (1960) introduced the concept of "bounded rationality"—a sort of selective ignoring—as the appropriate way to process impossibly large amounts of data. To do otherwise would be irrational rationality! Whether or not decision makers ought to strive for optimization is a matter of debate. The observation that human beings often do not optimize, however, is widely accepted. Thus suboptimizing strategies are often considered rational. A satisfying strategy (see Simon, 1960), for example, is demonstrated by the investment entrepreneur who simply selects an alternative that will yield an advantageous return rather than comparing this particular alternative with all possible investment opportunities. To facilitate acceptance of change in a bureaucracy, administrators often opt for a series of incremental satisfying decisions rather than push for a radical optimizing strategy.

Part of this controversy appears to evolve from a misunderstanding, or at least a restrictive definition of utility. It is certainly not dollar value. If we keep in mind General Bullmoose's famous dictum, "Time is money," the distinction between optimizing and satisfying begins to blur. The investment entrepreneur who seizes upon an opportunity for a 20 percent return may be optimizing to a greater extent than a hypercautious colleague who commits vast amounts of time investigating alternatives that at best might yield a negligibly higher return.

In Uncertain Decisions

In riskless decisions the probabilities are equal to 1; in risky decisions they are less than 1. But in both cases they are *known*. Thus the maximization of utility and expected utility rules are easily applied and defended. What rule should the decision maker adopt when the probabilities of obtaining various utilities are unknown? The *maximin* rule dictates that we select the alternative with the largest minimum payoff. This rule makes sense in two-person games in which your opponent is out to get you. It is also the rule of choice if we sincerely believe in Murphy's law ("If something can go wrong, it will") and O'Toole's commentary on Murphy's law ("Murphy was an optimist"). However in other situations *maximin* can be disadvantageous. For example, if it were applied in a risky decision, the certainty of making a dollar would be judged superior to the 90 percent chance of making one hundred dollars and losing nothing.

Although *maximin* pessimistically assumes that the worst will happen when the probabilities are unknown, *maximax* optimistically dictates that we select the alternative with the largest maximum payoff. Hurwicz (cited in Fishburn, 1966; Miller & Starr, 1967) suggested qualifying this choice with a "coefficient of optimism" wherein "1" and "0" would be tantamount to complete optimism and pessimism, respectively.

There are a variety of other rules pertinent to the making of uncertain decisions to which Fishburn (1966) and Miller and Starr (1967) have written very lucid introductions. If we recall the concept of subjective probability, however, the distinction between risky and uncertain decisions may be academic. In real life we are rarely if ever certain or uncertain about the probabilities of receiving utilities from the alternatives placed before us.

Thus, when confronted with a seemingly uncertain decision, the SEU model would suggest culling our pertinent experiences, affixing probability estimates according to our best "guesstimate," and then adopting the maximization of expected utility rule.

Interrelationships Between the SEU Model and Other Psychological Theories

Classical decision theory did not emerge in an isolated academic vacuum. Its subject matter is human behavior, specifically the study of why certain responses are selected when others are possible. As such it has much in common with other psychological theories. Feather (1959) has provided an illuminating cross-reference between the language of the SEU model and major theoretical constructs in the work of Atkinson (1957), Lewin (1943; also Lewin, Dembo, Festinger, & Sears, 1944), Tolman (1955), and Rotter (1954). Because much of this material is of only historical interest and marginal relevance, it will not be reviewed here. The reader will note in table 4.2, however, that these other psychological theories contemporaneous with

TABLE 4.2. Cross-reference of the SEU model with other psychological theories

Theorist	Concepts	Resultant
Edwards	Subjective probability x utility	SEU
Atkinson	Expectancy x (motive x incentive value)	Resultant motivation
Lewin	Subjective probability x valence	Force (weighted valence)
Rotter	Expectancy and reinforcement value	Behavior potential
Tolman	Expectation, need-push, valence	Performance vector

Source: Adapted from N. T. Feather, "Subjective probability and decision under uncertainty," *Psychological Review* 66 (1959), pp. 150-64. Copyright 1959 by the American Psychological Association. Reprinted by permission.

early work on the SEU model used similar concepts in explaining choice behavior. Apparently the SEU model has prevailed, probably because of its theoretical parsimony.

Utility is sometimes referred to as benefit or gain. Synonyms for negative utility are cost, risk, and loss. Highly relevant to this book are the numerous conceptual similarities that exist between the languages of classical decision theory and behavioral counseling. Utility and reinforcement, for example, have a number of common properties. Varying amounts of utility or reinforcement may accrue from the choice of a particular alternative. But negative utility or punishment can occur as well. Utilities differ with individuals; so does the designation of what is reinforcing or punishing. In riskless decisions a given amount of utility is certain. The same is true with reinforcement delivered on a continuous schedule. In decisions made at risk the probability of utility resulting is less than 1, as is the probability of reinforcement on an intermittent schedule. A strong relationship undoubtedly exists between our subjective probability estimates and the kind of reinforcement schedule we have been exposed to in the course of our lives.

There are other commonalities between the SEU model and behavioral counseling. Although conceptually classical decision theory permits a decision to exist prior to its implementation, in point of fact SEU researchers confirm their hypotheses by observing subsequent behavior. Behavioral research likewise focuses on the response alternative selected in the context of prevailing utilities. It would thus appear that although the languages of classical decision theory and behaviorism are considerably different, their subject matter is similar. Myriad direct translations can be readily made (see Lea, 1978). Progress in the development of each perspective could probably be enhanced by a dialogue between the two camps. For example, SEU researchers might learn much about the formation of irrational utility by studying the work of behaviorists. Clients of behaviorists, in turn, would be less likely to make a poor choice if their counselors had more than a passing acquaintance with classical decision theory.

Summary

Classical decision theory rests on the concepts of value and probability. Value refers to the desirability of an outcome or object and closely resembles the behavioral concept of positive reinforcement; negative value corresponds to punishment and indicates an outcome or object is undesirable. Values may be either objective (numbers representing physical quantities, for example) or subjective (numbers representing any individual's preferences). Subjective value is known as utility. Utilities vary with individuals and situations. Although economic theory has had much to say on how utilities ought to be measured, personal decision making is best facilitated by utilities quantified by simple self-report scales.

Probability refers to the likelihood that a given event will occur. To avoid the ambiguities inherent in using words to describe probability, mathematicians have developed a symbolic language that gives the appearance of an objective discipline. But the assignment of probabilities to the nonrepeatable events that characterize human decision making must be considered a subjective process.

All classical decision-making models are based on the interaction between four possible permutations of objective and subjective value and probability, but only one permutation—subjective value and subjective probability (known as the SEU model)—is given serious consideration today.

In riskless decisions (where the outcomes are certain) maximization of utility is the appropriate decision-making rule. In risky decisions (where the probabilities are less than 1) maximization of expected utility is the primary rule. Because some decisions may require the processing of impossibly large amounts of information, suboptimizing strategies (such as simply selecting an advantageous alternative) may be appropriate. In uncertain decisions (where the probabilities of obtaining various utilities are unknown) either the *maximin* or *maximax* rules may be applied, depending upon the degree of optimism or pessimism felt by the decision maker. Because probability estimation for nonrepeatable events is a subjective process, the distinction between risky and uncertain decisions may be academic. The SEU model calls for culling our pertinent experiences, affixing probability estimates according to our best "guesstimate," and adopting the maximization of expected utility rule.

Classical decision theory has much in common with other psychological theories, particularly the language of behavioral counseling. The next chapter illustrates the SEU model with a number of decision-making concerns, identifies some problematic assumptions of this model, and discusses alternative perspectives currently receiving attention.

5

Current Topics in Decision Theory

Classical decision theory continues to nourish considerable scholarly activity in fields such as administrative science, business economics, and operations research. Unfortunately, relatively few of these academic endeavors pertain to the conduct of counseling. The reader is invited to get the "big picture" from exhaustive reviews by Becker and McClintock (1967), Rapoport and Wallsten (1972), and Slovac, Fischhoff, and Lichtenstein (1977). Lest we wander too far afield, this chapter will be highly selective in the choice of topics discussed. Initially, I will explore recent attempts to apply the SEU model to several counseling concerns. Next I will point out some problematic assumptions that have caused the SEU model to undergo assault from a number of directions. As an alternative to the SEU perspective, Janis and Mann (1977) have developed the conflict model of decision making, which draws heavily from the literature of information processing and social psychology. Their work merits extensive coverage; particularly relevant are the intervention strategies they recommend. Finally, I will briefly review Greenwald's (1973) direct decision therapy, which apparently emerged outside the formal study of decision making.

Clinical Illustrations of the SEU Model

There have been numerous recent attempts to interpret such clinical problems as cigarette smoking, compulsive neurosis, criminal behavior, and occupational choice and their resolution in the language of classical decision theory. It is too early to judge whether these translations will improve treatment programming. At present most of these academic excursions traverse on long theoretical highways through widely scattered and impoverished towns of data.

Cigarette Smoking

Mausner (1973) points out that there is a puzzling discrepancy between the extreme difficulty counselors find in helping people quit smoking and the fact that some twenty-nine million individuals have given up the habit without professional assistance. This discrepancy led him to explore decision-making processes in smoking cessation apart from the study of treatment programming (see also Mausner & Platt, 1971; Vinokur, 1971). In one study Mausner (1973) examined the relevance of the SEU model by means of a psychometric pretest. Essentially all subjects were asked to indicate the value they placed on a wide variety of outcomes pertaining to smoking or not smoking. They were also instructed to give an estimate of their expectation that these outcomes would occur if they continued to smoke or if they stopped. Thus Mausner was able to calculate SEUs for smoking and not smoking on all subjects before treatment.

Mausner found that those subjects who reduced their smoking by half a pack or more following treatment had significantly higher SEUs for stopping than those subjects whose smoking behavior remained unchanged. In contrast, no differences emerged between the two groups on SEUs for continuing to smoke. Mausner concluded that "people make the decision to stop smoking not because they have a fear of the consequences of continuing to smoke, but because they have an increased expectation of benefits from stopping" (1973, p. 120). (It is interesting to note that weight loss and dental hygiene decisions may be governed by similar expectations. See Evans, Rozelle, Lasater, Dembroski, and Allen, 1970; Horan, Baker, Hoffman, and Shute, 1975; Horan, Smyers, Dorfman, and Jenkins, 1975.)

Mausner's (1973) study can be criticized on a variety of methodological grounds. Reduction was defined by self-report; there was no follow-up, and verified abstinence was not a criterion (see Horan, Hacket, and Linberg, 1978; and Horan, Westcott, Vetovich, and Swisher, 1974). Nevertheless, the psychometric pretest, despite its crudity, does suggest that clients' decision-making processes concerning their smoking may influence their responsiveness to treatment programming.

Compulsive Neurosis

Carr (1974, p. 311) defines compulsion as "a recurrent or persistent thought, image, impulse, or action that is accompanied by a sense of subjective compulsion and a desire to resist it." After reviewing a number of deficiencies in various contemporary views of compulsions, he suggests that classical decision theory concepts may be relevant. In the first place, Carr maintains that his own psychophysiological research indicates that compulsive neurotics show abnormally high estimates of the probability that unfavorable events will occur. This probability estimate multiplied by the subjective cost of the event yields an index of threat that the reader will note closely resembles the concept of SEU (subjective probability times utility). Carr then asserts that "compulsive behaviors develop as threat-reducing activities, effective through their lowering of the subjective probability of the unfavorable outcome" (1974, p. 316). In other words, the client chooses compulsive behavior as a strategy for reducing the (erroneously) high likelihood that unpleasant events will follow. This would, of course, suggest that counseling interventions ought to be directed toward lowering these estimates (that is, reducing the disparity between objective and subjective probability). Unfortunately, Carr has few recommendations to make in this regard.

Criminal Behavior

Broadhurst (1976) has neatly summarized Cohen's (1970) contention that criminal behavior can be explained in terms of the SEU model:

Cohen (1970) shows that the criminal decision depends neither on the certainty of being caught nor on the severity of the punishment—both of which can to some extent be estimated from official statistics—but on the interaction of *subjective* probability of being caught, *subjective* probability of punishment if caught and convicted, *subjective* severity of expected punishment, and *subjective* probability of enjoyment of the loot irrespective of discovery, detention, and punishment, making in all a complex SEU . . . .

The criminal offender is taking a gamble, staking his freedom and reputation against his subjective probabilities of gain and punishment, and hence his behavior is susceptible to analysis in decision theory terms (p. 281).

The Broadhurst-Cohen analysis appears quite germane to planned crimes, particularly white-collar crime such as tax evasion and embezzlement wherein the perpetrator has considerable time for deliberation. The SEUs involved in some forms of street crime, however, may be geometrically more complex, unstable, and unmeasurable. A victim's defensive behavior, for example, may produce impulsive criminal aggression that in turn alters the likelihood and severity of punishment. The SEU model assumes the panicky criminal deliberately takes these shifting probabilities and utilities into account.

   In any event, the suggestion that criminal behavior can be explained in terms of classical decision theory has not been fortified by any convincing research data. This omission is largely due to the impractical experimental requirement that a criminal's decision-making processes be tapped prior to the crime. Moreover, it is difficult to conceptualize what forms of counseling intervention might flow from an SEU perspective of illegal activity. If it can be shown that some forms of crime do pay, criminal behavior may appear to be inherently more "rational" than law-abiding behavior.

Occupational Choice

Kaldor and Zytowski (1969) propose that a theory of occupational choice can be derived from the tenets of classical decision theory. They contend that there are three determinants of occupational choice: the chooser's occupational utilities (preferences), the availability of resources (for example, college tuition), and the anticipated consequences of employing given resources in various occupations with differing potential for gratification. One chooses an occupation that allows for maximization of net gain. Kaldor and Zytowski readily acknowledge some crippling limitations of their model. For example, it assumes that the individual has complete knowledge of occupational possibilities, utilities, and consequences. (Counseling strategies others have developed to shore up these assumptions are discussed in subsequent chapters.) Moreover, their model has generated relatively little research activity.

Other Clinical Illustrations

Broadhurst (1976) suggests numerous other applications of formal decision theory to clinical concerns such as abortion, alcoholism, and gambling. In her opinion the future will find us all considering behavior change in terms of utilities and probabilities. My own perspective on the destiny of classical decision theory is less optimistic. Let us now examine why.

Some Problematic Assumptions of the SEU Model

A quick reading of basic decision theory literature might leave the impression that here is a very relevant technology, the application of which has been shamefully neglected by counselors who are in the business of helping people arrive at decisions. Such an accusation, however, would be at most only partly correct because some assumptions of classical decision theory seem to defy application.

One assumption, for example, concerns the generation of possible alternatives to a decision-making problem. Decision theory leaves no room for what might loosely be called creativity (behaviorists prefer to speak of new or novel responses). The process by which we arrive at viable alternatives is ignored; classical decision theory demands that all possible alternatives already be at hand. In practice, however, the generation of possible alternatives requires a substantial amount of counselor time and effort. Many clients are not even aware that the stress they are experiencing can be operationally defined as a choice problem much less have any idea of the options open to them.

Decision theory also requires that the alternatives be independent; that is, the utilities and probabilities of one alternative (or a new alternative) should not influence another alternative. In real life, however, this may not always hold true. Generally, I prefer prime rib to shrimp, and I will invariably order it from a list of edible alternatives. But if I should notice only one beef entry on a menu laden with fish specialities, my choice is very likely to change.

The concept of transitivity has also been a problem for decision theory. Transitivity means that my preferences can be ordered. If I prefer to marry Susan over Rachel and Rachel over Laura, then logically I must prefer Susan over Laura. Yet May (1954) conducted an experiment of this nature in which 27 percent of the subjects gave intransitive choice triads; Lauras were preferred to Susans!

Furthermore, decision theory does not deal with the problem of maladaptive utility formation. For example, peer influence strongly contributes to the development of favorable drug attitudes (Horan, 1973e; Stone & Shute, 1976) and thus ultimately to the ingestion of illegal drugs. In the language of decision theory, a youth might decide to take drugs partly because of an inordinately high utility assigned to peer approval. Classical decision theory assumes that one's utilities are rational and ought not be tampered with. Yet all counseling theorists acknowledge the pervasive problem of self-defeating utilities (that is, values or secondary reinforcers) in various client populations.

Decision theory acknowledges the existence of "probability preferences," but again without comment as to their origin or rationality. Edwards (1954) has shown that individuals strongly prefer low probabilities of losing large amounts of money to high probabilities of losing small amounts of money. Unless this quirk of human nature is genetically determined, we must assume it is learned. One could undoubtedly blow a theoretical bubble out of the laws and schedules of reinforcement to account for such preferences, but I am loath to do so. Probability preferences are useful in explaining why people make a decision, but they can muddy the water in terms of which decision ought to be made.

We not only prefer certain probabilities to others, but our species also errs in probability estimation. Preston and Baratta (1948) found that individuals not privy to objective probability information consistently over-estimated low probabilities and underestimated high probabilities. It would thus appear that barring another genetic predisposition, our probability-estimating behavior is very much subject to the laws of learning. And depending upon what kind of reinforcement schedule we have been exposed to, these estimates might well be consistently erroneous and thus lead to maladaptive decision making.

A final difficulty also arises from the probability component in decision theory, namely, the potentially wide variance between objective and subjective probability. If our client was considering marriage to a thrice-divorced current alcoholic, we would no doubt assume that our client's subjective-probability-for-future-happiness estimate differs from a probability estimate we might assign. On the other hand, who knows that situation better than our client? We are "wrong" in our subjective probability estimates only if we fail to react to new information via Bayes's theorem; initial estimates by clients or counselors are neither defensible nor refutable. Cohen and Hansel (1958) have shown that subjective probabilities are very much influenced by age and experience. But the packaging of age and experience for delivery to the decision-making client remains a problem for the counselor. Other assaults on the SEU model are lucidly discussed by Fishburn (1972).

The Conflict Model of Decision Making

Apart from the problematic assumptions of the SEU model, which diminish its relevance to counseling, it might also be said that classical decision theory provides a highly reductionistic view of how we make—or ought to make—decisions. The theory is not necessarily "wrong," but further explication of its key concepts could enchance its usefulness. What factors, for example, underlie our assignment of utility values to the consequences of various alternatives? Under what conditions do these values shift or solidify? Why do we ignore pertinent information? And why do we make irrational decisions?

Various fields of inquiry have much to say in response to these questions. Studies in attitude change (Brehm, 1968; McGuire, 1960, 1969), cognitive dissonance (Festinger, 1957), conformity (Asch, 1952), and commitment (Kiesler, 1971) are particularly pertinent. Janis and Mann (1968, 1977) have developed a theory of decision making that draws heavily on this literature. They have labeled their work "a conflict model of decision making." The distinction between hot and cold decisions, the concept of vigilant information processing, and several coping patterns in deciding are major theoretical components of their model. I will briefly review these components before turning to their very important work on the development of intervention strategies for decision-making counseling.

Hot and Cold Decisions

"Cold" decisions are made in a calm detached state. Utility values are generally low and easy to calculate. The choice of a bank in which to open a checking account or what to wear on a routine day at the office, for example, would rarely be expected to evoke strong emotions. Such decisions are easily fitted into the language of classical decision theory discussed in the last chapter. In contrast, Abelson (1963) speaks of "hot cognitions"—those aroused by vital concerns such as health and safety. Janis and Mann (1977) believe their conflict model of decision making is particularly pertinent to decisions made in the presence of hot cognitions, "when human beings are required to make decisions on highly ego-involving issues" (p. 46). Hot decisions occur in the context of stress; utility values are generally high and difficult to calculate. Examples might include one's choice of career, marriage partner, or medical intervention for a serious illness.

As with temperature conditions in the physical sciences, the terms "hot" and "cold" applied to decisions reflect differences in degree rather than process. The language of classical decision theory still applies to hot decisions. Utility, by definition, is subjective value. Hot cognitions simply make utility more volatile from the standpoint of measurement. Janis and Mann's emphasis on hot cognition, however, underscores their concern with vital personal decision making rather than the artificial or trivial sort that seems to typify much experimental work in this area.

Vigilant Information Processing

Janis and Mann (1977) have postulated seven procedural criteria they consider necessary for making "high-quality" decisions. Their notion of a quality decision bears a strong resemblance to the concept of effective or adaptive decision making introduced in chapter 1. Recall that the adaptiveness of a decision depends upon the behaviors that precede the decision rather than the events that follow it. Janis and Mann characterize the orientation of an individual meeting all seven of the following criteria as "vigilant information processing":*

The decision maker to the best of his ability and within his information-processing capabilities

1. thoroughly canvasses a wide range of alternative courses of action;
2. surveys the full range of objectives to be fulfilled and the values implicated by the choice;
3. carefully weighs whatever he knows about the costs and risks of negative consequences, as well as the positive consequences, that could flow from each alternative;
4. intensively searches for new information relevant to further evaluation of the alternatives;
5. correctly assimilates and takes account of any new information or expert judgment to which he is exposed, even when the information or judgment does not support the course of action he initially prefers;

---

*Use of the word "vigilance" in the context of decision and stress occurred before the work of Janis and Mann. Broadbent (1971), for example, devotes two full chapters to its explication. Most of this material, however, deals with advanced topics in perceptual psychology, particularly signal detection theory, one of the many subspecialties of decision making of marginal relevance to counseling.

6. reexamines the positive and negative consequences of all known alternatives, including those originally regarded as unacceptable, before making a final choice;
7. makes detailed provisions for implementing or executing the chosen course of action, with special attention to contingency plans that might be required if various known risks were to materialize. (p. 12)

Vigilant information processing is not an all-or-nothing affair. Janis and Mann suggest that each of these criteria could be considered as an item on a scale with a possible rating of, say, from 0 to 10. "Thus if a decision maker focuses exclusively on one course of action that someone recommends, spends no time at all thinking about what the alternatives might be, and asks no one in his social network to suggest alternatives, his score on the first criterion would be zero" (1977, p. 12). Failure to display a vigilant information-processing orientation would be reflected by a low rating on each of the seven criteria. Higher scores suggest varying degrees of vigilance. A major tenet of the conflict model is that such vigilance scores are predictive of postdecisional satisfaction or regret.

The seven criteria for vigilant information processing represent a fairly practical synthesis of what has been written about how to make a good decision. Most such formulations, however, rest on only face validity; that is, what has been postulated seems reasonable, but data existing beyond the theoretician's armchair has not or cannot be collected. Janis and Mann's suggestion that the behaviors preceding a decision can be quantified and related to postdecisional outcomes poses exciting research possibilities. The work, however, remains to be done.

Coping Patterns in Deciding

One of the most interesting features of the conflict model is its graphic depiction of coping patterns underlying our rational and irrational decisions. Psychological stress, resulting from the prospect of losing or failing to gain utility, is a hingepin variable. Extremely low stress or extremely high stress is likely to produce defective information processing; intermediate levels of stress, on the other hand, permit vigilant information processing.

Stress occurs whenever we are confronted with negative feedback or positive opportunities. Stress or lack of it breeds five basic patterns of coping, four of which often result in defective decision making: (1) *Unconflicted adherence* follows the decision maker's evaluation that the risks for not changing are negligible. Because little or no stress has been generated, the decision maker does not become vigilant in appraising the situation. (2)

Unconflicted change may result when the decision maker recognizes that the risks are high for not changing and low for changing. Some stress is generated and a choice is made without a thorough canvassing of the alternatives. (3) *Defensive avoidance* exists when the decision maker believes the risks for changing and not changing are both serious and further believes that prospects for finding a good solution are unrealistic. Stress is high and pursuit of new possibilities is prematurely curtailed. (4) *Hypervigilance* is akin to panic. The risks for changing and not changing are serious. Although a good solution may exist, the decision maker feels there is insufficient time to find it. Stress is high and an alternative is hastily selected without careful consideration of possible consequences. (5) *Vigilance*, in contrast to the first four coping patterns, will often result in effective decisions. The risks for changing and not changing are high, but the decision maker feels there is hope for and sufficient time to find a satisfactory solution. Stress is moderate and an alternative is selected only after a thorough search and appraisal. Figure 5.1 depicts the five patterns of deciding and the conditions leading to them.

In order to assist individuals with decision-making concerns, Janis and Mann and their associates have developed a number of intervention strategies and culled several others from the social psychology literature. These interventions are grouped into two categories: strategies for challenging outworn decisions and strategies for improving the quality of decision making.

Challenging Outworn Decisions

Janis and Mann recommend five intervention strategies for challenging outworn decisions. The first four are cognitive confrontations; the last is an emotional confrontation. Properly speaking, these are for the most part attitude-change procedures rather than decision-making counseling techniques and are relevant only insofar as they can be useful in changing poor decisions presently in effect.

Socratic Dialoguing. McGuire (1960) maintained that our cognitive superstructures are assembled in such a way that inconsistent thoughts can be neatly tucked away in separate compartments. Socratic dialoguing involves asking a person to state how he or she feels, believes, and behaves with regard to a particular topic and why. McGuire reported that the procedure causes people to display more logical consistency. The counseling implications are obvious. Counselors who encourage clients to verbalize their thoughts about particular topics or decisions presumably should also foster increased cognitive consistency. Ironically, this phenomenon has not

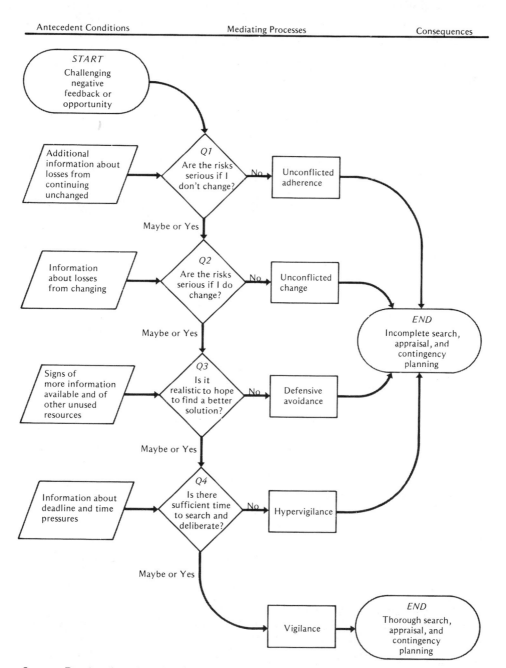

Source: Reprinted with permission of Macmillan Publishing Co., Inc. from *Decision making: A psychological analysis of conflict, choice, and commitment* by Irving L. Janis and Leon Mann. Copyright © 1977 by The Free Press a Division of Macmillan Publishing Co., Inc.

FIGURE 5.1. Conflict model of decision making

received any analog research attention in the counseling literature despite many counselors' widely professed allegience to "talking out cures."

Insight Induction. Katz, Sarnoff, and McClintock (1956) developed a two-stage process for shifting prejudice. First they provide subjects with information on how prejudice develops; then they "force insight" by presenting a case history of a student demographically similar to the subjects and illustrating how prejudicial attitudes were formed in the course of this student's life. Whether insight or modeling-plus-experimenter-demands causes the attitude shift is, of course, debatable. This procedure has much in common with the modeling research discussed in chapters 2, 3, and 9. For the moment, suffice it to say that counselors who present models of faulty decision making may cause clients to question the adequacy of their own decision making, especially if the faulty models suffer adverse consequences.

Induced Cognitive Dissonance. According to Festinger (1957) dissonance between two cognitions is psychologically distressing. Dissonance exists when "the obverse of one element would follow from the other" (p. 13). Individuals experiencing such a disparity are motivated to seek a state of consonance, which can be achieved by making their cognitive, affective, and motor behaviors consistent with each other. Rokeach (1971) has observed that dissonance can be induced by exposing "a person to information designed to make him consciously aware of states of inconsistency that exist chronically within his own value-attitude system below the level of his conscious awareness" (p. 453). Theoretically, either the value or the decision could change; but according to Rokeach, because "values are determinants of attitudes as well as behavior," (p. 471), the latter occurrence would be expected.

Rokeach has produced some rather impressive decreases in racial prejudice with this technique. Moreover, induced cognitive dissonance has caused student drug attitudes to become more conservative (Swisher & Horan, 1972). If we look at Rokeach's concept of value from the perspective of utility, the phenomenon is readily explainable by the SEU model of decision making: We select alternatives with the highest utility-probability product. Should we discover new utilities inherent in other alternatives, our decisions are likely to change. In practical terms, if a counselor can identify an unknown or at least unverbalized value (reinforcer) present in a given client that is inconsistent with the holding of an outmoded decision, the decision will be effectively challenged.

The Awareness-of-Rationalizations Technique. Reed and Janis (1974) developed this procedure to make smokers aware of their self-defeating excuses for persisting in their decision to smoke. Essentially, eight common rationalizations are presented to smokers one at a time (for example, "It really hasn't been proven that cigarette smoking is a cause of lung cancer"). Interviewers then ask the smokers a number of questions designed to uncover the tendency to rely on each such excuse. Once the rationalization tendency is exposed, the subjects are given didactic information refuting their rationalizations.

Reed and Janis report that the procedure resulted in changed attitudes about smoking; however, their behavioral data, which would imply changed decisions about smoking as well, are difficult to interpret and unconvincing. The reader may have noticed that the awareness-of-rationalizations technique bears a strong resemblance to independently developed cognitive behavioral counseling procedures discussed in chapter 3. Under the name of cognitive restructuring, it serves as a treatment component in various comprehensive behavioral programs (for example, Hackett & Horan, 1977; Mahoney, 1973).

Emotional Confrontations Via Role Playing. This procedure evolved from Janis and Mann's observation that ineffective decisions can change after a dramatic emotion-arousing experience. Relatives of lung-cancer patients, for example, often realize their own personal vulnerability and quit smoking. Most of the work on emotional role playing has also occurred in the context of smoking decisions. Essentially, the technique requires that heavy smokers play the role of persons told by their physicians that they have lung cancer. The procedure is strikingly similar to another independently developed technique known as covert sensitization (see chapter 3) except that the soliloquies are generated by the client rather than the counselor.

Theoretically, one might argue that emotional role playing may be more powerful than covert sensitization because it allows for increased relevance and less "tuning out" of the aversive image. Kazdin's (1975) modification of covert modeling, which calls for clients to describe their imagery aloud, is also procedurally similar. Although a variety of studies (for example, Mann, 1967; Mann & Janis, 1968) suggest that emotional role playing is effective in changing smokers' attitudes, again the behavioral data on smoking reduction, although statistically significant, has not been clinically or operationally impressive by today's standards (see Horan, Hackett, & Linberg, 1978). Toomey's (1972) study provides a faint degree of support for the use of emotional role playing in challenging the drinking decisions of chronic alcoholics.

Improving the Quality of Decision Making

The foregoing interventions are designed to jolt clients out of poor deci-
sional ruts. Janis and Mann (1977) suggest three other techniques for helping clients become vigilant information processors on the road to
high-quality decision making.

Balance Sheeting. Balance sheet procedures in decision making really
date back to the "moral algebra" of Benjamin Franklin described in chapter
1. Many variations of this theme exist, some of which will be covered in
subsequent chapters. The Janis and Mann version involves setting up a grid
for each alternative, as depicted in figure 5.2. In the two columns the counselor and client jointly identify all the positive and negative consequences
(pros and cons) pertaining to the rows, which consist of four utility categories: gains or losses for self, gains or losses for others, self-approval or
disapproval, and social approval or disapproval. Balance sheets such as this
one are widely employed as a means of reducing the possibility of over-
looking important information in decision-making problems.

Most users of the technique accept it on face validity, but Janis and
Mann are to be commended for conducting a series of empirical studies
showing that use of their version of the balance sheet results in reduction of
postdecisional regret and increased adherence to the decision (for example,
Hoyt & Janis, 1975; Mann, 1972). My own clinical experience, however,
suggests that a red flag or two be raised in regard to their choice of utility
categories. Many clients, for example, place an inordinately high value on
social approval, and decisions made in pursuit of this hollow reinforcer
may ultimately prove self-defeating. Moreover, the specific components of
self-approval for other clients may be equally problematic. Nevertheless,
counselors with a sensitivity to the issues underlying the cognitive restructuring procedures discussed in chapter 3 may use this balance sheet quite
effectively.

Outcome Psychodrama. This procedure requires clients to project
themselves into the future and enact scenarios involving the consequences
of having chosen various alternatives. The technique closely resembles
emotional role playing, but instead of being used for challenging outworn
decisions, outcome psychodrama is intended to foster vigilant information
processing prior to choosing. Essentially, clients are stimulated to think
about and vividly experience what would happen if they, for example, got a
divorce or picked a particular career. Janis and Mann report several favorable case study illustrations and suggest that outcome psychodrama can
enhance the effectiveness of the balance sheet procedure by adding new

TYPES OF ANTICIPATION	ALTERNATIVE COURSES OF ACTION					
with examples from research on career conflicts of lawyers	Alternative 1 (e.g., job with Department of Justice)		Alternative 2 (e.g., job with a Wall Street firm)		Alternative 3 (e.g., private practice in a small town)	
	+	−	+	−	+	−

A. Utilitarian gains or losses for self
  1. Personal income
  2. Interest value of daily work
  3. Opportunity to live in a preferred city
    ·
    ·
  n						

B. Utilitarian gains or losses for significant others
  1. Social status for family
  2. Reducing political corruption in community
  3. Advancing civil rights for nation
    ·
    ·
  n						

C. Self-approval or -disapproval
  1. Moral considerations pertaining to ethical legal practices
  2. "Ego ideal" of being an independent thinker
  3. Self-image as defender of innocent people
    ·
    ·
  n						

D. Social approval or disapproval
  1. From wife (or husband)
  2. From close friends
  3. From a national pro-fessional organization
    ·
    ·
  n						

The cells in this schematic grid should be visualized as being filled with positive (+) and negative (−) entries of varying magnitude depicting the strength of the incentives to accept or reject each alternative. The purpose of filling out the grid is to predict vulnerability to subsequent setbacks by identifying the main sources of conflict. Ordinarily the grid is set up with rows representing the alternative courses of action; the rows and columns are reversed in this table in order to list examples of subcategories within each of the four types of anticipations.

Source: Reprinted with permission of Macmillan Publishing Co., Inc. from *Decision making: A psychological analysis of conflict, choice, and commitment* by Irving L. Janis and Leon Mann. Copyright © 1977 by The Free Press a Division of Macmillan Publishing Co., Inc.

FIGURE 5.2. Balance sheet

entries. However, no controlled experimental evaluations of outcome psychodrama, either alone or in conjunction with other techniques, have been carried out.

Emotional Inoculation for Postdecisional Setbacks. The purpose of this procedure is to help clients implement or at least remain committed to a particular alternative after making a vigilant decision. Emotional inoculation (Janis, 1971) involves three steps: (1) calling attention to impending losses and risks (that is, education about the probability of a rough road ahead), (2) encouraging clients to work out ways of reassuring themselves about the ultimate success of the particular alternative (that is, informal coping skills training), and (3) providing new information on how to handle potential setbacks (that is, more education and coping skills training).

The reader will note this technique's very strong resemblance to Meichenbaum's (1972, see also Meichenbaum & Turk, 1976) stress inoculation paradigm, which was reviewed in chapter 3. Except for one interesting study (Langer, Janis, & Wolfer, 1975) emotional inoculation has not been subjected to experimental scrutiny. The utility of stress inoculation, however, is becoming fairly well established (for example, Hackett, Horan, Buchanan, & Zumoff, 1978; Horan, Hackett, Buchanan, Stone, & Demchik-Stone, 1977; Schlichter & Horan, 1978).

Janis and Mann's comprehensive endeavors did not emerge under the rubric of any particular counseling theory. Hence their conflict model of decision making is reviewed here rather than in subsequent chapters devoted to perspectives and procedures with psychoanalytic, existential, rational, or behavioral counseling overtones. Before turning to the work of Greenwald (1973), another independent, it is significant to note that most of the important intervention strategies Janis and Mann recommended or developed are compatible with the emerging cognitive-behavorial point of view.

Greenwald's Direct Decision Therapy

Greenwald's (1973) book entitled *Direct Decision Therapy* arose not from a formal study of decision theory but rather from reflections on his own life and the lives of his patients. Greenwald contends that all problems in living have implicit payoffs. For example, he once asked a young hospitalized psychotic woman what the advantages of being crazy were. "She replied, 'There are lots of advantages.' She then listed the advantages: 1) She never had to worry about a job; 2) She didn't have to worry about dates . . .; 3) She could do and say anything she wanted" (p. 167). Essentially, then, neuroses and psychoses do not just happen upon us. We choose to adopt them because of myriad secondary gains (reinforcers).

Greenwald maintains that the therapy process first involves clarification of whether the client wants to change or remain the same. If the client decides that the payoffs for not changing are no longer adequate, direct decision therapy then proceeds to an exploration of alternatives and consequences. For example, the young psychotic woman mentioned above decided that she wanted to get out of the hospital and asked how she could be released.

I said, "It's easy. All you have to do is act sane. The only difference between you and us [the staff of the hospital] is that you act crazy and we act sane. If you want to get out, act sane."

She was going out on a weekend pass with her family. She said, "I'm going to tell them I'm going to be sane."

I said, "Do you know what will happen?"

She assured me, "They'll be happy."

So I told her, "Don't be so sure. In fact, now they will think you're really crazy." (1973, p. 168)

As is obvious in the case of this young woman, implementation of the decision to change may be difficult. Greenwald thus distinguishes between a wish to change and a decision to change. The latter demands hard work on the part of the client and a good deal of support from the therapist.

It is unfortunate that Greenwald chooses to lace his work with naive assaults on behavioral counseling. In one preposterous example he accuses behavioral counselors of wiring electric shock machines to the refrigerators of obese clients with the unintended outcome "some people get so addicted to the shock that they eat in order to get it" (1973, p. 296). Apart from these occasional lapses in scholarship, however, Greenwald's perspective on how many problems in living occur and become entrenched is highly compatible with the behavioral point of view. Certainly, his description of the reinforcers sustaining the young woman's psychosis could have been written by an ardent behaviorist.

Although Greenwald is correct in underscoring the notion that the decision to change is up to the client (at least outpatient clients), he presents no data to support his contention that a change will occur once such a decision is made. In fact, considerable evidence to the contrary exists. For example, witness the common failures of clients in both control and experimental treatments for weight loss and cigarette addiction in spite of their apparent decisions to change (Lichtenstein & Danaher, 1977; Stunkard & Mahoney, 1976). The effectiveness of Greenwald's model could be dramatically enhanced by supplementing his decision-making orientation with empirically validated techniques for helping clients implement their desired alternatives. Without such ancillary therapeutic activity, Greenwald's direct decision therapy stands as a monumental tautology: Clients change because they have decided to change. If they fail to change, it is because they really have not decided to change. We might wonder what, then, is a decision to change apart from the post hoc occurrence of changed behavior?

SUMMARY

There have been several recent attempts to apply the SEU model to counseling concerns such as cigarette smoking, compulsive neurosis, criminal behavior, and occupational choice; but certain assumptions of the SEU model diminish its relevance to counseling. As an alternative Janis and Mann offer the conflict model, major theoretical components of which include the distinction between hot and cold decisions, the concept of vigilant information processing, and coping patterns in deciding.

The conflict model includes five attitude change strategies for challenging outworn decisions, four of which (Socratic dialoguing, insight induction, induced cognitive dissonance, and the awareness-of-rationalizations technique) are cognitive confrontations and the last (emotional confrontation via role playing) makes use of heavily affective material. Three additional techniques (balance sheeting, outcome psychodrama, and emotional inoculation) focus on helping clients become vigilant information processors and improve the quality of their decision making.

Greenwald's direct decision therapy, based on a widely accepted premise that problems in living have implicit payoffs (reinforcers), initially involves determining whether the client wants to change or remain the same. Greenwald's contention that change will occur once the client decides to change is contraindicated, for example, by research in weight loss and cigarette addiction.

So far in this book we have explored the languages of behavioral counseling and formal decision theory and have seen the compatibility of basic concepts and current work in both fields. In upcoming chapters this perspective will be supplemented with the views of various schools of counseling, but in the next chapter we turn to the pervasive problem of ethics in the conduct of decision-making counseling.

6

Ethical Issues in Decision-Making Counseling

In books on counseling, ethical matters, if discussed at all, are often relegated to a final chapter, almost as a dutiful afterthought. The importance of ethics in decision-making counseling, however, warrants early treatment.

Ethical issues in counseling abound. Topics such as accountability, confidentiality, fees for service, and so forth could easily be included in our ethical discussion. However, my intention is not to cover every possible issue. Readers interested in pursuing a larger perspective might start with the ethical guidelines published by the American Personnel and Guidance Association and the American Psychological Association (APGA, undated; APA, 1967, 1972). Instead, in this chapter I will discuss two questions that are highly relevant to the conduct of decision-making counseling: Is there always a "right" choice? and What are the ethical limits of counselor input in client decisions?

To answer the first question, I will begin by examining the sandy foundations on which ethical models are constructed. From this ground-level viewpoint we shall see that ethical laws are often of limited use in dictating the "right" alternative. It will also be apparent that this question is confounded by the fact that the word "right" has multiple meanings. Many decisions have little to do with ethics and the use of this word simply clouds the fact that the judger and the judged may have differing utilities.

My answer to the second question begins with an observation of the relatively unpublicized problem of intrusive counselor utilities that seem to permeate much of what goes on in the name of counseling. Although behaviorists unjustifiably get much of the blame, no school of counseling is free from this potentially insidious phenomenon. After a brief exploration of counselor input in traditional behavioral counseling and the learning mechanisms for that input, I will offer a few guidelines for the conduct of decision-making counseling. Let us now examine these questions in greater detail.

Is There Always a "Right" Choice?

The attempt to achieve something as close as possible to certain knowledge of right and wrong seems to be the aim of all ethical reflection. We might substitute for this right-wrong dichotomy the concepts good-evil, moral-immoral, valuable-valueless, appropriate-inappropriate, and so forth; semantic antics are irrelevant. No one seems to dispute the desirability of obtaining such knowledge, but there is certainly conflict over who has the pipeline to "the way, the truth, and the light."

The passage from a description of human events to a prescription of ethical conduct is risky. It requires a series of often unwarranted assumptions that even the most cursory examination of ethical evolution would reveal as significantly based on a rather unbalanced blending of maladaptive thinking, religious dogmas, and social lubricants. Differences in the proportion of these components seem to account for the myriad ethical beliefs and opinions that surround us today.

Be that as it may, the ethicist (someone who is vocationally preoccupied with moral matters), first assumes that there is a natural law ("right" way of behaving) or ontological system, which can be approximated in terms of an ethical code through the rigorous application of inductive and deductive processes. This is analogous to the thought pattern of the physical or social scientist who presumes that this is not a universe of chance, that organic and inorganic substances operate according to certain laws, and that knowledge of these laws can be had and organized into some sort of reflectively derived superstructure or model.

The ethicist then begins to formulate a series of "self-evident" primary propositions such as "Goodness consists in the satisfaction of desire" (naturalism), or "Man's ultimate goal is happiness" (Thomistic realism). More links are subsequently added to this deductive chain in the form of secondary and tertiary principles. All of this is done within the bounds of logic and reason; Venn diagrams might even be offered as mathematical proof. The process is fascinating, but why is it that we have such contradictory opinion, for example, on ethical solutions to a problem pregnancy? The answer lies with "that whore—Reason" as Voltaire so aptly described it.

A cornerstone of reasoning (and hence of the model-building process) is the syllogism, which in its simplest form consists of a major premise, a minor premise, and a conclusion. It is perfectly possible to have a totally valid (logical) syllogism with a conclusion that is entirely erroneous because the initial premises are never proven but only assumed to be true. Such is the phenomenon that enables the paranoid to be a paragon of logic.

Physical and social scientists overcome this difficulty by subjecting their models to a simple "truth" criterion, namely, "Does it work?" Models are judged "good" or "bad" by their effectiveness in a strictly pragmatic sense. Thus, if we can show that the explosive metal sodium when combined with the deadly gas chlorine yields the harmless and vital substance called table salt, we have an idea that Dalton's atomic model gives us a pretty "good" (workable) insight into the way things really are. Ethicists have no such criteria; what is "good" or "bad" is only the subjective hunch of what seems reasonable, plausible, or nice.

Ethics in Client Decisions

Given the rather arbitrary foundations of ethical models, it would be folly to assume that we can inductively arrive at immutable ethical generalizations ("natural law") governing all kinds of behavior and thus dictating "right" choices. Every moral principle has its exceptions. For example, "Thou shalt not kill," whether chiseled in stone, induced, or assumed to be self-evident, becomes in practice "Thou shalt not kill" except in defense of oneself, in defense of another, in protection of one's property, in times of war, or in cases of capital punishment.

Moral objections to adultery have been dismissed as arbitrary by a number of mental health professionals in favor of "civilized extramarital adventure" (Ellis, 1973). Nevertheless, our legal system, which in theory reflects the will of the majority, considers adultery unequivocally wrong. Are there exceptions to this principle? To a conservative audience, is adultery ever "right"? Consider the decision of Mrs. Bergmeier:

As the Russian armies drove westward to meet the Americans and British at the Elbe, a Soviet patrol picked up a Mrs. Bergmeier foraging food for her three children. Unable even to get word to the children, and without any clear reason for it, she was taken off to a prison camp in the Ukraine. Her husband had been captured in the Bulge and taken to a POW camp in Wales.

When he was returned to Berlin, he spent weeks and weeks rounding up his children; two (Ilse, twelve, and Paul, ten) were found in a detention school run by the Russians, and the oldest, Hans, fifteen, was found hiding in a cellar near the Alexander Platz. Their mother's whereabouts remained a mystery, but they never stopped searching. She more than anything else was needed to reknit them as a family in that dire situation of hunger, chaos and fear.

Meanwhile, in the Ukraine, Mrs. Bergmeier learned through a sympathetic commandant that her husband and family were trying to keep together and find her. But the rules allowed them to release her for only two reasons: (1) illness needing medical facilities beyond the camp's, in which case she would be sent to a Soviet hospital elsewhere, and (2) pregnancy, in which case she would be returned to Germany as a liability.

She turned things over in her mind and finally asked a friendly Volga German camp guard to impregnate her, which he did. Her condition being medically verified, she was sent back to Berlin and to her family. They welcomed her with open arms, even when she told them how she managed it. When the child was born, they loved him more than all the rest, on the view that little Dietrich had done more for them than anybody.

When it was time for him to be christened, they took him to the pastor on a Sunday afternoon. After the ceremony they sent Dietrich home with the children and sat down in the pastor's study to ask him whether they were right to feel as they did about Mrs. Bergmeier and Dietrich. Should they be grateful to the Volga German? Had Mrs. Bergmeier done a good and right thing?*

The foregoing does not mean that ethical generalizations are irrelevant to a client about to make a decision. The collective judgments of moral philosophers and the wisdom of the ages have more than just minor utility. Fletcher (1966) has articulately argued for a situational approach to ethics in which moral principles are considered valid except when their application would reflect a lack of *agapé* (the New Testament "normative ideal of 'love' " [p. 15]) for our fellow man. Kierkegaard (1954) expressed similar sentiments when he maintained that any break with an ethical universal should be made in "fear and trembling" rather than in the callous arrogance of power. Thus ethical principles are to be taken seriously but not dogmatically.

Essentially, then, ethics is hardly a certain science. Moreover, there is a good deal of debate over what kinds of behavior are to be judged unethical. And finally, even commonly accepted ethical generalizations are subject to exceptions and extenuating circumstances. Thus ethical laws are of limited use in dictating the "right" choice.

---

*From *Situation ethics*, by Joseph Fletcher. Copyright MCMLXVI, W. L. Jenkins. Used by permission of The Westminster Press.

Client Choice Problems Outside the Realm of Ethics

Ethical considerations may or may not be present in client decisions. For example, a terminally ill patient debating suicide would undoubtedly undergo a good deal more ethical introspection than an individual contemplating the choice of wardrobe for a cocktail party. Curiously enough, the English language permits us to use the word "right" to describe an alternative in both of these decisions.

Ethical considerations have little or no bearing on many client decisions. Choice of an academic major or professional career, for example, is basically outside the realm of ethics (unless, of course, an unethical profession like "hit man" is a possibility). To speak of a "right" decision in cases such as these is a misnomer; no moral principles are involved. Other utilities such as making money or pursuing interests rather than "rightness or wrongness" are part of the decision.

The use of the term "right" here apparently represents a concept similar to that of a good decision (that is, a decision with a favorable outcome) discussed in chapter 1. In any event, before such judgments can be made it is important to look at who is doing the judging. For example, Blocher (1974) describes the case of a senior high school girl with a recurring fantasy about setting off on a trip across the country in the company of another girl and implies that this would be a very poor decision. Others might agree, particularly those counselors who feel that students should go right to college. On the other hand, some counselors might argue that the benefits of such a trip would certainly outweigh any slight delay in completing her education. In contrast to such authoritative opinion, has anyone thought to ask the girl (Horan, 1975)? As Herr (1970, p. 3) correctly observes, "The problem is that judgments about whether or not a decision is a 'good' one are typically made not by the chooser but by some external expert. Consequently, such judgments may have no relationship to anything that the decision-maker himself values." Gardner (1965) has succinctly described the dangers of "self-renewal," that is, believing what was good for us must be good for everyone else. In reality who are we to say that a trip is "wrong" and college is "right" for a daydreaming high school senior—or anyone, for that matter?

Whitehead (1938, p. 15) once commented, "The simple-minded use of the notions 'right or wrong' is one of the chief obstacles to the progress of understanding." This remark is particularly pertinent to the conduct of decision-making counseling. Problems of choice permit few if any "right" answers.

What Are the Ethical Limits of Counselor Input in Client Decisions?

My conversion to cognitive-behaviorism came late in my graduate training. I was given a heavy and exclusive dose of orthodox Freudianism in my clinically oriented masters program and during my doctoral work in counseling I became deeply immersed in a sort of Rogerian-Sullivanian existentialism. I have observed that "client manipulation" is not a practice restricted to so-accused "Machiavellian" behaviorists. The issue is every bit as real and, I might add, potentially more insidious, in nonbehavioral approaches to counseling (London, 1967).

Two Personal Vignettes

The first patient assigned to me for a diagnostic workup during my clinical internship at a county mental hospital was a thirty-one-year-old female who might briefly be described as experiencing auditory hallucinations and requiring periodic custodial care for the past decade. The woman's husband had suffered a broken neck and consequent paralysis from the waist down only a few months before her latest admission to the hospital.

My role in her rehabilitation program was to administer a number of projective and psychometric tests and from these data I was supposed to compose what I now believe amounted to an anthropomorphic Freudian fairy tale for the benefit of the attending psychoanalyst, who would probably never read it. In the terms of the prevailing view, "ego" was losing a long-standing battle with "id" and "superego" was trying to prevent my client's recovery. I believe I labeled her a "chronic undifferentiated schizophrenic with paranoid features"; however, such name calling had little to do with understanding her condition.

As luck would have it, this particular patient was brought to the attention of a general staff meeting. Though I was delighted that the attending analyst had in fact read my report, I was totally appalled at his treatment approach. "The basic problem," he began, "is that she's a Catholic. Were she not, she could decide to get a divorce." Then after farming her children out to foster homes, she would be free to frequent the local pubs, where an ample supply of men could be found to fulfill her presently frustrated sexual needs.

In proclaiming that a career of bar hopping was "better" than the job of caring for an invalid husband and children, the analyst revealed a set of ethical values. In cringing at his prescription, I revealed my own. However, the fact that the analyst would in all likelihood covertly attempt to manipulate the client into deciding to abandon her religion and family is much more worthy of comment than our respective differences (Horan, 1974d).

Another rude awakening to the relatively unpublicized problem of intrusive counselor input occurred during a "personal growth group" that I attended early in my career. Group members were predominantly agnostic; there were, however, several active Protestants and Jews. The sole practicing Catholic member volunteered a concern. His wife was an atheist and, having had three children, now wanted to use contraceptives. Though he, too, wanted no more children, he objected to contraceptives on religious grounds. But what was he to do? (The issue of birth control was considerably more troubling to Catholics of a decade ago.)

I watched in utter amazement as Solomon Asch (1952) must have done years before in his conformity-pressure studies. In regard to birth control, the utilities of the group were in complete harmony with those of the wife. After a good deal of anxious squirming, the Catholic member was "led down the road to self-discovery" and found that his "real values" were, after all, similar to those of the group! Recognizing this conversion to the group point of view as such and nothing more, I protested, but apparently not very loudly or at least not convincingly. I have no doubt what the decision would have been had the group been composed of priests and nuns.

Counselor Input in Traditional Behavioral Counseling

Whether we like it or not, human behavior is subject to learning principles that existed long before contemporary behavioral scientists named and described them. Throughout history parents, governments, and religious institutions have attempted to apply these heretofore unnamed principles to influence their charges' behavior. In a sense, then, there is nothing new about the idea of modifying someone's behavior; however, the technology for doing so is rapidly improving.

The application of every counseling theory calls for deliberate counselor-caused changes in client behavior (London, 1967; Skinner, 1971). Few counselors, regardless of their theoretical orientation, would seriously consider their counseling successful if their juvenile delinquent clients continued to steal and be physically assaultive. But the fact that counselors attempt to modify client behavior does not make it ethical to do so without certain constraints. Let us now turn to the issue of counselor input in contemporary behaviorism.

The terms behavior modification, behavior therapy, and behavioral counseling are often used interchangeably. Separate definitions have been suggested but little agreement has resulted (Franzini & Tilker, 1972; Lazarus, 1971). Although the following distinctions may seem arbitrary and only to add to the confusion, they do make it easier to deal with the question of ethics.

Behavior Modification

In behavior modification the client does not have the freedom to terminate the counseling relationship. The client may wish to continue (and would thus simplify the behavior modifier's task); on the other hand, he or she may actively resist. Generally speaking, ethical objections are almost never voiced when behavior modification is applied to specialized populations where there is virtually unanimous social consensus that the troublesome behaviors ought to be changed. For example, some autistic children will literally chew their shoulders to the bone or pummel their heads with their fists until they go blind or deaf unless they are restrained. Few would question the ethics of a counselor attempting to reduce such self-destructive behavior. Likewise, no one would morally object to teaching a retarded individual how to use a toilet.

On the other hand, when there is not virtually unanimous social consensus on the undesirability of a particular behavior (that is, when its maladaptiveness is not self-evident), behavior modification programs should come under serious ethical scrutiny. For example, a prison behavior modifier might justifiably be asked, "Just what does constitute 'good grooming' and why is it worthy of being reinforced?" (see Emery & Marholin, 1977; Winkler, 1977). The issue is further confounded by the fact that some of what goes on in the name of behavior modification is thoroughly disgusting to professional behavior modifiers. In a recent television program on delinquency, for example, an "expert" confidently described how roping a child to a bed—spread eagle—for a week supposedly modified the child's aggressive behavior. Although other such examples exist (see Cotter, 1967; Horan, 1973f; Krasner, 1971), there are relatively few instances of "credentialed" behavior modifiers involved in unethical programming.

Behavior Therapy and Behavioral Counseling

Behavior therapy and behavioral counseling are essentially synonymous terms. Clients see the counselor on a voluntary basis and are free to terminate the counseling relationship at any time. Although the counselor does help clarify the client's concerns, the choice of counseling goals and their order of priority are entirely up to the client, as is the decision to work toward their attainment. Furthermore, when several behavior-change strategies are equally viable, the counselor will invariably implement the strategy the client prefers.

At first blush, then, it would appear that behavioral counseling is essentially a scientific enterprise outside the domain of ethics. The client makes all the decisions about how, when and even if to proceed and the expert counselor, having been exposed to a good deal of behavioral research, simply distills from the literature the most promising behavior-change strategies. Then, client willing, the counselor proceeds to help the client work toward his or her goals, not the counselor's.

In practice, however, this ethical neutrality is illusory. The conduct of behavioral counseling is every bit as open to intrusive counselor input as is nonbehavioral counseling. The psychoanalyst favoring bar hopping and family abandonment could just as easily have been a behaviorist subtly pushing the client to this therapist-preferred alternative. The personal growth group could very well have been composed of behaviorists whose line of questioning would lead the Catholic member to decide in favor of birth control. The simple application of a counseling strategy to assist a client in attaining a goal may be as ethically neutral as a laboratory investigation of nuclear fission, but the counselor's input into the client's decision to work toward a particular goal is a matter for close ethical scrutiny, as is a politician's deployment of nuclear weaponry.

Learning Mechanisms for Intrusive Counselor Input

Counselor attention has proved to be a very powerful positive reinforcer. Some of the classic studies have shown that attention in the form of head nods or words like "good" or "uh huh" can cause significant increases in the kinds of client verbalization that follow—plural nouns, hostile words, and statements of opinion, (for example, Greenspoon,1955; Verplanck, 1955). In reviewing thirty-one studies of this sort, Krasner (1958) reported a majority of positive results. This line of research has been applied to more clinically relevant client behaviors occurring outside the counseling interview (Krumboltz & Thoresen, 1969).

Even Carl Rogers (1961), who detests this process, acknowledges that it can occur in the counseling interview. Ironically, Rogers himself—the father of nondirective counseling—makes effective use of verbal positive reinforcement (empathy and warmth) in his own counseling. Truax (1966) conducted a microscopic analysis of a sample of twenty therapy sessions between Rogers and a client. He conclusively showed that throughout the course of therapy (a total of eighty-five sessions) Rogers differentially reinforced those kinds of client statements seen as desirable in client-centered counseling theory.

To illustrate the potential insidiousness of this phenomenon, perhaps another personal digression is in order: In spite of the fact that vocational adjustment is one of the best general indexes of mental health (Lofquist & Dawis, 1969), helping clients resolve educational-vocational choice concerns carries relatively little prestige among many counselors. I have occasionally observed counselors and counseling students essentially ignoring (extinguishing) client discussion of career choice concerns to save time, as they put it, for "more important personal topics." Any verbal hints of other problems in living like sex, loneliness, or depression were heavily reinforced by counselor attention. Many clients initially without such problems discovered they had had them all along, but their vocational concerns were never addressed!

The fact that the counselor serves as a powerful role model is another source of serious ethical contamination in decision-making counseling. Counselors have a good deal of status and prestige in the eyes of their clients (if not their employers). Clients are very likely to adopt the values and imitate the behavior of their counselor. Is a homosexual client likely to choose heterosexuality if he or she knows that the counselor is leading a contented gay life-style? Is divorce a more probable alternative if the marriage counselor is divorced? Conversely, we might expect married or heterosexual counselors to exert a similar modeling influence on the decision-making behavior of their clients. (See Krumboltz and Varenhorst, 1965, for further illustration and discussion.)

Ethical Guidelines for Counselor Input in Client Decisions

All of the foregoing indicates that counselors, knowingly or not, may have the power to shape a client's decision in a particular direction. Unless the counselor is in fact absolutely neutral or uncertain about which alternative promises to be most advantageous to the client, it is unlikely that any client's decision will be totally free of this influence. Ethical counselor conduct, then, would call for giving all viable alternatives in a choice problem a "fair hearing" and deliberately withholding any reinforcement for implementing a particular alternative until after the client makes the decision favoring that alternative. Furthermore, when counselors find themselves strongly believing in or opposing a particular alternative, they are probably ethically obliged to refer the client to another counselor or at the very least to discuss their biases with the client, temper them as such, and foster information gathering on all sides of the question.

Many generalizations, including the foregoing ethical proclamations, have their exceptions. It is not uncommon to find clients giving serious thought to maladaptive alternatives. Are counselors obliged to provide a mantle of rationality for clearly crazy options? Probably not. But first of all counselors should be aware that immediately to dismiss such alternatives as preposterous may jeopardize the counseling relationship. (cf. Heubusch & Horan, 1977). The client may terminate prematurely. If the alternative is obviously disadvantageous, this will in all likelihood become apparent as decision-making counseling progresses.

Even if the "craziness" of a particular option is not readily apparent to the client, it would not necessarily be unethical for the counselor deliberately to steer the client away from a maladaptive course of action. In fact one might argue that a counselor would be remiss in not attempting to dissuade a client from pursuing an obviously unethical alternative such as physical assault on another person. However, counselors should not take this highly situational prerogative lightly; direct influence in a client decision ought to be the exception rather than the rule.

In forming guidelines for counselor input, we might recall that in behavior modification little cause for ethical concern exists if there is virtually unanimous informed social consensus on the inappropriateness of a particular target behavior. For example, no one would question the ethics of a mental health professional attempting to eliminate an autistic child's self-mutilating activity. We might cautiously extend this ethical guideline to the conduct of decision-making counseling as well. Counselors may actively discourage certain alternatives and possibly even promote others, to the extent that a hypothetical everyman would not object. Whether this everyman should be the counseling profession or the public at large is a matter for debate. Taking a cue from other professions, I am inclined to opt for the former, being fully aware of the dangers of elitism and in either case the pitfalls inherent in establishing concepts like adaptiveness or insanity by consensual validation. On the other hand, the collective judgments of an informed peer group are certainly more meaningful than the potentially capricious opinions of any one member. Thus counselors who find themselves subtly promoting alternatives that would not be endorsed by the counseling profession at large, and doing so in the guise of impartial decision making, may well be behaving unethically.

On other occasions a client may ask a counselor for direct advice. Should the counselor refuse to provide it? Probably yes. In the first place, decision-making counseling ought to equip the client with a framework for making future decisions as well as with a resolution of the present choice conflict. I am reminded of the old aphorism: Feeding a hungry man will bring him back each night; teaching him to fish will make him self-sufficient. Second, any advice would be dispensed from the counselor's perception of what is reinforcing rather than from the client's vantage point. Finally, counselors who offer advice are likely to be held accountable in case of an unfavorable outcome. This liability might be worth the risk if counselors in fact could make better decisions than the clients themselves; however, no data exists to support such a contention.

On the other hand, if the client fully accepts the responsibility for making the decision but sincerely wonders what the counselor would do if confronted with a similar choice problem, it would seem rather unfair to deny the client access to this information. This sort of counselor self-disclosure might be occasionally permissible, but the counselor's choice of alternatives should be treated as simply a piece of information, not as the best possible course of action.

SUMMARY

There are two ethical questions pertinent to the conduct of decision-making counseling. To answer the first question, "Is there always a 'right' choice?", we must first examine how ethical laws are formulated. Ethics is not a certain science; there is unresolvable debate about what kinds of behavior are to be judged unethical. And even commonly accepted ethical generalizations are subject to exceptions and extenuating circumstances. Thus, ethical laws are of limited use in dictating the "right" choice. Moreover, many client decisions do not involve ethical matters at all; use of the word "right" may confuse the simple fact of differences between client and "expert" utilities.

In considering the second question, "What are the ethical limits of counselor input in client decisions?", we must be aware of the pervasive problem of intrusive counselor utilities in all schools of counseling. Differential attention and modeling factors are possible learning mechanisms for intrusive counselor input.

Ethical guidelines for counselor behavior in decision-making counseling include considering all viable alternatives, withholding reinforcement for implementing an alternative until the client has freely selected one, possibly referring a client to another counselor if the counselor strongly opposes or endorses one of several adaptive alternatives (due to idiosyncratic utilities), intervening only when an alternative is obviously unethical or maladaptive, and treating counselor preference (if at all) as incidental information rather than as the appropriate course of action.

This discussion of ethical issues in decision-making counseling closes the first part of the book. Part II builds on the foundations of part I in reviewing dynamic, rational, and behavioral approaches to decision-making counseling as well as pertinent problem-solving literature.

COUNSELING
THEORY AND
DECISION MAKING

7

Dynamic Approaches to Decision-Making Counseling

The classification of counseling theories is not an easy task. According to London (1967) all schools of psychotherapy can be neatly fitted into a dichotomy: insight versus action approaches. Harper (1959) at the other extreme, has written a book entitled *Psychoanalysis and Psychotherapy: 36 Systems.* Still another method identifies psychoanalytic, existential, rational, and behavioral as the four major schools of thought. There are some difficulties with this latter method, however. Both psychoanalytic and existential counselors place a good deal of emphasis on dynamic motivation. Behaviorists value (though to lesser extent) the "reinforcing" relationship qualities posited by the existentialists. And counselors in all of the camps behave "rationally" at least on occasion. Overlap notwithstanding, I will discuss counseling theory and decision making from this fourfold perspective. This chapter will focus on the psychoanalytic and existential approaches. Specifically, we will explore decision making as it is treated in the psychoanalytic therapy of Freud, the existential counseling of Rogers, and the quasi-existential approach of Carkhuff. Chapters 8 and 9 will deal with the rational and behavioral points of view.

The Psychoanalytic Therapy of Freud

Background

In attempting to account for why human beings behave as they do, Freud (1963, 1967) invented the topographic and structural models of personality. The topographic or "iceberg" model consists of two levels, the conscious and the unconscious. Just as 90 percent of an iceberg is hidden below the water surface, so likewise most human behavior results from unconscious motivation. When unconscious material attempts to enter the conscious level, a "censor" function (repression) pushes it back or lets it through in disguised form.

The structural model of personality is composed of id, ego, and superego functions. The id is a sort of seething cauldron of all that is unholy in the human condition, a vast reservoir of erotic and aggressive impulses, all unconscious, seeking immediate discharge in the environment. The ego's primary purpose is to keep the lid on the id. It does this—not very well, incidentally—through a series of defense mechanisms, the deployment of which are strictly unconscious. For example, homosexuality is taboo in this culture. Should a man experience an erotic id impulse toward another man ("I love him"), the ego uses the defense "reaction-formation" to change this impulse to its opposite ("I hate him"). Because hating for no good reason is also socially unacceptable, the ego, through another defense mechanism, "projects" this impulse onto the other person ("He hates me"). Thus in psychoanalytic theory homosexuality is an underlying cause of paranoia. The last component of the structural model is the superego, which keeps us feeling guilty whenever we fail to live up to parental expectations.

At birth the infant is all id. The ego grows out of an interaction between the id and the environment. For example, "wimpering" is an early ego technique designed to get food. (More sophisticated maneuvers are needed later on). The superego arises out of the relationship between the child's ego and the same-sex parent. A boy, fearing castration from his father as punishment for his incestuous impulses toward his mother, "introjects" the value system of his father. Introjection is a defense mechanism that literally means the boy "swallows" the image of his father, thereby destroying the threat. But because we are what we eat, the boy becomes just like dad! (If the reader has difficulty swallowing this explanation, a similar process is reflected in the saying "If you can't beat 'em, join 'em"). Be that as it may, according to psychoanalytic theory, young girls feel they have already been castrated, hence they do not strongly introject parental values. Thus women are less moral than men. (Though Freud was not the first male chauvinist, he did help put an academic dressing on the doctrine of male superiority.)

Human beings operate on two principles. The pleasure principle suggests that we are basically hedonists and wish to do whatever feels good. But such indiscriminant activity is likely to bring on dire consequences, hence the reality principle posits that we act to maximize pleasure while minimizing pain. For example, the id demands that the hungry child take a cookie. The ego, recalling mama's prohibition against snacking before dinner, wards off the eating impulse and takes solace in the fact that obedience will probably merit two cookies after dinner. The superego explains why the child does not take a cookie even when there is no chance of being caught.

Decision Making

Though much of the ego's role is unconscious (for example, deployment of defense mechanisms), what little energies are left over after keeping the id in check may be devoted to conscious activities. Perceiving the environment and developing verbal and motor skills are ego tasks. Rational thinking, including decision making, is also the ego's responsibility.

Although the problem of indecisiveness has been subjected to considerable etiological speculation (Fenichel, 1945), psychoanalytic writers have not formally discussed the process of decision making per se. The reality principle—maximizing gain while minimizing costs—would seem to tie Freudian views of decision making to classical decision theory, however, the psychoanalytic approach is colored by a heavy emphasis on unconscious motivation. In other words, much of what we decide to do is not rational at all; "rationalized" would be a better word.

Illustrations of the role of unconscious motivation abound in the psychoanalytic literature of vocational choice. Early writers such as Jones (1923), Zillboorg (1934), Hendrick (1943), and Brill (1949) all argued that or provided case examples in which id impulses found release in one's choice of career. Sadism, for example, might be "sublimated" (expressed in a socially acceptable manner) in the work of a butcher or surgeon. Forer (1953) and Small (1953), and later the "Michigan School" (Bordin, Nachman, & Segal, 1963) expanded on these conceptualizations and provided them with a slight degree of empirical support.

If much of what we decide to do, then, is the result of unconscious determinants, how can psychoanalytically oriented counseling facilitate the making of good decisions? The answer is very little short of a complete personal psychoanalysis—a very long and expensive procedure. (Several sessions a week at $75 or more per session for a number of years is not atypical.) Free association, dream analysis, interpretation, and transference (responding to the analyst as a parent) are all involved in this painfully slow process of total personality reorganization.

The development of insight is the major goal of psychoanalytic counseling, that is, what was previously unconscious becomes conscious. "Where id was, ego shall be" (Freud, 1963). As the result of this insight, there is a redistribution of psychic energy. The ego becomes more powerful because it no longer has to commit the bulk of its resources to defending against id impulses. A stronger ego, then, is better able to make decisions in accord with the pleasure and reality principles.

Essentially, psychoanalytic theory has provided counselors with a very colorful explanation of how people decide or remain indecisive. Unfortunately, however, counselors are left empty-handed. On an ad hoc basis there is little they can do to help clients choose between a number of existing alternatives.

The Existential Counseling of Carl Rogers

Background

In contrast (and partially in reaction) to Freud's contention that the core of the human personality is, at best, asocial, Carl Rogers (1959, 1961) sees people in a much more positive light. We are told that human beings are endowed with certain powers of autonomy, creativity, and rational choice. The prime motivator is called the "organismic valuing process" (a sort of good id), which, if provided with the proper kinds of environmental support, will propel the individual into a "self-actualizing" lifestyle. Self-actualization is seen as an ideal way of living rather than an inert state.

Unfortunately, our quest for self-actualization is hampered by the adoption of "conditions of worth." In order to maintain the goodwill of significant others—primarily our parents—we buy into their value system. To be a worthy son or daughter, one must think and feel in a certain prescribed manner. The conditions of worth then function in much the same manner as Freud's superego. In any event, the individual is left with two competing value systems—his or her own naturally good values and the possibly artificial values of significant others. This dissonance produces a good deal of anxiety, which may cause people to seek help in counseling.

Just as the organismic valuing process and the conditions of worth mirror the constructs id and superego, Rogers uses the term "self-concept" in a manner somewhat similar to Freud's definition of ego. The self-concept consists of reflected appraisals of significant others. It is basically what we think of ourselves and consequently governs how we will act. For example, if we are labeled (accurately or inaccurately) as juvenile delinquents, we will come to think of ourselves in that manner and begin to act accordingly.

Decision Making

A poor self-concept coupled with the adoption of artificial values would certainly impede the making of a good decision. The individual's organismic valuing process—from which all good decisions flow naturally—becomes diverted from its goal of self-actualization. Decisions made to please others or to comply with a faulty-unfavorable self-image are not to one's own best advantage.

Thus in both the Freudian and Rogerian frameworks decisions are made on the basis of not entirely rational or conscious factors. Furthermore, unless we are self-actualized, our decisions may produce even more distress and discomfort. There is one recourse, however, and that is to immerse ourselves in Rogerian psychotherapy.

Rogers (1961) has postulated that three conditions are "necessary and sufficient" for therapeutic change to occur. In the first place the counselor must be *genuine*. Synonyms for this concept include congruent, authentic, transparent, and nonexploitive. Being genuine implies that the counselor must be aware of his or her own feelings and not be afraid to allow the client to see them. Rogers labels the second condition *unconditional positive regard*, also known as therapist warmth, liking, prizing, or *agapé*. This nonpossessive, nonerotic love must also be nonjudgmental; that is, the counselor must have high regard for the client regardless of what is said or done. The third and final condition is *empathic understanding*, also referred to as sensitivity or simply empathy. Of the three conditions, this is perhaps the most crucial. It implies the ability to see the world through the client's eyes, to recognize fully and accurately the client's feelings, and to convey to the client that he or she is, in fact, being understood.

Rogers argues that such a relationship allows clients to abandon their conditions of worth without experiencing loss of support or any other dire consequences. They are thus free to get in touch with their own values—those of their organismic valuing process. And as a by-product of this counseling atmosphere, they come to think of themselves in more favorable terms. At last self-actualized clients can be trusted to make their own decisions, and these decisions will be adaptive: "I find that increasingly such individuals are able to trust their total organismic reaction to a new situation because they discover to an ever-increasing degree that if they are open to their experience, doing what 'feels right' proves to be a competent and trustworthy guide to behavior which is truly satisfying" (Rogers, 1961, p. 189).

Apart from providing these "necessary and sufficient" relationship conditions, then, Rogers has nothing to offer a client seeking help with a decision. In practice he may even ignore such requests. For example, in a filmed interview (Rogers, 1968), Rogers is asked by Gloria, a divorced client, if she should be honest with her daughter in acknowledging her sexual relationships with men. Later in the interview she wonders whether she should be more discriminating about sex partners. Rogers never deals with Gloria's questions; the interview evolves into a discussion of her relationship with her father. Rogers's responses mirror her indecision.

Building on the foundations of Rogerian self-concept theory, however, a number of vocational choice theorists (for example, Super, Starishevsky, Matlin, & Jordaan, 1963; Tiedeman & O'Hara, 1963) have argued that decision-making ability in later years can be enhanced by early favorable developmental experiences, which culminate in an improved self-concept. But apart from this "preventative" approach, the counselor is still left without a specific strategy for helping clients resolve pressing choice problems. Apparently, then, Rogerian existential theory, like psychoanalytic theory, has little to offer the client facing a decision short of complete immersion in intensive psychotherapy.

The Quasi-Existential Approach of Carkhuff

Background

Carkhuff began his career as a sort of Rogerian apologist. He and his early associates (Berenson & Carkhuff, 1967; Carkhuff & Berenson, 1967; Truax &

Carkhuff, 1967) earned prominence by picking apart the "psychotherapy is not effective" phenomenon. Carkhuff acknowledged this finding to be generally true; that is, the average mental health scores of those exposed to psychotherapy did not differ from those who had not been so exposed. But on closer inspection, although the mean scores remained the same, the variances differed widely. In other words, some people got better, others got worse. Subsequent research purported that the presence of the Rogerian relationship qualities was directly related to the phenomenon of getting better. Counselors who were genuine, warm, and empathic produced therapeutic gains in their clients. The clients of counselors lacking these attributes suffered even greater setbacks. When highly trained counselors were found to be deficient in these qualities, Carkhuff abandoned the use of the term "counseling" in favor of "helping" and encouraged the use of paraprofessionals into roles previously held by credentialed counselors (Carkhuff, 1969a, 1969b).

Carkhuff's approach to counseling has steadily drifted away from its Rogerian foundation. To the three Rogerian dimensions he added two more qualities distilled from the Gestalt counseling literature (for example, Perls, 1969). These were *immediacy* ("what goes on between us right now") and *confrontation* ("telling it like it is"). Still another quality, *concreteness* ("being specific"), reflects the influence of behaviorism. Carkhuff labeled the six qualities "facilitative conditions" and claims they are the *sine qua non* of effective counseling (Carkhuff, 1971).

Though he does not acknowledge it in print or in public, Carkhuff's approach to counseling has been accelerating recently in a behavioral direction. In a speech to the American Educational Research Association, Carkhuff (1973a) described working with a youngster upset by the fact that his family would soon be moving to a strange town. This concern boiled down to a specific problem of potential loneliness, which in turn suggested the making of friends as a counseling goal. Carkhuff provided an operational definition of a friend that met all of Mager's (1962) criteria for well-written behavioral objectives. Carkhuff then suggested that the making of friends was a complex skill that could be learned (shaped!) in successive steps. It was clear that a technique like behavioral rehearsal would be the predominant conseling strategy.

Decision Making

Prior to the aforementioned speech, Carkhuff (1973b) published a very popular paperback entitled *The Art of Problem-Solving*. This book suggests a four-step process for helping clients resolve problems of choice.

The first step is called "developing the problem." Here the counselor's focus should be on exploring the problem and trying to understand the client's frame of reference. The Rogerian relationship-listening qualities are of paramount importance, as Carkhuff believes that the goal of counseling (reaching a decision) flows from a comprehensive understanding of the client.

Carkhuff labels the second step "breaking down the problem." At this time alternative courses of action are generated and values are ordered into a hierarchy. Carkhuff's use of the term value here is somewhat cryptic. It does not closely correspond to the notion of value or utility in classical decision theory. Nor does it resemble the concept of value reflected by various psychometric procedures and devices (cf. Katzell, 1964). For example, in working with a fictitious woman client, Carkhuff identifies the following as "values" to be considered in choosing how to spend her work life: children, husband, job, school, housework, miscellaneous, finances. Thus for Carkhuff values do not mean abstractions like honesty, prestige, achievement, unselfishness, and so forth. Nor do they strictly speaking suggest gains and costs or positive and aversive consequences. As stated, they seem to represent factors to consider in making a decision. Only by an intuitive leap can we translate them into anything akin to values. For example, "children" might really represent "not spending a desired amount of time with my children"—a perceived aversive consequence of a particular alternative.

The third step in Carkhuff's decision-making paradigm is called "considering courses of action." This step involves a close examination of those values and alternatives that promise the highest degree of fulfillment. The counselor is allowed to suggest values and alternative courses of action when the client cannot, a proviso that represents a radical departure from Rogerian theory.

Carkhuff labels the final step in helping clients reach a decision "developing courses of action." Both choosing and implementing courses of action are involved. The conceptual basis of this step resembles the "moral algebra" of Ben Franklin (see chapter 1) and the balance sheet procedures of Janis and Mann (1977; see chapter 5). The specific decision-making grid Carkhuff suggests (see figure 7.1) apparently evolved from the vocational decision-making work of Katz (1966), which will be discussed in chapter 8. In Carkhuff's grid the various alternative solutions to the choice problem are represented along the horizontal axis and values are depicted on the vertical axis. Because values may be stronger in some individuals than others, provision is made for "weighting." For example, Carkhuff's client rated children as +8, husband and job each as +5, school as +4, housework as +3, miscellaneous as +2, and financial as +1. (Similarly, with someone facing an occupational choice, "prestige" might be double the rating assigned to "salary" or vice versa.) Then one or two plus or minus signs are entered under the alternatives according to whether they allow expression of the corresponding value. A mathematical index of this expression can be obtained by multiplying the value's weight by the number of plus or minus signs under each alternative. Finally, by summing these weight-expression products under each alternative, the most promising alternative emerges as the one with the highest total score.

Value Hierarchy	Courses of Action							
	I Get babysitter	II Get house-keeper	III Quit job	IV Quit school	V Build-up	VI Cut-down	VII Husband's help	VIII Teachers' aide
1. Children (+8)	−−(−16)	++(+16)	++(+16)	+(+8)	+(+8)	+−(0)	+(+8)	+(+8)
2. Husband (+5)	+(+5)	++(+10)	++(+10)	+(+5)	+(+5)	+−(0)	++(+10)	+(+5)
3. Job (+5)	+(+5)	+(+5)	−−(−10)	+−(0)	+(+5)	+−(0)	+(+5)	++(+10)
4. School (+4)	+(+4)	+(+4)	+−(0)	−−(−8)	+(+4)	+−(0)	+(+4)	+(+4)
5. Housework (+3)	+(+3)	+(+3)	++(+6)	+(+3)	+(+3)	+−(0)	+(+3)	+(+3)
6. Misc. (+2)	+(+2)	+(+2)	+−(0)	+−(0)	+(+2)	+−(0)	+(+2)	+(+2)
7. Financial (+1)	−(−1)	−(−1)	−−(−2)	+−(0)	0(0)	+−(0)	0(0)	0(0)
	+2	+39	+24	+8	+27	0	+32	+32

Source: R. R. Carkhuff, The art of problem solving, (Amherst, Mass.: Human Resource Development Press, 1973-b).

FIGURE 7.1. Decision-making grid

Close inspection of Carkhuff's decision-making grid quickly reveals the classic "error of misplaced precision." It does the astronaut little good to have a landing gear sensitive enough to deposit him on a postage stamp if his booster rocket will not bring him anywhere near the moon! Although the most fulfilling alternative in the Carkhuff grid emerges in a mathematical cloak, the foundation garments are completely subjective. Determination of both the values and alternatives, as well as the assignment of weights and estimates of expression, are entirely figments of the joint client-counselor imagination that need to be fortified by information-seeking behaviors.

Katz's (1966) model, which apparently stimulated Carkhuff's thinking, was not similarly troubled. Katz recommended using an a priori, factor-analytically based value taxonomy. The levels of the value and the expression possibilities were also empirically based. For example, if a client values a particular salary and must choose between several job possibilities, there are statistical tables to which one might turn in order to estimate the probability of making that salary in each occupation under consideration.

Difficulties with his model notwithstanding, Carkhuff does deserve accolades for exploring the concept of decision making in counseling apart from the area of vocational choice. Although much has been written on decision making and vocational development (for example, Herr, 1970; Herr & Cramer, 1972), very few counseling theorists have extended vocational choice paradigms to include other problems in living. Carkhuff has provided us with a seminal model for further consideration.

Summary

Dynamic approaches to counseling include Freud's psychoanalysis, Rogers's existential counseling, and Carkhuff's quasi-existential "helping" interventions. Freudian theory stresses the importance of unconscious motivation; posits a three-part model of personality structure (the id, ego, and superego); and suggests, as does classical decision theory, that we act to maximize pleasure while minimizing pain. Psychoanalytic writers have not formally discussed decision-making counseling, but because of the extraordinary role of unconscious motivation, it would appear that to enter psychoanalysis and gain "insight" is the only way to facilitate rational choice.

Rogers posits a prime motivator called the organismic valuing process, which leads to self-actualization unless it is hindered by the adoption of artificial conditions of worth. The self-concept, formed from reflected appraisals of significant others, governs how we act. A poor self-concept or the adoption of artificial conditions of worth impedes naturally good decision making. Immersion in Rogerian counseling with a genuine counselor who provides unconditional positive regard and empathic understanding allows clients to get in touch with their own values, think of themselves in more favorable terms, and consequently make good decisions. Thus Rogers responds to client choice problems as he would any other client problem in living.

Carkhuff's helping model adds three other qualities to the Rogerian dimensions (immediacy, confrontation, and concreteness), all of which are called facilitative conditions and deemed essential for effective counseling. Unlike Freud and Rogers, Carkhuff specifically addresses the topic of decision-making counseling with a four-step intervention package: developing the problem, breaking down the problem, considering courses of action, and developing courses of action. The last step employs a decision-making grid that apparently evolved from grids used in vocational counseling, but Carkhuff's model suggests wider application. Carkhuff's willingness to provide direct assistance to clients with choice problems has much in common with rational approaches to counseling reviewed in the next chapter.

Rational Approaches to Decision-Making Counseling

Rational approaches to decision-making counseling are much more accommodating to the language of formal decision theory than are either the psychoanalytic or existential points of view. In rational counseling choice problems are defined as such; alternatives are weighed in the light of new information; and the counselor actively helps the client implement a plan of action. My use of the label rational counseling might suggest that a fairly unified school of thought exists, but such is not the case. Counseling theorists who operate under the rational rubric comprise a fairly heterogeneous group. This chapter is restricted to those theories most relevant to the conduct of decision-making counseling. Specifically, I will review the contributions of Ellis, trait and factor theorists, Gelatt, and Katz.

Ellis's Rational Emotive Therapy

Background

Albert Ellis is one of the most colorful and controversial figures in the counseling profession. He is by self-proclamation a psychotherapist, a sexologist, and a sexual libertine; however, his model of counseling—termed "rational emotive therapy"—can be viewed separately.

Ellis (1962) believes that understanding human misery (neurosis) is as simple as ABC. "A" represents an activating event or antecedent stimulus that may produce a particular self-verbalization or belief at "B." These beliefs can be either rational (B_r) or irrational (B_i). "C" refers to our consequent emotional response. Any sustained negative emotion—neurosis—is always the result of an irrational belief about "A." For example, a girl is jilted by her boyfriend ("A"). She then seeks therapeutic help after finding herself in the throes of a depression lasting several months ("C"). This depression can only be the result of illogical thinking at "B." Such self-defeating self-talk usually takes the form of "Isn't it horrible that he's done this." "I can't live without him." "His jilting me proves that I'm a worthless person," and so forth.

In 1973 Ellis added D and E to his formulation. "D" refers to the therapist's task of actively disputing these irrational beliefs and serving as a frank counterpropagandist for a more rational perspective. Our jilted client should be saying things to herself such as "I don't like being dumped on, but it's hardly catastrophic. My adequacy or worth as a human being doesn't depend one iota on his opinion of me. In fact, I'm probably better off finding out about his deceptive streak now before committing any more of my life to him." As a result of more rational thinking, our client finds herself with a new effect, that is, emotional freedom at point "E." Ellis also stresses the importance of homework assignments; in this case our client should be actively pursuing some of the many other "fish in the sea" (Ellis, 1965, 1966).

There is ample research supporting Ellis's hypothesis that certain kinds of self-verbalizations may produce untoward emotional responses (Nawas, 1970; Rimm & Litvak, 1969; Veltin, 1968). Furthermore, Ellis's work has spawned a good deal of behavioral reconceptualization (see chapter 3). In spite of the clinical utility of Ellis's formulations, however, there are certain epistemological problems inherent in any belief system purporting to be rational. In the 1960s one could easily construct a logically tight rationale for continued involvement or withdrawal of American forces in Vietnam. If we assume that all cats have feathers and that all feathered creatures are dogs, we can mathematically prove that all cats are dogs. Logic does not demand "true" assumptions.

Rational emotive therapy rests on the assumption that all sustained negative emotion (neurosis) is the result of illogical thinking. This of course would imply that Hitler's guilt, if he had any, should be seen as irrational and possibly dismissed by his counselor with the old saw "to err is human!" Grief at the loss of a loved one, a less farfetched example, would likewise be construed as the end product of illogical drivel. Conversely, counselors never try to dissuade clients from feelings of happiness that arise from "irrational" thinking. For example, feeling proud of a task well done is as inherently illogical as feeling miserable about a failure if we view adequacy from Ellis's perspective.

Nevertheless, much human misery is caused or at least accompanied by irrational thinking. Ellis has provided us with a useful therapeutic tool, if not a faultless epistemology.

Decision Making

In his earlier writings Ellis (1962) does not explicitly talk about a framework for making decisions, but he does argue rather convincingly for a life-style based on a long-range, social hedonism. All of us should guiltlessly seek out and enjoy harmless physical sensations (such as sex and gustatory pleasures); but, because we will probably not die tomorrow, some degree of moderation in our eating, drinking, and merrymaking may be a safer course of action.

In addition to stressing the concept of future consequences of our actions, Ellis emphasizes the equality between self-interest and social interest; that is, what is good for us is also good for our culture: "There is a very good answer to the question why one should love one's neighbor, or at least why one should take care not to harm him: namely, that only in so doing is one likely to build the kind of society in which one would best live *oneself*" (1962, p. 323). This doctrine is, of course, akin to the classic economic theory of "enlightened self-interest." By paying his workers five dollars per day, Henry Ford ensured they would have enough money to buy his automobiles.

But though Ellis does present a philosophy on which all decisions to act ought to be grounded, his credo is relatively abstract, so the dictates of what specifically constitutes rational behavior are open to wide interpretation. Furthermore, in his classic text Ellis (1962) does not provide the counselor with a technology or even a procedural description for helping clients resolve a decision.

In a more recent book, *The Civilized Couple's Guide to Extra-Marital Adventure,* which was designed for lay reading (no pun intended), Ellis (1973) addresses these issues indirectly. We are told, for example, that "civilized adultery" may be a very rational activity. In fact the opening chapter is entitled "Extramarital adventure: Almost everybody is doing it." In a subsequent chapter ("To be or not to be an extramarital adventurer: That is the question") Ellis examines a number of factors to consider before making such a decision. These include gauging and analyzing your motives, dealing with feelings of shame and guilt (You shouldn't have any; they're irrational!), and using a "hedonistic calculus" in which facts are considered along with the advantages and disadvantages of each alternative. Finally, should one decide to embark on a course of extramarital adventure, one must make another decision—should one be honest with one's spouse? After marshaling the opinions of numerous experts, Ellis generally recommends "no" (for reasons that, incidentally, may or may not be entirely rational).

Thus Ellis does recommend engaging in a number of preparatory steps prior to making a decision. The gathering of relevant information and the consideration of advantages and disadvantages are components that tie Ellis's views to those of most other decision theorists. But though some of the components may be present, the process is rather incomplete and unsystematic. No formal sequence of counselor activities is provided.

Ellis does apparently allow for the possibility of more than one "rational" choice. However, it is rather difficult to read his book on extramarital sex and come away with the notion that monogamy could ever be anything but a stifling compromise.

Finally, there is the matter of intrusive counselor values—a factor that cannot be dismissed as irrational drivel (see chapter 6). Ellis's system demands that the therapist directly attack the client's irrational beliefs, a procedure most counselors—behaviorally inclined or otherwise—would support from a cost-benefit perspective. Although the irrationality of certain client self-statements may be obvious to everyone, just what constitutes a rational substitute may not be at all clear. Ellis is not above advice giving or arguing for a particular alternative such as secrecy from one's spouse in the matter of extramarital sex. But Ellis's utilities may differ widely from those of his clients and other rational emotive counselors.

Essentially, then, Ellis has provided the counselor with a very useful framework for removing clients from discomforting emotional states. Although his conceptualizations have stimulated much behavioral counseling theory, research, and practice, his work only indirectly and imperfectly addresses the topic of decision-making counseling.

Trait and Factor Counseling

Background

People differ. Some are aggressive; others are submissive. Some smile frequently; others frown. Some are intelligent; others are not. There are approximately eighteen thousand words in the English language that are descriptive of such human conduct (Allport, 1961). Over the past century the trait psychologist has been primarily concerned with boiling down this enormous number of descriptive adjectives into a more manageable quantity. For example, a list containing the words outgoing, sociable, gregarious, friendly, and attention seeking might be reduced to a single entity such as extraversion. Just as the chemist Mendeleff developed the periodic chart that now defines and differentiates a mere hundred and five elements out of literally billions of compounds in the earth's crust, the trait psychologist likewise seeks a taxonomy or master list of elemental words thought to be descriptive of all human conduct. But success has been elusive, there are nearly as many trait taxonomies as there are trait psychologists.

Traits are often equated with needs and factors, but there are important differences. Need theories of personality are essentially prescientific in that they purport to explain a phenomenon when all they actually do is label it. For example, to claim that a client slashed his or her wrists because of "masochistic needs" provides the illusion of explaining why the suicidal act occurred. All that can actually be said is that the client behaved in a self-destructive manner. Likewise to argue that one studies to meet achievement needs or explores to satisfy curiosity needs would be equally redundant.

Trait theories are much less grandiose. They do not purport to explain a behavior pattern but only to describe it. The focus is primarily on whether or not a word such as "aggressive" is an adequate descriptor of human conduct. How the individual got that way is a speculative matter. A trait is a name for a particular class of similar behaviors that can further be defined in terms of a continuum and the familiar bell-shaped curve. Nearly all psychometric tests, which measure traits, are constructed in such a way that most people will have an "average" amount of a given trait, with relatively few people at either extreme. An individual scoring high on the trait "dominance," for example, might be expected to behave frequently in a dominant manner, at home, at play, and at work. Most trait theorists believe that human individuality can be explained in terms of one's unique pattern of traits (Allport, 1961; Cattell, 1965; Eysenck, 1961; Guilford, 1959).

Need and trait theories of personality often rest on armchair speculations rather than empirical foundations. Factor theories are a little more sophisticated. Factors are traits derived from a statistical manipulation called factor analysis, which essentially examines the relationship between various pieces of data and sorts out, so to speak, variables that are similar, dissimilar, or not related. Unfortunately, computer output depends upon input; factor analysis reflects only that portion of reality it ingests. Thus to view personality from the perspective of factor analysis may be akin to looking at the universe from the bottom of a well.

Although the trait approach to the study of personality has broad popular appeal, its theoretical and empirical status has been closely scrutinized by Mischel (1968, 1973) and found wanting. Apart from abilities related to intelligence, human beings are remarkably inconsistent. Mischel argues rather convincingly that trait theories do not give enough credence to environmental and personal variables, which are more powerful predictors of behavior. The so-called "dominant" individual, for example, might be submissive in another situation or the same situation interpreted differently.

Decision Making

For the first half of this century decision-making counseling was not conceptualized apart from vocational guidance, which in turn was inextricably bound with trait approaches to personality. For example, Frank Parsons (1909, p. 5), the father of the vocational guidance movement, recommended that the worker make the following assessments prior to choosing a vocation: "(1) a clear understanding of yourself, your aptitudes, abilities, interests, ambitions, resources, limitations, and their causes; (2) a knowledge of the requirements and conditions of success, advantages and disadvantages, compensation, opportunities, and prospects in different lines of work; (3) true reasoning on the relations of these two groups of facts." Parsons was essentially arguing that the individual possesses a number of traits. Likewise, the qualities of various jobs can be thought of as a similar set of traits. Decision-making counseling, then, is simply finding a compatible match between client traits and job traits.

Subsequent technological developments increased the ease and precision with which people could be matched with jobs. Interest and ability tests were developed; vast amounts of employment information were condensed and attractively packaged. Computers were then called in to assist if not replace the counselor as receipt of a success-probability statement for various job alternatives became the principle component of decision-making counseling.

Although trait psychology still permeates many sectors of the vocational guidance field, the "cutting edge" of the profession has adopted a much broader perspective. The choice of an occupation is no longer seen as a static event occurring at a single point in one's life. Rather career education (Herr, 1969) should be an integral part of the student's academic program. To ease the transition from student life to the world of work, our educational curricula from kindergarten through high school or beyond ought to be systematically providing informational and personal competence experiences germane to the making of satisfactory career decisions (Herr & Cramer, 1972).

At this point it would be easy to digress into a detailed description of career education programming, but this material has been fully covered by other authors (for example, Borow, 1973; Byrne, 1977; Herr, 1974; Herr & Cramer, 1972; Horan, in press; Osipow, 1968). Though it may well be the principal preoccupation of school-based counselors, helping clients choose a career alternative is only one of an infinite number of decision-making counseling concerns. The trait approach to personality has had some utility in career decision-making, but extrapolations beyond this domain have not been attempted.

Gelatt's "Conceptual Frame of Reference"

Background

H. B. Gelatt has been a pioneer in the application of formal decision theory to counseling practice. In a 1962 article he decried the absence of a theoretical framework for secondary guidance services and suggested this void was the greatest deterrent to research and development in the field. Gelatt believed that decision theory offered the most promising conceptual frame of reference for counseling.

Decision Making

Gelatt (1962) observed that all decisions have essentially the same characteristics. In the first place there is an individual who must make a decision. Second, there are two or more possible courses of action. Finally, we presume that the decision is to be made on the basis of information. Building on the work of Bross (1953) and Cronbach and Gleser (1957), Gelatt suggested there were essentially two kinds of decisions: terminal decisions, which are final, and investigatory decisions, which call for additional information. An investigatory decision recycles until it results in a terminal decision.

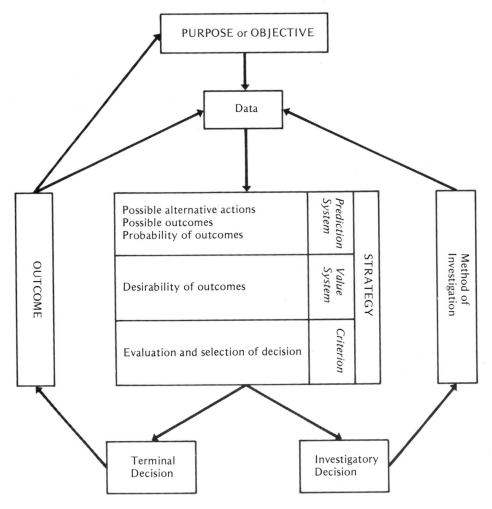

Source: Harry B. Gelatt, "Decision Making: A Conceptual Frame of Reference for Counseling," *Journal of Counseling Psychology* 9 (1962), pp. 240-45. Copyright 1962 by the American Psychological Association. Reprinted by permission.

FIGURE 8.1. Conceptual model of decision making

The components of Gelatt's (1962) conceptual model are depicted in figure 8.1. Gelatt illustrates these components with the common problem of educational planning. The client's objective is to select an appropriate program of courses; the counselor's role is to help the client decide in a systematic manner. In the predictive system the decision maker assesses the possible alternatives, outcomes, and probabilities. Therefore test results, previous course grades, interests, and the relation of this decision to future choices are examples of possibly relevant data. In the value system the decider determines the desirability of the various outcomes. Gelatt is careful to distinguish between the desired and the desirable. Valuing is a subjective process that differs with individuals and circumstances. (Recall the discussion of utility in chapter 4.) In the criterion strategy the client must weigh the information obtained in the prediction and value systems before selecting a terminal or investigatory decision.

Gelatt's conceptual model was elaborated somewhat in a subsequent publication (Clarke, Gelatt, & Levine, 1965), but the task remains for future authors to explicate fully the implications of formal decision theory for the making of personal decisions.

Katz's "Papier-Mâché Mock-Up"

Background

Martin Katz is a staff member of the Educational Testing Service in Princeton, New Jersey, who has a strong background in psychometrics, trait psychology, decision theory, and vocational development. In 1966 he put together a remarkably creative model for making static educational or occupational choices. Though Katz refers to his model as a "papier-mâché mock-up," his humility is uncalled for. The model is an excellent application of classical decision theory to the field of career decision making. Though Katz's (1966) original writing is not well known, its influence on subsequent thinking is obvious.

Decision Making

Katz suggests that career choices ought to begin with an examination of our values. Although conceptualization and research on the topic of values is primitive in comparison to other domains, such as interests or aptitudes, for the moment our self-study can be aided by any one of a number of factor-analytically based value inventories, which can provide us with a list of values relevant to our decision.

Katz feels that values have three properties: *dimension, magnitude,* and *importance.* The dimension of a value is simply its name, such as income, autonomy, or altruism. Magnitude means the amount or level of a value. Income, for example, consists of several possible salary levels. Importance refers to a scaling or weighting of our respective values. For instance, salary might be much more important to us than autonomy.

Katz's decision-making model is illustrated by the grid for Joe Doe depicted in figure 8.2. The first three columns are devoted to value properties. Dimension A is the value income; B through E represent other values. The magnitudes A_1, A_2, A_3, A_4, A_5 might represent yearly incomes in thousands of dollars. The boldface type on A_3 means that income range is a "value threshold" or salary Joe Doe specified as acceptable. In the importance column one hundred points (an arbitrary but convenient number) are distributed in such a way that for Joe Doe A_3 would be worth as much as B_1 and C_2 together. We should note that initial entries are rarely final. Katz suggests massaging these figures until we are content with the numerical constellation. An important counselor function is to point out intransitives (values that do not add up to one hundred). The entire exercise should serve to "clarify our values" as well as prepare us for a decision.

The next component of career decision making is to identify our options (alternatives). Four options are depicted on Joe Doe's grid (W, X,Y,Z). These might represent, for example, the four curricula open to students at his school. When large numbers of alternatives are possible, Katz recommends preliminary screening or clustering of the options into broad areas. This condensation process makes the model more manageable. The client can make a specific choice within a given cluster later.

The likelihood that a particular value magnitude can be accommodated by a given option is called the "strength of return coefficient." In Joe Doe's grid, Katz uses a "standard five" scale where five represents the fact that more than 92 percent of the people in occupation W received at least the threshold income A_3. Coefficients of 4, 3, 2, or 1 would signify 69–92 percent, 33–68 percent, 9–32 percent, and less than 9 percent, respectively. Normative salary data are not difficult to obtain. Estimating the strength of return for other values, however, is a very imprecise matter. (Recall the discussion of subjective probability in chapter 4.)

The next step in Katz's model is to multiply these coefficients by the importance scores assigned to the respective value magnitudes. For example, the importance score for A_3, 30, multiplied by the coefficient of 5 pro-

Illustrative chart for Joe Doe										
VALUES			OPTIONS Strength of return							
			W		X		Y		Z	
Dimension	Magnitude	Importance (sum = 100)	Coefficient	Product	Coefficient	Product	Coefficient	Product	Coefficient	Product
A	A_1 A_2 A_3 A_4 A_5	30	5	150	2	60	4	120	2	60
B	B_1 B_2 B_3	20	4	80	5	100	5	100	3	60
C	C_1 C_2	10	5	50	1	10	3	30	1	10
D	D_1 D_2	5	5	25	3	15	1	5	1	5
E	E_1 E_2 E_3 E_4	35	3	105	2	70	3	105	4	140
Sum of value returns				410		255		360		275
Joe's probability of success				0.7		0.8		0.7		0.5
Expected value				287		204		252		137.5

Source: Martin R. Katz, "A model of guidance for career decision making," *Vocational Guidance Quarterly* 15 (Washington, D.C.: APGA, 1966), pp. 2-10. Copyright 1966 American Personnel and Guidance Association. Reprinted with permission.

FIGURE 8.2. Decision-making grid

duces a product of 150. This product is known as the "value return." Taking the sum of the value returns for each option tells us which option will allow the greatest expression of our values. For Joe Doe alternative W, with a score of 410, appears most promising at this point.

Because option W has the greatest sum of value returns, Joe Doe might be tempted to make a decision on the basis of this data. But Katz's model goes one step further. Information on the probability of entry or success or both in a given option might be available or easily obtained. For example, test scores or academic records can tell us the probability of our being accepted and retained in a particular university or curriculum. If we have such information, we now multiply the sum of value returns for each option by the appropriate probability of success estimate. This maneuver produces an "index of expected value," which thus dictates the appropriate choice. Option W is still Joe Doe's best bet. (See also Hills, 1964.)

Some counselors may reject Katz's model on the basis that it treats decisions as static whereas vocational development might better be construed as a continuous process. Katz (1966, pp.8–9) responds to this criticism quite well: "Decisions, whether long-range or short-range, tentative or binding must still be made . . . at various choice-points. . . . The numbers produced in the bottom row of this model have no permanence. They reflect the individual's reasoned state of mind interacting with available information at a given moment in time. . . . At appropriate intervals, and certainly whenever there is some likelihood that change has occurred, Joe can go back to the starting point." Thus the model is ideally suited for making firm, short-range decisions such as what curriculum to enter. Long-range decisions, such as what ultimate career to choose, can be tentatively made and revised at a later date, pending new values, options, and information.

Although Katz's model is appropriate for use in the vocational choice arena, it suffers many of the same limitations of classical decision theory when applied to other client choice problems. The values pertaining to the myriad decisions of life do not exist in listed, much less factor analyzed, form. Nor are there tables to which we can turn for precise probability information about value realization in the infinitely large legion of life's alternatives.

Summary

Rational approaches to decision-making counseling are generally more accommodating to formal decision theory than are dynamic approaches, but counseling theorists who operate under the rational rubric make up a fairly heterogeneous group. Ellis views neurosis (sustained negative emotion) as a consequence of irrational beliefs about various events. Rational emotive therapists actively dispute these beliefs in order to help their clients achieve emotional freedom. Although there is evidence that self-verbalizations can cause emotional responses and that rational emotive therapy can provide counselors with a useful framework for relieving some forms of client distress, Ellis's work is only indirectly and imperfectly applicable to decision-making counseling.

Trait and factor personality theory was initially applied to decision-making counseling in the context of vocational guidance, which historically focused on matching the traits of an individual with the traits of a job. Current views stress the need to provide informational and personal competence experiences germane to the making of satisfactory career decisions.

Gelatt suggested that decision theory offered the best conceptual frame of reference for counseling. Noting that decisions involve a decision maker and at least two alternatives, Gelatt distinguished between terminal decisions that are final and investigatory decisions that call for more information. The components of Gelatt's model include a prediction system, a value system, and a criterion.

Katz's "papier-mâché mock up" is a direct application of classical decision theory to the domain of career choice. His model employs a grid that considers expression probabilities of designated value levels (corrected by importance scores) in several possible alternatives. The career alternatives that allow the greatest value expression can then be corrected by probability of success estimates. Though ingenious, Katz's model suffers the same limitations as classical decision theory when applied to other choice problems.

The foregoing rational modes of treating client choice problems differ in the extent to which they incorporate concepts from classical decision theory. Moreover, in subsequent chapters we shall see that formulations from the behavioral-counseling and problem-solving literatures can dramatically enhance the effectiveness of the rational approach.

Behavioral Approaches Decision-Making Counseling

The tone of this chapter differs considerably from the preceding two chapters on counseling theory and decision making. In contrast to decision-making procedures that evolved from psychoanalytic, existential, and rational approaches to counseling, behaviorally based strategies have been subjected to considerable experimental scrutiny. The data-gathering proclivity of behaviorists will soon become apparent.

The principles and procedures of behavioral counseling have already been surveyed in chapters 2 and 3. In this chapter I will review the impact of behavioral counseling strategies on decision-making behaviors. For ease in discussion I have classified the myriad studies into five categories: (1) experiments on the influence of verbal conditioning, (2) comparative studies of verbal conditioning and modeling, (3) projects exploring permutations of modeling procedures, (4) simulation studies, and (5) evaluations of comprehensive programming procedures. Most of the research in this area has focused on vocational choice problems. A final category is comprised of decision-making research with other client concerns. Before delving into this review of research, I feel it is appropriate to point out some general differences between behavioral counseling and other approaches and to reiterate the compatibility of behavioral counseling with classical decision theory.

General Differences Between Behavioral Counseling and Other Approaches

In contrast to the psychoanalytic approach covered in chapter 7, behavioral counseling is characterized by a strong emphasis on client goal attainment and a clear specification of the client and counselor behaviors that are presumed to lead to it. For example, in psychoanalytic counseling the counselor would see the presenting problem of test anxiety as merely symbolic of a deeper conflict like fear of being castrated. In practice the counselor essentially would ignore the presenting problem and direct the counseling operations toward the development of client insight (that is, conversion of the client to a psychoanalytic interpretation of life). Success in psychoanalytic counseling requires only the development of insight, which may or may not be followed by reduction of the presenting problem. On the other hand, the behavioral counselor would, client willing, identify the reduction of test anxiety as a counseling goal (though other goals might also be designated). The counselor would then employ one of the standard behavioral techniques for anxiety reduction, such as desensitization or cue-controlled relaxation. Behavioral counseling would not be considered successful until the client's test anxiety was reduced to a clinically insignificant level.

Differences between existential and behavioral approaches to counseling are not quite as extreme. Whereas a Rogerian counselor might define a counseling relationship characterized by counselor congruence, regard, and empathy as "necessary and sufficient" for client progress, a behavioral counselor would be somewhat more skeptical. Initially, the behavioral counselor would ask how these relationship qualities might be defined in terms of what the counselor actually does. Ivey's (1971) work provides an excellent partial answer. Empathic counselors, for example, exhibit the clearly definable "attending behaviors" of eye contact, postural position, and verbal following. The behavioral counselor would probably endorse these relationship qualities as "necessary but insufficient" for client progress. Certainly a positively reinforcing relationship can facilitate the discovery of client problems and accelerate goal attainment, but the behavioral counselor would argue that as with medicine, there ought to be more to the practice of counseling than a good couch-side manner.

Differences between rational and behavioral approaches to counseling are more subtle. In working with the presenting problem of test anxiety, for example, a rational emotive counselor would first identify the irrational self-statements containing exaggerated consequences of failing a test (for example, "That would prove I'm a worthless person!"). The rational emotive counselor would then point out their absurdity and suggest a more appropriate private monologue. Behavioral counselors, particularly those with an appreciation for the material contained in chapter 3, might approach this problem in a similar manner. Unlike the exclusively rational counselor, however, the behavioral counselor would be free to augment this cognitive intervention with more traditional behavioral programming.

Behavioral Counseling and Classical Decision Theory

The goal of behavioral decision-making counseling, is obviously the making of a decision. Behavioral counselors assume that a favorable outcome is more likely if the client engages in a number of preparatory behaviors prior to choosing. The counselor's major tasks are to stimulate and reinforce these client behaviors. Classical decision theory supports this active counselor role. Recall from our discussion of Bayes's theorem in chapter 4 that the more information we have about objective probability, the greater the likelihood of agreement between objective probability and our own subjective probability estimate. Some of the preparatory behaviors in behavioral decision-making counseling involve the gathering of probability information. Thus to the extent that classical decision theory can be used to facilitate adaptive decision making, behavioral decision-making counseling does likewise.

As seen in chapter 5, the language of classical decision theory is severely limited when applied to real-life client concerns. Behavioral counseling offers a more expansive model in which classical decision theory might be viewed as a subset. It would perhaps be more accurate to say that behavioral counseling offers the *promise* of a more expansive model. In point of fact, behavioral counselors have had relatively little to say about procedures for helping clients resolve choice problems. The principle exception to this observation is the work of John D. Krumboltz and his students at Stanford University. Most of their writing has been in the area of career choice. Essentially, Krumboltz and his students began with classical decision theory and immersed it in a general decision-making counseling model. Their model consists of eight concrete steps or operations behavioral counselors ought to accomplish with clients facing problems of career choice. (Krumboltz & Baker, 1973; Krumboltz & Thoresen, 1964):

1. Defining the problem and the client's goals
2. Agreeing mutually to achieve counseling goals
3. Generating alternative problem solutions
4. Collecting information about the alternatives
5. Examining the consequences of the alternatives
6. Revaluing goals, alternatives, and consequences
7. Making the decision or tentatively selecting an alternative contingent upon new developments and new opportunities
8. Generalizing the decision-making process to new problems

It is important to realize that these operations need not necessarily be followed in the above order. Rather, they ought to be considered priorities. The sequence for accomplishing them might vary somewhat from client to client.

Other authors have developed similar conceptual models for decision making and problem solving. Their work will be reviewed and synthesized in subsequent chapters. Krumboltz's paradigm is illustrated here largely because of its representativeness and also because it stimulated the vast majority of the research reviewed in this chapter. Most of the research on behavioral decision-making counseling has been restricted in focus. Armed with the assumption that the need for alternative generating and information gathering is self-evident, behavioral researchers have endeavored to apply concepts from operant and social learning theory to the fostering of such client behavior.

Verbal Conditioning in Decision-Making Counseling

In a seminal study Ryan and Krumboltz (1964) attempted to determine if counselors could use verbal approval (expressions such as "good" or "fine") to influence clients' deliberation and decision statements. Deliberation statements involved a tentative weighing of alternatives (for example, "I want to look over the general requirements before I plan my course"). Decision statements pertained to conclusions that had been reached in the past, alternatives that had been rejected, or decisions that had been reached during the counseling interview (for example, "I am spending more time studying now"). Sixty male students were randomly assigned to one of two counselors and one of three treatments: (1) decision responses reinforced, (2) deliberation responses reinforced, and (3) decision-deliberation responses not reinforced. Each student was seen in a twenty-minute individual counseling session that was divided into operant, treatment, and extinction periods. Ryan and Krumboltz found that deliberation and decision statements increased during the reinforcement period but declined when reinforcement was withdrawn. Moreover, the counselors were differentially effective; that is, one of the counselors was clearly superior in terms of producing the desired changes. Furthermore, on a projective story-telling test those clients who had been reinforced for making decision responses continued to do so at a higher rate than those clients exposed to the other treatments. Finally, none of the clients indicated an awareness of the response-reinforcement relationship during their interviews.

This 1964 study by Ryan and Krumboltz is important in a number of respects. In the first place it was a dramatic illustration of the verbal conditioning phenomenon (for example, Greenspoon, 1955; Krasner, 1958; Verplanck, 1955) in an applied setting. Moreover, it showed that counselors had the capacity to influence their clients' decision-making behavior at least within the context of a counseling interview. Several unsettling issues remain, however. Why, for example, did the two counselors who were trained to a high degree of reliability in recognizing deliberation and decision responses prove to be differentially effective? There is a logical problem inherent in this study as well. During extinction periods deliberation and decision responses decreased. However, on the generalization measure comparatively high rates of these behaviors still remained. Presumably, one would expect little or no generalization from extinguished behavior. Moreover, the adequacy of the generalization measure (a projective test) is certainly open to question. Does counselor verbal reinforcement produce changes in active client behavior outside of the interview? Finally, although the clients were not aware that they were being verbally conditioned, perhaps the same or even greater changes in decision-making behaviors could have been effected by mere advice giving on the part of the counselor.

Subsequent studies conducted by Krumboltz and his students focused on the fostering of information-seeking behavior in clients through the use of verbal reinforcement and modeling procedures. These will be reviewed below. Several of the questions raised by the Ryan and Krumboltz (1964) study were answered in the next decade by Samaan and Parker (1973), who compared the effects of verbal-reinforcement counseling and advice-giving counseling on the frequency of information-seeking responses within the interview and the frequency and variety of information-seeking behavior outside of the counseling interview. Information-seeking responses within the interview included expressions of past, present, active, or intent for future seeking of relevant information. Information-seeking behaviors outside of the interview consisted of writing, reading, talking, self-information, visiting, listening, and job exploration. The latter was assessed through interview questionnaires, of which a sample of ten were found to be 87 percent valid. Four counselors administered the two treatments (and a no-treatment control) to fifty clients in two individual counseling sessions one week apart. Verbal-reinforcement counseling resulted in significantly more information-seeking responses within the interview and marginally ($p<.10$) greater information-seeking behavior outside of the interview. Generalization was evidenced under verbal-reinforcement counseling by a marginally significant correlation ($p<.10$) between information seeking within and outside of the interview.

Although the verbal conditioning phenomenon in laboratory settings is well documented, the Ryan and Krumboltz (1964) and Samaan and Parker (1973) studies specifically suggest that verbal reinforcement can promote certain client decision-making behaviors within a counseling interview and that there may be generalization of these behaviors outside of the interview. Moreover, verbal reinforcement is substantially superior to advice giving.

Verbal Conditioning and Modeling in Decision-Making Counseling: Comparative Research

The topic of verbal conditioning raises the ire of many nonbehaviorists. Degrading analogies between counselors rewarding clients with praise and laboratory technicians reinforcing rats with food pellets are occasionally drawn. What is frequently overlooked, however, is the fact that behaviorists did not invent verbal reinforcement. They have only sought to describe it, illustrate it, and employ it when helping clients resolve their problems. In any event, although verbal conditioning was a popular research topic in the 1950's and early 1960's, its importance in counseling—and indeed to human learning in general—soon paled in the light of modeling theory and research (Bandura, 1969).

After the Ryan and Krumboltz (1964) project that showed the influence of verbal conditioning on clients' deliberation and decision responses, Krumboltz and his students began a stream of studies attempting to increase internal and external information-seeking behavior of clients faced with career decisions. The latter would occur within three weeks after counseling and was assessed by experimentally blind interviewers. Such behavior was quantified in terms of frequency and variety (for example, talking to three different people employed in a considered occupation and reading two articles about that occupation would yield a frequency score of five and a variety score of two). Random samples of these questionnaires were objectively verified and in all studies adequate validity was reported.

In the first project (Krumboltz & Schroeder, 1965) fifty-four eleventh-grade students were stratified on sex and then randomly assigned to one of nine counselors and one of three treatments. In the reinforcement counseling treatment the counselors verbally and nonverbally reinforced their clients for engaging in any information-seeking behavior. The model-reinforcement counseling treatment was similar with one exception: Prior to counseling the client heard a fifteen-minute audiotape that depicted a male student facing a decision-making concern and requesting relevant information. The taped counselor expressed approval of the student's information-seeking comments and led the student to consider other relevant information. In a no-treatment control condition clients were not contacted prior to the final assessment. Krumboltz and Schroeder found that although the effects of the experimental treatments on information-seeking behavior within the interview were negligible, both reinforcement and model-reinforcement counseling produced more external information-seeking behavior than was displayed by clients in the no-treatment control condition. Further analysis revealed that the male and female clients responded differentially to the experimental treatments. Reinforcement counseling was significantly effective with female clients but not with male clients on the frequency and variety measures. On the other hand, males in the model-reinforcement group carried out a greater variety of information-seeking behaviors than did males in the reinforcement group; no significant differences appeared for the females. Because the model tape was of a male student and because seven of the nine counselors were female, Krumboltz and Schroeder speculated that counselor and model sex-effects contributed to the pattern of results. In other words, information seeking by the female clients may have been largely due to the presence of a reinforcing female counselor, whereas the male clients were more influenced by the male model tape.

Krumboltz and Thoresen (1964) subsequently conducted a replication and extension of the publication-delayed Krumboltz and Schroeder (1965) project. They randomly assigned 192 eleventh-grade clients who were stratified on sex and participating school to one of the following treatment conditions: (1) individual model reinforcement, (2) group model reinforcement, (3) individual reinforcement, (4) group reinforcement, (5) individual control film discussion, (6) group control film discussion, and (7) inactive control group. In contrast to the earlier study, which examined only individually administered verbal-reinforcement and model-reinforcement counseling, this study also explored possible differences between individual and group counseling modes. Moreover, study design was improved by the addition of a placebo control procedure. Again the authors found the model-reinforcement treatment to be more effective with males than the reinforcement treatment, but there was no significant difference among females. Taken as a whole, the individual and group counseling modes were equally effective, although some counselors in certain schools were better with groups and others were better with individuals. In a further analysis of the data, Thoresen and Krumboltz (1967) found that counselor reinforcement of information-seeking responses within the interview was positively correlated with client information seeking outside of the interview.

In an attempt to determine if the foregoing findings held true with nonurban youth, Meyer, Strowig, and Hosford (1970) randomly assigned 288 eleventh-grade males and females from six high schools in rural Wisconsin to verbal-reinforcement and audio-model-reinforcement counseling in group and individual counseling modes. A no-treatment control and another condition involving a filmed model in the context of group-reinforcement counseling were also included in the design. The model counselors were male, but model clients were the same sex as the students. All behavioral counseling procedures were found to be equally effective but superior to the no-treatment control procedure in terms of producing increases in frequency and variety of information-seeking behavior. Moreover, in contrast to the Krumboltz and Schroeder (1965) and Krumboltz and Thoresen (1964) projects, Meyer and his associates found that female students participated in more information-seeking behavior than did males receiving similar counseling treatments in the same school.

In a related study Atkinson (1971) randomly assigned forty-six male and forty-eight female high-achieving tenth graders to one of nine counselers and one of four treatment conditions: (1) verbal-reinforcement counseling, (2) videotape-model-reinforcement counseling, (3) role-playing-reinforcement counseling, and (4) control discussion counseling. Student-initiated actions such as interviewing a resource person or looking through college catalogs constituted the major dependent variable. Both verbal- and model-reinforcement counseling were superior to the control treatment. Role-played-reinforcement counseling was not. Moreover, model-reinforcement counseling produced more student activity than the role-played-reinforcement treatment. The models were of the same sex as the students and the results held true for both sexes.

Generally speaking, comparative research on verbal-reinforcement and model-reinforcement decision-making counseling has not been extensive. Two of the four studies employed no-treatment control groups, which can be used to illustrate that something happened but shed relatively little light on why. Simple attention, instructions, or suggestions from the counselor, for example, might produce comparable effects. In any event, the studies as a whole suggest that both verbal-reinforcement and model-reinforcement techniques can produce information seeking by students. Furthermore, no differences appear when these treatments are immersed in the context of group or individual counseling. Clear superiority of model-reinforcement over verbal-reinforcement counseling has not been demonstrated. There is some indication that same-sex models may enhance the effectiveness of model-reinforcement counseling; however, the outcome data in the studies reviewed so far have not been consistent in this regard. Moreover, the factors that contribute to the success or failure of certain counselors using these techniques remain unknown.

Permutations of Model-Reinforcement Decision-Making Counseling

Armed with data that verbal-reinforcement counseling could accelerate clients' decision-making behavior and that the addition of models offered the promise of increased effectiveness, Krumboltz and his students began to take a closer look at the role of model characteristics in promoting change. In both the Krumboltz and Schroeder (1965) and Krumboltz and Thoresen (1964) studies female students proved to be nonresponsive to the model-reinforcement treatment that depicted a male model. Krumboltz, Varenhorst, and Thoresen (1967) then randomly assigned fifty-six female high school juniors from seven schools to video-model-reinforcement counseling, directions control treatment, or no treatment at all. The model counselor's prestige and attentiveness were experimentally manipulated as well, but without effect. Retrospectively the authors concluded that the model counselor's characteristics were probably less important than those of the model client. In any event they did find that the female clients who observed female models performed more information-seeking behavior than did the female clients in either control treatment. (Recall that similar results were later reported by Meyer, Strowig, and Hosford, 1970, and Atkinson, 1971.)

Next, Thoresen, Krumboltz, and Varenhorst (1967) examined the effect that the sex of the model counselors, model clients, and actual counselors had upon male and female clients. Ninety-six male and female high school juniors were randomly assigned either to audio-model-reinforcement counseling, in which all possible model counselor-client and actual counselor-client sex combinations were varied, or to active and inactive control conditions. They found that (1) model-reinforcement procedures were more effective than control procedures for males but not for females, (2) male students responded best when males were in all other roles, and (3) female students were most affected by a male counselor presenting either an all-male or an all-female model tape. Thus, although the results of these studies appear consistent for male clients, the effects of model-reinforcement counseling on female clients are not quite as predictable.

Thoresen and Krumboltz (1968) then conducted two more studies in which male models of varying athletic and academic skill were exposed to male clients displaying similar levels of proficiency. In the first study forty-eight students of self-reported high, medium, or low athletic success from two schools were assigned to one of two counselors and either a high, medium, or low athletic success model. In the second study seventy-two students of self-reported high, medium, or low academic success from three schools were assigned to one of three counselors and either a high, medium, or low academic success model. Highly skilled athletic models were most effective in producing information seeking by the students; variations in the academic success model yielded insignificant differences.

In a massive follow-up to these two studies, Thoresen, Hosford, and Krumboltz (1970) exposed models of high, medium, and low success in athletic, academic, and social endeavors to 189 students similarly categorized. Moreover, aspired success levels were also taken into account. Although several subanalyses of the data replicated previous work, some puzzling interactions occurred. Moreover, the experimental students did not consistently seek more information than control students who participated in their school's traditional guidance program (for example, a "career day"). Thus this ambitious study lent little support to the utility of model-reinforcement counseling.

Stilwell and Thoresen (1972) investigated the effect of the model's ethnic group on attitudes toward vocational education, interest in various occupations, and information-seeking behavior. They randomly assigned 68 Mexican-American and 179 non-Mexican-American tenth-grade boys from two schools to one of the following treatments: (1) Mexican-American model videotape, (2) non-Mexican-American model videotape, (3) audio-tape control (formed from the soundtracks of the two video-tapes), and (4) script control (presentation of a written dialogue from the experimental treatments). The non-Mexican-American model was most effective in producing positive attitudes toward vocational education; however, interest in various occupations was fostered best by models of similar ethnic background. Unfortunately, no differences in actual information seeking resulted between experimental and control conditions.

More promising findings were reported by Wachowiak (1972), who randomly assigned sixty undergraduate males to one of eight male counsel-ors and one of three treatment conditions: (1) model-reinforcement coun-seling, (2) traditional (trait and factor) counseling, and (3) no-treatment control. Model-reinforcement counseling resulted in greater certainty-of-academic-major ratings than did traditional counseling, which in turn pro-duced higher ratings than the control condition. These differences were still apparent at six- and twelve-week follow-up periods. An identical results pattern was found on a satisfaction-with-major variable except that at twelve weeks differences between the traditional and control treatments washed out. Finally, on the Vocational Decision-Making Checklist (Harren, 1964) both model-reinforcement and traditional counseling resulted in sig-nificant improvement in comparison to the no-treatment control condition but did not differ from each other.

Similarly, Fisher, Reardon, and Burck (1976) randomly assigned twenty-one male and twenty-one female college students to one of three career information treatments, two of which differed only in terms of the presence or absence of a model-reinforced videotape. The third treatment consisted of alternate informational materials. Fisher and his associates were concerned with types of information seeking (the write, observe, read, listen, visit, and talk categories adapted from Stewart, 1969) and frequency of these behaviors. The model-reinforcement treatment produced greater type and frequency scores than did either of the other two treatments. Female observers showed increases in types of information seeking while male observers displayed increases in the frequency of such behavior. Because the model tape depicted a male counselor and client, these dif-ferential effects are difficult to interpret; but the overall pattern lends sup-port to the utility of model-reinforcement procedures in decision-making counseling.

Following laboratory evidence that vicarious reinforcement can enhance a model effectiveness (see Bandura, 1969), LaFleur and Johnson (1972) sought to investigate this phenomenon in an applied context. One hundred and forty tenth- and eleventh-grade students were randomly assigned to active control or to cartoon booklet treatments in which the model was or was not reinforced. Performance of modeled behaviors (infor-mation seeking via postcards, library books, invited speaker, counselor conference), knowledge of these behaviors, and interest in seeking informa-tion were assessed before and after treatment. Although the modeling treat-ments did not differ from each other, both were superior to the active control condition on all criteria.

It is difficult to draw firm conclusions from the array of studies described above. In the first place different researchers employed different outcome measures. Moreover, the use of no-contact or minimal-contact con-trol groups can help a very impractical effect reach statistical significance. Finally, attempts to replicate important findings are conspicuously absent from the literature or are disappointing. In spite of these interpretative cautions, however, most of the studies do suggest that model-reinforcement counseling is an effective means of promoting student information seeking. Care should probably be taken to match the sex of the model with the sex of the client. It is not clear whether video models are more potent than audio models. Although there is laboratory evidence suggesting that models should be similar to the observers, successful by observer standards, and reinforced for engaging in the modeled behavior, applied research studies in decision-making counseling have been too few and sporadic to verify these principles. Excellent illustrations of the considerations involved in constructing model tapes can be found in Stewart (1969) and Hamilton and Bergland (1972).

Simulation Strategies

Few of us would buy a new pair of shoes without trying them on for size. Yet many individuals enter or prepare for entry into various careers knowing relatively little about the day-to-day rewards and punishments inherent in them. Provision of such "real" information is the major purpose of the *Job Experience Kits* (1970) developed by Krumboltz and his students (Krumboltz, Baker, & Johnson, 1968; Krumboltz, Sheppard, Jones, Johnson, & Baker, 1967). One such kit describes the work of a police officer (Krumboltz & Bergland, 1969), another, the job of an appliance serviceman (Nelson & Krumboltz, 1970). In the accountant kit (Krumboltz & Sheppard, 1969) the student becomes immersed in the detective work of an accountant searching for evidence of fraud.

Basically, the materials are self-contained, programmed learning experiences that also happen to be easily readable and attractively packaged. Information on a particular career is supplied and followed by problem-solving activities of gradually increasing complexity. Thus students can work vicariously at a number of jobs before choosing and committing themselves to a particular kind of work.

The kits are based on research activity, not on mere marketing considerations; as part of their development they were experimentally compared to control treatments in which students were provided with similar information but in a different manner. In summarizing the empirical status of these kits, Krumboltz and Baker (1973) report that the materials consistently produced more declared interest and more overt occupational information seeking than did the control treatments. Moreover,

a) Students tended to explore not only the occupations for which they solved problems but in addition a greater number of different occupations than did students who experienced the control treatments. b) Girls tended to out-perform boys in information seeking, especially in the lower socioeconomic schools. c) Students in the problem-solving groups exhibited more knowledge of work expectations and estimates of job satisfaction than did control students. d) Students who worked problem-solving kits made more requests to work on additional kits than did control subjects. e) Varying the number of correct answers necessary to have the students' performance labeled "successful" had insignificant effects on the criterion measures. f) Students given their choices of kits to work with were more active information seekers and expressed more positive attitudes toward those occupations than did students who did not receive their choices of materials. g) Students given specific questions to use in their information quests achieved higher scores on occupational information tests than did students who received only general guidelines. h) Students who were notified that they would be asked questions about the information they had gathered achieved higher scores on occupational information tests than did those who were not notified. This effect was especially marked among students who did not receive their choices of kits. i) Added realism in the kits (use of an actual ammeter in the Electronic Technician Kit instead of a diagram) significantly increased several criterion responses (Hamilton & Krumboltz, 1969). j) Eleventh graders tended to seek more information than ninth, tenth, or twelfth graders.*

The Life Career Game (Boocock, 1968) is another popular simulation technique designed to prepare students "for intelligent career-decision making." In a series of case studies and quasi experiments, Boocock (1967) and Varenhorst (1969) reported very favorable effects. Unfortunately, these optimistic findings have not held up under controlled experimental investigation (Johnson & Euler, 1972; Swails & Herr, 1976). Even incorporation of a specific decision-making strategy did not enhance the game's effectiveness (Munson, Horan, Miano, & Stone, 1976). Although these evaluative efforts in turn might be criticized on the basis of insensitive assessment devices or low interest levels on the part of the student participants, the value of the Life Career Game remains experimentally unconfirmed.

---

*John D. Krumboltz, and R.D. Baker, "Behavioral counseling for vocational decisions," in *Career Guidance for a New Age*, ed. H. Barrow (Boston: Houghton-Mifflin, 1973.) pp. 268-69.

Toward More Comprehensive Programming

Most of the studies reviewed so far in this chapter demonstrate that a specific procedure can result in a statistically significant increase in a particular behavior. For example, a group of Irish-American students who observe an Irish-American student athlete visiting a career library can be expected to visit that library in greater numbers than a similar group of Irish-American students who have not observed the model. At least such will likely be true for the male students! Studies that show such differences are useful illustrations of behavioral principles. The fact that most of these treatments can be administered in less than an hour attests to the power of these principles. But in a practical sense adaptive decision making demands more than many of these information-seeking behaviors imply. Thus researcher and practitioner attention gradually shifted toward the development of more comprehensive programming.

Thoresen and Hamilton (1972) randomly assigned eighty eleventh-grade male students to one of three experimental treatments or one of two kinds of control conditions: (1) video-presented peer social modeling, (2) group counseling with structured stimulus materials, (3) peer social modeling combined with structured stimulus materials, (4) attention placebo control, and (5) delayed treatment control. Unlike previous work, this study focused on ways of assisting students in processing information as well as seeking it. Moreover, four counseling sessions were conducted instead of the typical one or two. Treatment effects were evaluated by a pre- and post-assessment of knowledge of how to obtain and use relevant career information, identification and use of a variety of information in a simulated career exploration situation, and frequency and variety of career exploratory behaviors performed outside the treatment setting. Thoresen and Hamilton found that on the knowledge test peer social modeling and the combined modeling and materials treatments were superior to both control treatments. The materials alone treatment was not. However, on the simulation test all three experimental treatments were better than the control treatments. Unfortunately no significant differences were found on frequency and variety of career exploratory behaviors. In contrast to previous work using these two variables, a more powerful treatment resulted in a weaker effect. The authors explain this paradox by suggesting that the pretest may have diminished the utility of the assessment device.

More equivocal findings were reported in a similar project by Bergland, Quatrano, and Lundquist (1975). They randomly assigned eighty male eleventh-grade students to one of two counselors and one of four treatment conditions: (1) structured group interaction, (2) videotaped models, (3) videotaped models and structured interaction, and (4) delayed treatment control. They employed numerous dependent measures but found no significant differences on any of them. Bergland and his associates speculated that the particular group of students used in this study may not have been appropriate because they were not seeking help, they were vocationally well experienced, and many had already made career choices.

In marked contrast to both of the above studies, Evans and Cody (1969) reported very promising findings. They randomly assigned sixty eighth-grade students (thirty males and thirty females) to one of three treatment conditions. In the guided practice condition the students listened to a tape-recorded presentation of a decision-making strategy adopted from Bross (1953) and Gelatt (1962). Then they observed a videotaped model of a male student being assisted by a male adult in the working through of a problem in decision making. Replays of the model tape were used to teach the decision-making strategy. The students were then seen individually by one of five male counselors, who guided them in practicing the strategy until they were able to implement the strategy successfully without assistance in three consecutive training problems. The nonguided condition essentially amounted to a placebo control in which the setting, problems, and adult attention remained constant. A no-treatment control group was also employed. Evans and Cody reported that on an immediate posttraining test both male and female students in the guided practice condition were significantly superior to those in the other two conditions in implementing the decision-making strategy. Such an outcome is not especially remarkable, however, in view of the fact that the assessment and training tasks for the guided practice treatment were similar. But it is noteworthy that this superiority continued to be apparent in a thirteen-day follow-up, during which they also found that the decision-making skills had transferred to dissimilar situations.

Later Smith and Evans (1973) conducted a similar project with thirty-six male and thirty female college students. The experimental guidance program consisted of training in Bross's, (1953) decision-making strategy in conjunction with identification of the students' values, interests, and traits. Weekly activities included listening to audiotapes, a large group meeting, and a small group counseling session over a five-week period. This experimental program was contrasted with traditional individual vocational counseling and a no-treatment control. Scores on the Vocational Decision-Making Checklist (Harren, 1964) were higher for the experimental program than for individual counseling, which in turn was superior to no treatment at all. No differences between the two counseling procedures were apparent on a student evaluation form that purported to tap completeness of and satisfaction with counseling.

Essentially then, adaptive decision making requires more than the simple gathering of information; for example, clients must also learn how to process this information. Research attention thus shifted away from "one-shot" modeling-reinforcement treatments toward the development of more comprehensive programming. Studies by Evans and his colleagues suggest that decision-making strategies can be learned and retained in the context of counseling.

Behavioral Decision-Making Counseling in Other Areas

Considering the relevance of decision-making counseling to the problems clients present to behavioral counselors, the lack of systematic research and development activity in this area is both surprising and disappointing. The work of John Krumboltz, his advisees, and in turn their advisees constitutes most of what little has been done. Moreover, the Krumboltz legacy has been largely restricted to only one aspect of decision-making counseling, vocational choice. Except for a few sporadic endeavors, no research data exists on how to help clients resolve other choice problems. A few evaluated attempts to apply decision-making counseling to mental patients, alcoholics, and delinquent and nondelinquent youth are reviewed below.

Mental Patients

Olson and Greenberg (1972) immersed several aspects of decision-making counseling into the context of a token economy program designed to improve the personal functioning of chronic mental patients. Seventy-four institutionalized mental patients were assigned to either no treatment, placebo treatment, or an incentive treatment that used cash and canteen privileges to reinforce the patients for participating in groups formed to help them plan and administer their own treatment (the groups wrote progress reports on their members containing recommendations for treatment programming). Group leadership was rotated and therapist control was gradually phased out, so the groups became relatively autonomous decision-making bodies. The incentive condition produced a greater percentage of attendance at activities, more townpasses taken, and a larger number of days spent out of the hospital. The nursing staff, which may have been resistant to the concept of increased patient responsibility, rated the placebo condition more favorably.

Olson and Greenberg do not indicate whether they employed a replicable decision-making model, and their study might be critiqued on methodological grounds, including nonrandom assignment of patients to treatment conditions. Nevertheless, the study does suggest that giving patients responsibility for making decisions about themselves and reinforcing them for exercising this responsibility may bring about improvements in other areas of personal functioning.

Alcoholics

Most alcoholism treatment programs are based on the a priori decision that complete abstinence is the only viable counseling goal. Controlled drinking, however, has been receiving considerable attention in recent years as a possible treatment goal (for example, Addis & Horan, 1975; Hedberg & Campbell, 1974; Sobell & Sobell, 1973; Wilson & Rosen, 1976). Such programs may allow a client to choose between abstinence and controlled drinking, but relatively little has been written about the specific decision-making counseling process that ought to underlie the client's choice.

One notable exception to this pattern is the pilot work of Feldman (1976), who developed a relatively explicit decision-making counseling strategy for use with alcoholics and applied it to a group of ten inpatients in a residential alcoholic rehabilitation facility in rural Pennsylvania. Nine patients previously admitted and recently discharged from that facility served as controls. Feldman attempted to evaluate his program on the basis of a questionnaire administered by a caseworker one month after treatment. Satisfaction with life and continuity of employment were the major dependent variables, but experimental mortality was so high in the control group that statistical analysis was not possible. Defining success as completion of the treatment program, sobriety, and availability for follow-up assessment and defining failure as dropping out of the treatment program, intoxication, or lack of availability for follow-up assessment, Feldman reported an 80 percent success rate for the experimental group compared to only 22 percent for the controls. Of course, Feldman's work can be critiqued on numerous methodological grounds (nonrandom assignment of subjects, brief follow-up period, a posteriori definitions of success and failure, and so forth); nevertheless it is a promising early attempt at applying behavioral decision-making counseling to an alcoholic population.

Delinquent and Nondelinquent Youth

Russell (1977) has extended the vocational decision-making work of his mentors at Stanford to the development of a booklet and audiotape treatment package designed to provide delinquent youths with skills needed to resolve problems of choice (see also Russell & Thoresen, 1976). The initial quasi-experimental phase of his work involved pre- and posttesting a group of five delinquent children who proceeded through the decision-making materials. After treatment the children were able to generate an average of 4.4 alternatives in a simulated choice problem; prior to treatment they had been able to identify only an average of 2.9 alternatives. Russell then randomly assigned thirty-four elementary schoolchildren either to his experimental treatment of four hours duration or to no treatment at all. Those students exposed to the decision-making materials generated significantly more alternatives. Russell's attention then shifted to a microscopic inspection of those children helped least, so that refinements in his package could be made.

Branca, D'Augelli, and Evans (undated) also attempted to develop and evaluate a behaviorally based program for teaching decision-making skills to elementary schoolchildren. Their program consists of six forty-minute weekly sessions during which the students were "guided" through decisions faced by a simulated family. In contrasting their program with a control treatment on a "decision-dilemma questionnaire," however, they found no significant differences in decision-making ability.

Russell's positive results with juvenile delinquents need to be tempered by the realization that he employed a no-treatment control group. On the other hand, the generally disappointing results Branca and her associates reported need to be viewed in the light of the fact that they used a "powerful," commercially available self-concept-enhancement program as a placebo control. Both research endeavors must be considered as pilot work—promising but in need of revision, refinement, and reevaluation.

Research Status of Behavioral Decision-Making Counseling

The behavioral approach to decision-making counseling essentially involves the immersion of several aspects of formal decision theory into a more general counseling framework. Krumboltz's eight-step paradigm, which includes alternative generating and information gathering as key components, is a typical conceptual model. The goals of such counseling are the making of a decision and the learning of the decision-making process by the client. The counselor serves as a teacher, stimulator, reinforcer, and modeler of relevant client activities.

Behavioral decision-making counseling has not been evaluated intact.

In other words, we do not know from a research standpoint whether a client who experiences a particular decision-making counseling model will in fact gain an increased likelihood of making a good decision. Most behavioral researchers and practitioners have assumed that the worth of such models is self-evident. This risky but understandable assumption is fortified by the writings of well-known counseling scholars, supported by formal decision theory, and difficult to disprove. Nevertheless, behavioral decision-making counseling ought not be exempt from rigorous empirical scrutiny.

What we do know about behavioral decision-making counseling is that there are a number of principles and procedures counselors can adopt in order to accelerate certain client behaviors thought to be prerequisite to the making of an adaptive decision. For example, counselors who cue and reinforce their clients for information gathering can be relatively assured that such will happen. Even this assurance, however, must be tempered by the realization that counseling research standards have stiffened in recent years. All the early studies reviewed in this chapter were rigorous and highly credible from a historical perspective, but today increasing attention is being paid to the concept of experimental control (see Jacobson & Baucom, 1977; Kazdin & Wilcoxon, 1976). For example, research studies that purport efficacy for counseling treatments on the basis of comparisons between no treatment or weak placebo treatments must be interpreted with caution. Unfortunately, much of what we know about behavioral decision-making counseling is based on noncautious interpretation. This does not mean that the research evidence here is weaker than in other areas of counseling, but rather that all counseling research must respond to advances in experimental methodology. Research studies conducted in previous eras thus must be viewed with a healthy skepticism.

Summary

Behavioral counseling differs from the psychoanalytic approach primarily in terms of its emphasis on client goal attainment and on specification of client and counselor behaviors presumed to lead to such goals. It differs from the existential approach in viewing the relationship qualities as necessary but insufficient for client progress. Current practice of behavioral counseling has much in common with rational counseling except that rational interventions may be supplemented with more traditional behavioral programming for any given client problem.

Classical decision theory can be viewed as a subset of a behavioral approach to resolving client choice problems. Behavioral counselors assume that if their clients engage in a number of preparatory behaviors prior to choosing, the decision will be more likely to result in a favorable outcome. The counselor's major task is actively to foster such client behaviors.

Some research has shown that verbal reinforcement can promote certain decision-making behaviors of clients within a counseling interview and that there may be generalization of these behaviors outside of the interview. Moreover, verbal reinforcement is reportedly superior to advice giving.

Comparative research on verbal reinforcement and model reinforcement counseling has neither been extensive nor tightly controlled. Clear superiority of model reinforcement counseling has not been demonstrated. Moreover, the factors that contribute to the success or failure of certain counselors using these techniques remain unknown.

Many studies have shown that the various permutations of model reinforcement counseling can increase student information seeking. Care should probably be taken to match the sex of the model with the sex of the client. Although there is laboratory evidence suggesting that models should be similar to observers, successful by observer standards, and reinforced for engaging in the modeled behavior, applied research studies in decision-making counseling have been too few and sporadic to verify these principles.

Simulation strategies foster information gathering and permit tentative implementation of alternatives without committment. The *Job Experience Kits* have been favorably evaluated; the Life Career Game has not.

Adaptive decision making demands more than the simple gathering of information. More comprehensive approaches to decision-making counseling have received some support.

The research of John Krumboltz, his advisees, and in turn their advisees constitute most of the work done in behavioral decision-making counseling. Moreover, the Krumboltz legacy has been largely restricted to vocational choice concerns. There have been a few attempts to extend this work to mental patients, alcoholics, and both delinquent and nondelinquent children.

Many behavioral counseling strategies can promote the display of behaviors pertinent to adaptive decision making. Future research in this area needs to incorporate recent improvements in evaluation methodology and to demonstrate the practical utility of behavioral decision-making counseling.

This concludes the review of dynamic, rational, and behavioral approaches to resolving client choice problems. The next chapter focuses on problem-solving literature that has strong implications for decision-making counseling.

Pertinent Problem-Solving Literature

The literature on problem solving does not appear to be bounded by time or space. Historical figures such as James (1890), Thorndike (1898), and Dewey (1933) were contributers and current areas of inquiry include such diverse topics as creativity training and teaching computers to play chess. In his 1966 review, Davis remarked that research in human problem solving has a well-earned reputation for being the most chaotic of all categories of learning. "It is almost definitional of laboratory problem-solving experiments that virtually any semi-complex learning task which does not clearly fall into a familiar area of learning can safely be called 'problem solving' (p. 36)." Duncan (1959) voiced a similar lament in an earlier review, and the word "chaotic" remains an apt descriptor today.

The decision-making and problem-solving literatures overlap to a considerable extent; indeed, some authors use the terms interchangeably (see Krumboltz & Thoresen, 1976, pp. 368-414). Others view decision making as merely a subset of problem solving; for example, D'Zurilla and Goldfried (1971) reduce decision making to a single component in a five-stage general model of a problem-solving process. Still other authors (for example, Brinkers, 1972; Janis & Mann, 1977; Lindley, 1971) treat decision making as a fully autonomous entity. The reader is invited to adopt whatever conceptual framework seems clear and feels comfortable. My own theoretical bias is to set decision making in bold relief as an academic discipline and as a counseling strategy. However, there are a number of concepts in the amorphous problem-solving literature that have a direct bearing on the conduct of decision-making counseling. This chapter is a concession to their relevance.

Some Definitional Difficulties

As with other concepts in education and the social sciences, dictionary definitions of "problem" abound. Thorndike's (1898) early definition is still widely quoted: "A problem exists when the goal that is sought is not directly attainable by the performance of a simple act available in the animal's repertory; the solution calls for either a novel action or a new integration of available actions" (cited by Sheerer, 1963, p. 118). More recently, Skinner (1966, p. 225) said as much in fewer words: "A question for which there is at the moment no answer is a problem." Arguing that the terms "question" and "answer" are restricted to verbal problems, Davis (1973, p. 12) suggests, "A problem is a stimulus situation for which an organism does not have a ready response." Then, taking a cue from Dewey (1938) and Hoffman (1961), Davis adds that the stimulus situation cannot permit the problem solver the option of avoiding or ignoring the problem. Thus "problems" that we don't have to solve aren't problems.

Counseling problems might be conceptualized in a similar manner. A client has a problem when he or she feels called upon to act but does not know which action is appropriate. What to do about a troubled marriage or how to cope with an intrusive supervisor are typical of the myriad problems clients bring to counselors. However, problems studied in experimental laboratories, for example, how to build a coat rack out of two sticks and a "C" clamp (Maier, 1945), are usually free of agonizing emotional concomitants.

No one has as yet offered a universally acceptable definition of a problem. This lack of a firm conceptual groundwork, however, has not impeded the erection of theoretical skyscrapers. Mahoney (1974) muses that workers in this field seem to have less difficulty describing their tree than their forest. To be sure, such is the case with many if not most concepts in education and the social sciences. Wechsler and Binet may differ in their definitions of intelligence, but researchers who operationally define intelligence in terms of a particular test score can readily communicate with one another. Unfortunately, the problem-solving literature includes a vast array of operational definitions for problem situations and problem-solving performance, each with a host of shortcomings (see Gagné, 1964).

Behavioral Perspectives of Problem Solving

Alexander Bain first used the words "trial and error" to describe thinking in 1855, four years before Darwin published his work on natural selection (Campbell, 1960). Almost five decades later, Thorndike (1898, 1911) attempted to demonstrate in the laboratory that animals solve problems through trial and error learning. A caged hungry cat permitted to see and smell a dish of food will exhibit a variety of seemingly random behaviors. Inefficient responses—those that do not lead to the food, such as scratching the floor or biting the cage bars—will gradually extinguish. After a number of trials and errors the cat may "accidently" turn a latch that grants access to the food. This reinforced response will eventually prevail.

It is important to note that the early problem-solving behavior of Thorndike's cat was not random but rather the result of genetic predisposition or prior learning or both. Such behavior might be termed "blind" in that the correct solution is unknown. Moreover, turning a latch is a response not likely to be in the cat's repertoire; so this problem will be harder to solve than another involving, for example, pulling a string. Similarly, because of a rooting tendency, a pig is more likely to solve a problem that requires raising a small platform than is either a cat or a dog (Maier & Burke, 1967).

Campbell (1960) extended Thorndike's trial and error perspective on animal problem solving to include creative thought and other knowledge processes in human beings. His central tenets are as follows:

1. A blind-variation and selective-retention process is fundamental to all inductive achievements, to all genuine increases in knowledge, to all increases in fit of system to environment.
2. The many processes which shortcut a more full blind-variation and selective-retention process are in themselves inductive achievements, containing wisdom about the environment achieved originally by blind variation and selective retention.
3. In addition such shortcut processes contain in their own operation a blind-variation and selective-retention process at some level, substituting for overt locomotor exploration or the life and death winnowing of organic evolution. (p. 380)

Essentially, then, according to Campbell, we do not behave randomly when confronted with a problem but rather in accord with our individual learning histories. We exhibit a number of blind responses, and our environment lets us know which one is correct. Some of us may be better problem solvers than others because we have learned pertinent problem-solving skills via selective environmental reinforcement. Our environment will continue to exert a refining influence on such skill development. Moreover, vision and thought processes are efficient generators of blind responses that can be substituted for motor trial and error behavior so that we need not act out incorrect solutions when we "see" they will not work.

Campbell's point of view has much in common with those of other behaviorists. Blind variation in problem-solving behavior, for example, might be further explained in terms of Hull's (1952) habit-hierarchy mechanism. A problem situation evokes a sequence of solution responses, the order of which is determined by individual reinforcement histories. In other words, we first try what has worked well for us in the past. Should our initial efforts not prove successful, we may exhibit other behaviors that are lower in our response hierarchies. Maltzman (1955) and Staats (1966) elaborated upon Hull's work by including complex combinations of different habit hierarchies in explaining problem-solving behavior.

Skinner's (1966) operant analysis of problem solving greatly expanded Campbell's concept of selective retention. According to Skinner, when we reinforce a response, we increase its probability; this is simple operant conditioning. "Problems" arise, however, when reinforcement contingencies are complex:

For example, there may be no response available which satisfies a given set of contingencies. Or competing responses may be evoked—among them emotional changes which weaken the very response upon which reinforcement is contingent or destroy the power of the reinforcer. Or the contingencies may be satisfied only by a sequence or chain of responses, early members of which are too remote from the terminal reinforcer to be strongly affected by it until conditioned reinforcers have been set up. (p. 226)

Skinner contended that it would be easy to teach Thorndike's cat how to solve its problem by shaping the latch-turning response, but clearly this is not the thing to do if we are interested in teaching problem solving. The latter can be facilated, for example, by reinforcing the learning of rules that serve as discriminative stimuli orienting the problem solver toward an effective solution. (Such rules are very much akin to Campbell's, 1960, concept of processes that "shortcut" full blind variation and selective retention.)

Gagné (1970) echoed this theme when he suggested that effective problem solving rests upon previously learned rules. Given a problem situation, the learner tries out a number of such rules and tests their applicability. When he or she finds a particular combination of rules that work, not only is the problem solved but something new is learned—an entity not formally different from a rule. "It may be more complex, and it is surely new (to the learner), but it is a rule with the same properties of broad applicability as other rules" (p. 215).

Davis (1966, 1973) elaborated on the visual and thought processes that Campbell (1960) suggested may be substituted for motor trial and error behavior. In his 1966 review, Davis classified laboratory problem-solving tasks according to whether they called for overt trial and error or "implicit problem-solving activity." Most laboratory tasks such as anagram problems call for the latter (except when paper and pencil or letter blocks are provided). Davis (1973, p. 43) neatly summarized the research in this area in one sentence: "The problem-solver will think if he can, he will manipulate if he must."

Classical conditioning may also play a role in problem solving. Kendler and Kendler (1962) point out that problem solving involves both "horizontal" and "vertical" processes. Horizontal processes are best typified by long Skinnerian chains of behavior that occur over time. Vertical processes acknowledge the fact that such chains exist simultaneously and can interact. Serendipity, the art of finding one thing while looking for another, illustrates this interaction. The Kendlers believe that problem solutions often involve a vertical connection between a cue and a response from different chains. Davis (1973, p. 57) has provided an excellent example of this phenomenon: "A bat or porpoise may navigate by bouncing its voice off unseen objects. This information, viewed as a horizontal idea-chain, might suggest a solution for the parallel (vertical) stimulus problem of inventing a navigational aid for blind people."

At the risk of oversimplification, then, I will say the behavioral perspective is that problem solving is basically a trial and error enterprise. But trial and error should be interpreted in a broad sense to include not only physical activity but also seeing and thinking. Given a problematic situation, we normally try out a number of potential solutions, not randomly, but in accord with our learning histories—strongly reinforced responses are generally displayed first. In the course of our experience we will undoubtedly discover a number of problem-solving shortcuts or rules. Like the boxer who learns never to lead with a right, we can acquire these rules through trial and error (ouch!), or they may be transmitted by society. Sometimes experiences we have had in other areas suggest the solution to a problem (vertical processes).

Behaviorists do not have a monopoly on the problem-solving literature. Gestalt psychologists such as Köhler (1925) and Sheerer (1963) have been equally if not more prolific in contributing their views. Köhler stressed the importance of insight, contended that Thorndike's cats merely stumbled onto the solution through chance alone, and argued that true problem solving could occur only under favorable optical conditions. A chimpanzee, for example, after an hour of "fruitless" activity paused to survey its environment, then insightfully used a stick to rake in a banana placed just out of arm's reach. If Thorndike's cats could have seen the relationship between the latch and the access to food, they might have shown the sudden insightful behavior the chimpanzee displayed.

Since Köhler maintained that insight commonly occurred in animals, the concept hardly lends dignity to human beings (cf. Skinner, 1971). Moreover, the Gestaltists have been soundly criticized for a sentimental and theoretically foggy preoccupation with insight, which Campbell (1960) dismissed as merely the successful completion of a blind-variation cycle. (Recall that visual and cognitive trial and error can be substituted for overt activity. The chimpanzee more than likely tried out a number of potential responses in its "mind's eye" before discovering the stick-as-rake solution.) Furthermore, Campbell (1960, p. 390) asserted that when insight is "publicized as part of an ideology of creativity, it can reduce creativity through giving students a feeling that they lack an important gift possessed by some others, a feeling which inhibits creative effort and increases dependence upon authority."

On the other hand, the behavioral perspective has not yet really demonstrated its practical utility. Behavioral researchers have provided us with relatively consistent theorizing that is long on explanation but short on the generation of effective intervention strategies. Although many of the problem-solving treatments to be discussed below are compatible with the behavioral perspective, they did not originally flow from the pens of behaviorists.

Problem Solving and Counseling

Since D'Zurilla and Goldfried (1971) and Urban and Ford (1971) published their classic statements, numerous authors (for example, Dixon, 1976; Heppner, 1976; Mahoney, 1974; Spivack, Platt, & Shure, 1976) have emphasized the relevance of the problem-solving literature to counseling in general and behavioral counseling in particular. The interface between counseling and problem solving can be summarized as follows:

1. Client concerns may be conceptualized as problems analogous to the sort of problems studied in laboratory settings.

2. Problem-solving ability need not be defined as a psychometric trait subject to the same criticisms leveled by Mischel (1968, 1973) against other traits. Instead, problem solving might best be viewed as a generic term covering a number of individually identifiable and teachable skills.

3. Problem-solving techniques come from a diverse literature that includes, for example, creativity training. The designation of a particular intervention as pertinent to problem-solving counseling is based on demonstrated utility rather than theoretical fidelity. In other words, if a certain technique has been shown to produce a desired effect, it matters not that the technique originated with psychoanalysts, existentialists, behaviorists, or business executives. If need be, translations can be made at a later date.

4. Problem-solving skills clients acquire in the context of counseling for a particular concern may generalize to other concerns clients encounter in the course of their lives.

A wide variety of problem-solving strategies, ranging from fairly simple "tips" for the counselor to keep in mind to fully articulated treatment programs, have relevance to the conduct of counseling. Some of these interventions pertain more to the early stages of counseling, when the problem solver initially experiences a state of doubt or difficulty. Other interventions are designed to enable the client to generate a number of potentially effective solutions. Still others deal with all aspects of the problem-solving process. I shall discuss each of these categories in turn.

Early Interventions

D'Zurilla and Goldfried (1971) have reviewed a number of studies that suggest a particular kind of orientation attitude bears a strong relationship to problem-solving success. For example, Bloom and Broder (1950) found that less successful problem solvers tend to be impulsive, impatient, and quick to give up if they do not immediately find a solution. D'Zurilla and Goldfried assert that problem solvers ought to learn to accept the fact that problematic situations are to be expected by all and that effective coping is possible. Moreover, problem solvers need to recognize problematic situations when they occur and inhibit the tendency either to respond impulsively or do nothing at all. Presumably an Ellis (1962)-based counseling intervention would be useful in developing the appropriate general orientation.

Once the problem solver learns to "stop and think," D'Zurilla and Goldfried suggest the counselor's task is to help the client formulate the problem. Clinical problems, in contrast to those encountered in the laboratory, are usually ambiguous. The client will need to define the problem clearly in operational terms, separate relevant from irrelevant information, and identify the primary goals. Although D'Zurilla and Goldfried suggest that training programs like those developed by Karlins and Schroder (1967) and Crutchfield and his associates (Covington, Crutchfield, & Davies, 1966; Olton & Crutchfield, 1969) can help foster pertinent inquiry and formulation skills, most classroom programs of this sort are not applicable to individual counseling with adolescents and adults in distress. More appropriate perhaps would be a variety of strategies such as empathic listening (to extinguish anxiety), shaping of greater degrees of specificity in describing the problem, and model-reinforcement procedures to produce information gathering (see chapter 9).

A final early intervention strategy counters the well-known inhibiting influence of old habits in solving new problems (see Davis, 1973; Luchins, 1942; Taylor & McNemar, 1955). Such corrosive effects can be curtailed by simple instructions to respond in a creative manner (for example, Christensen, Guilford, & Wilson, 1957; Maltzman, Bogartz, & Breger, 1958; Rosenbaum, Arenson, & Panman, 1964). Similarly, Colgrove (1968, p. 1208) told her experimental subjects, "You have the reputation of being a very original person and of being good at coming up with answers to difficult problems. That is why Gus came to you. Keep this in mind while studying the problem." Her results indicate the mere suggestion that a person has the reputation of being an original thinker creates a mental set that upgrades the problem-solving performance.

Interventions for Generating Solutions

Maltzman's Originality Training

Maltzman (1960) conceptualized originality as nothing more than an operant that happens to be uncommon but relevant to a given stimulus situation. "Original" operants are subject to the same learning principles as are other operant responses. Moreover, according to Maltzman, the mere occurrence of an original operant may be sufficient for its reinforcement—the amount varying inversely with the initial probability of the response. (One's learning history is undoubtedly punctuated with instances of originality met with primary or secondary reinforcers or both.) Finally, Maltzman suggested that reinforcement of original responses could be expected to increase the general tendency to emit uncommon responses.

To enhance originality, Maltzman developed a standardized word-association training procedure in which he presented subjects with twenty-five stimulus words, one at a time, and asked them to respond as quickly as possible with the first word that came to mind. He then repeated the entire list five times with instructions to respond with a new word each time. The Maltzman technique has been subjected to a number of experimental investigations (Caron, Unger, & Parloff, 1963; Maltzman, Bogartz, & Breger, 1958; Maltzman, Simon, Raskin, & Licht, 1960; Penney & McCann, 1962; Rosenbaum, Arenson, & Panman, 1964), most of which are highly supportive, particularly when the training procedure is accompanied by instructions to "be original."

Freedman (1965) developed an interesting variation of the Maltzman technique. Basically, the subjects are given thirty seconds to produce as many free associations as possible to each word on a ten-word list. Although the Freedman procedure has produced higher creativity scores than control conditions, it has not been experimentally compared with the Maltzman technique.

The relevance of either the Maltzman technique or the Freedman variation to clinical problems has yet to be determined. Although both procedures have been experimentally examined, only psychometric outcome devices such as Guilford's (1950) Unusual Uses Test or Mednick's (1962) Remote Associates Test have been employed. Perhaps counselors who ask their clients to free associate (or who free associate *with* their clients) on what might be done to resolve a presenting problem would increase the likelihood of discovering a creative solution.

Brainstorming

In recent years the term "brainstorming" has become popularized and attention to its theoretical underpinnings and procedural guidelines has eroded. Brainstorming (Clark, 1958; Osborn, 1963) is a problem-solving procedure developed largely for use in industrial settings; but its relevance to counseling—particularly group counseling—is readily apparent. Correct use of the term requires close adherence to four general rules:

1. *Criticism is ruled out.* Group members are told to defer judgment on any member's ideas or suggestions. Potentially good solutions to a problem are more likely to emerge in an atmosphere of unconditional acceptance than one in which criticism (punishment) is possible or probable.
2. *Freewheeling is welcomed.* Participants are encouraged to offer wild ideas. The more unusual, bizarre, or offbeat the suggestions, the more likely the discovery of a truly original and useful solution. "It's easier to tame down than to think up" is a rule that evolves from the first rule because freewheeling cannot occur in a critical atmosphere. (The reader might note the similarity

between freewheeling and Maltzman's, 1960, procedure for training in originality.)

3. *Quantity is welcomed.* Group members are urged to think up as
   many solutions as possible. The greater the number of ideas, the
   greater the likelihood of useful ideas.
4. *Combination and improvement are sought.* In addition to offering
   ideas of their own, participants are encouraged to suggest how
   others' ideas can be improved upon and how two or more ideas
   can be integrated into a third idea.

Apart from the above rules, Osborn (1963) offers a number of experience-
based suggestions such as groups should consist of ten to twelve
members who are heterogeneous in training, background, and sex but as
equal in employment status as possible.

In the business world, where ideas are evaluated in terms of how
much money was made or saved, anecdotal evidence in favor of brainstorming is impressive: Sylvania Electric's popular flashcube originated
in a brainstorming session (Clark, 1958; Mason, 1960; Osborn, 1963).
Evaluation of ideas in the experimental laboratory, however, is more
problematic (see Davis & Manske, 1968; Davis & Roweton, 1968; Warren
& Davis, 1969). Studies on the efficacy of the various brainstorming rules
are generally favorable (for example, Bayless, 1967; Davis & Manske,
1966; Parloff & Handlon, 1964; Parnes, 1967). Unfortunately, much of the
applied research on brainstorming suffers from a lack of experimental
rigor, but its potential as a specific counseling procedure appears
promising.

Metaphorical Thinking

In a television comedy sketch George Gobel once dismissed a minor
problem in living as "just another barnacle on the sinking ship of
youth." In spite of his mournful affect, the audience roared with laughter
in appreciation of the unusual metaphor. Indeed, such metaphors seem
to be the hallmark of humor and most other forms of creative writing. At
least two problem-solving strategies capitalize on the close relationship
between creativity and metaphorical thinking.

The first, *bionics,* stresses the drawing of analogies between biological mechanisms and technological design (Papanek, 1969). Sonar capabilities in bats, for example, have strong implications for the solution of
naval engineering problems such as navigation and submarine detection.
The second, *synectics,* developed by Gordon (1961; see also Prince, 1968),
emphasizes three kinds of analogical thinking in problem solving: (1)
Direct analogy resembles bionics in that nature is often searched for
clues in solving problems. For instance the color-changing mechanism of

a flounder suggested a process by which roofs might automatically change color from heat-absorbing black in the winter to heat-reflecting white in the summer. (2) Personal analogy involves imagining oneself to be the problem-object. Given such a set, a question such as "What would make me change?" might lead to creative solutions. (3) Finally, fantasy analogy calls for farfetched solutions much akin to the freewheeling rule in brainstorming. Asking how a problem could solve itself may have led to the self-defrosting refrigerator or the self-cleaning oven.

Although anecdotal reports on the utility of metaphorical thinking in industrial problem solving abound, controlled experimental evidence is nonexistent. Undoubtedly many creative solutions attributed to bionics and synectics might just as well have been discovered by simply telling the problem solver to "be creative." Nevertheless, if properly evaluated, both procedures might prove to be quite useful.

The possibility that counseling procedures based on metaphorical thinking may be relevant to client problem solving has never been adequately articulated. In a discussion of cognitive restructuring Lazarus (1971) does suggest the "2-peach parable"—a metaphor designed to reduce sexual guilt. But here the problem solution, guilt reduction, is already known. I am prone to use another metaphor called "the hamster love story" as a counseling technique designed to stimulate alternative solutions to clients who invariably find themselves on the losing side of their dating relationships: My younger brother once raised three hamsters, two females and a male, in separate cages. When they were old enough to breed, he placed all three on the top of a coffee table. One of the females began actively to explore the new surroundings. She noticed the presence of the male but seemed more concerned about being her own hamster: Was there food and water up here? Where might shelter be found? The other female gave a number of nonverbal hamster cues indicating the desire for an immediate serious relationship. As the male hamster began active pursuit of the independent-minded female, I couldn't help but chuckle, "How human!" This metaphor invariably stimulates client thinking about more adaptive ways to handle present and future relationships. Moreover, it is equally appropriate for either sex and can be relevant to a number of marital problems as well.

Comprehensive Training Programs

ICPS Skill Training

Spivack, Platt, and Shure (1976) and their associates contend that psychological adjustment is essentially related to the development of five "interpersonal cognitive problem-solving (ICPS) skills":

1. *Sensitivity to interpersonal problems.* This general skill covers a variety of topics such as an awareness of the variety of possible problems that beset human interaction and an ability to examine oneself when relating to others.
2. *Ability to generate alternative solutions.* This skill parallels the process of brainstorming in that numerous alternatives are sought in the context of deferred judgment.
3. *Capacity for means-ends thinking.* One displays this kind of thinking by articulating step-by-step procedures for carrying out the solution to an interpersonal problem that includes recognizing obstacles that must be overcome and considering how others might react to the implementation of a particular solution.
4. *Capacity for consequential thinking.* This kind of thinking is reflected by considering the consequences of one's social acts in terms of their impact both on other people and on oneself. Essentially it implies the question: "What might happen as a result of my doing this?"
5. *Awareness of personal motivation and interpersonal continuity.* This general skill implies a recognition of one's motives in interpersonal conduct and a realization that current interpersonal events have a continuity with past events. For example, "I am unhappy because he is irritated with me. But maybe he is irritated with me because I ignored him today."

Although there appears to be considerable overlap in the general descriptions of the ICPS skills, Spivack and his associates have operationally defined most of these skills in terms of tests appropriate to various age groups. For example, alternative thinking in four- and five-year-olds is measured by the Preschool Interpersonal Problem-Solving (PIPS) Test (Shure & Spivack, 1974), which consists of asking the child to think of as many solutions as possible to a "peer" interpersonal problem (wanting a toy another child has) and an "authority" interpersonal problem (having broken mother's flower pot). With children nine to twelve years of age the measurement of alternative thinking consists of presenting seven problems having a greater degree of sophistication. For example: "Johnny wants his friend to go to the playground with him after school but his friend doesn't want to go. What can Johnny do to get his friend to go with him?" One's score on alternative thinking consists of the total number of relevant solutions offered. Other ICPS skills are measured in like fashion.

In their 1976 book Spivack, Platt, and Shure review a steady stream of studies on the ICPS model, beginning with those of the 1960s. Essentially they found that the absence of ICPS skills is strongly related to a wide variety of indexes of maladjustment, including, for example, delinquency and drug use. Consequently, they and their associates have developed and experimentally evaluated ICPS skill training programs for a diverse array of client populations, including a prevention program for kindergarten children, a treatment program for hyperactive children, a program for mothers of young children (ICPS skills-deficient children have ICSP skills-deficient mothers), a school program for third- and fourth-grade children, a school program for fourth- and fifth-grade children, a treatment program for chronic psychiatric patients, a group therapy program for young adults and adults, and a group therapy program for hospitalized psychiatric patients. A critical review of the individual studies supporting these programs would take us far afield. Suffice it to say that in general the programs have been shown to foster not only the development of ICPS skills but concomitant behavioral improvement as well. To encourage these skills, the programs employ a wide variety of techniques, including affect-identification (empathy training), behavioral rehearsal, cognitive modeling, cognitive restructuring, decision making, self-instruction training, simulation gaming, social reinforcement, videotape modeling, and vocabulary building on ICPS itself through didactic instruction.

Other Comprehensive Programs

Texts by Davis (1973) and Spivack, Platt, and Shure (1976) provide thorough coverage of a wide variety of problem-solving and creativity training programs. The interested reader is urged to peruse these sources for additional information on several of the strategies reviewed in this chapter and a number of other programs redundant or of marginal relevance to decision-making counseling.

The pertinence of comprehensive problem-solving training programs to clinical and educational concerns is receiving increased attention in the counseling literature. Jacobson (1977) developed a multicomponent program for the treatment of marital discord. Mendonca and Siess (1976) combined problem-solving and anxiety-management training in an attempt to reduce indecisiveness about career plans. Finally, Poitras-Martin and Stone (1977) translated the etherial jargon of "psychological education" into a skills-oriented problem-solving framework appropriate to sixth graders. All three of these recently developed comprehensive programs have produced positive effects.

Summary

The diverse literature on problem solving has been aptly described as chaotic; much of it overlaps with that of decision making. Some authors use the two terms interchangeably; others see decision making as a subset of problem solving. Still others (including the author of this book) treat decision making as an autonomous entity that needs to incorporate pertinent concepts from the amorphous problem-solving literature.

There is no universally accepted definition of "problem"; moreover, unlike counseling problems, most problems studied in laboratory settings are free of agonizing emotional concomitants. According to behavioral theory, problem solving is essentially a trial and error enterprise that includes not only physical activity but seeing and thinking as well. People confronted with a problematic situation can be expected to engage in a number of responses in accord with their learning histories. Problem-solving rules or shortcuts are also learned through trial and error, but sometimes the solution to a problem is suggested by experiences we have had in other areas.

Three categories of problem-solving interventions can be applied in the context of counseling: early interventions used, for example, to thwart impulsive responding and foster an appropriate problem-solving set; interventions for generating solutions, including originality training, brainstorming, and metaphorical thinking; and comprehensive training programs such as ICPS skill training.

With this chapter part II ends. Part III uses the preceding material to construct a cognitive-behavioral model of decision-making counseling.

SYNTHESIS

Toward Synthesis: The Components of Counseling, Problem Solving, and Decision Making

So far in this book we have seen that except for the area of vocational choice, behavioral counseling researchers generally have not bothered to develop a technology for helping clients improve the quality of their personal decision making. But behaviorists do not shoulder the blame alone. The other major counseling theories either ignore the topic of decision making or address it imperfectly. We have also seen that although the languages of behavioral counseling and classical decision theory permit a moderate degree of cross-referencing, much research in the latter field is irrelevant or inapplicable to counseling. Fortunately, however, the recent emergence of cognitive behaviorism, the evolution of new perspectives in decision theory, and the presence of pertinent work in the amorphous problem-solving literature all hold promise for the development of a technology to help clients resolve problems of choice.

In this chapter I plan to lay the foundation for an operational model of decision-making counseling. The model will be more fully explicated in the chapters to follow. For the moment I would like to focus on a general overview of the major components of counseling, into which descriptions of the various stage theories of problem solving and decision making can be neatly fitted. In confronting this task I am acutely aware of some painfully precise comments of my good friend and colleague, Kenneth W. Hylbert, to the effect that much of what passes for scholarship is simply the relocating of bones from one academic graveyard to another followed by capping them off with a new headstone. Readers more interested in synthesis than historical background may prefer simply to glance through the material in table 11.2 and skip ahead to the sections in this chapter entitled "General Summary of Counseling Models" and "A Summary Model of the Stages in Problem Solving and Decision Making."

An Overview of Counseling

Chapters 7, 8, and 9 were laden with counseling theory, which, as my students keep telling me, may be as helpful to the neophite counselor as romance magazines are to the novice dater. Neither dictates what to do after you say "hello." A number of authors have responded to the need expressed by many counselor trainees for a procedural road map pointing out where to go in counseling and how to get there. In this section I will briefly review three such responses that I feel are distinguished by their clarity and precision.

Winborn and Associates

Five faculty members in the counselor education program at Michigan State University (H. M. Burks, J. R. Engelkes, R. G. Johnson, N. R. Stewart, and B. B. Winborn) have collaborated in the development of a flowchart (figure 11.1) that depicts the essential ingredients of "systematic counseling" (Winborn, 1973). Their work is heavily influenced by what has come to be known as the "systems approach" (see Silverin, 1968). A system can be described as an integrated and related set of components organized to obtain a specific objective. Systematic counseling is essentially an attempt to dispel the counseling mystique by viewing counseling as a complex phenomenon that can be broken down into ten subsystems (or categories of counselor activities).

Subsystem one is defined as *counselor*. Much of the work on systematic counseling deals with the design and evaluation of curriculum materials for counselor training (see Horan, 1972a). These educational efforts are expected to produce counselors with high levels of competence and appropriate professional attitudes. Formally, subsystem one ends with a "practicum makes perfect" experience; however, professional growth should continue beyond graduation.

In subsystem two the practicing counselor *processes client referrals*, which may be received from a variety of environmental sources such as parents or school personnel. A walk-in client is a self-referral. If the referral is appropriate (for example, a type of concern within the counselor's expertise), the counselor informs the referral source about various ground rules such as confidentiality and the need for information and cooperation. If the referral is not appropriate, the counselor helps the client or referral source locate assistance.

Subsystem three may be optional, depending on if there is time to *prepare for* an *interview*. Preparation may not be possible with a self-referred client, for example, who immediately begins discussing a concern.

During subsystem four the counselor *explains* the *counseling relationship*. In the first interview all clients need to be informed, for example, about the purpose of counseling and the counselor's and client's responsibilities. Depending on the urgency of the client's concern, however, this information may be delayed until the end of the interview.

In subsystem five the counselor *constructs* a *model of client concerns*. This involves identifying the concerns, selecting those appropriate for counseling, gathering further information on the concern (including establishment of a baseline), and, finally, verifying with the client whether the model of concerns corresponds to the client's actual problems in living.

During subsystem six the counselor and client must jointly *decide* on a *goal for counseling*. Answers to questions such as "What would you like to be able to do after counseling that you cannot do now?" suggest the general goals of counseling. Specific goals should be stated in observable terms, including designations of essential conditions and criterion levels (Mager, 1962). Counseling goals, if achieved, imply elimination of the client's concerns. If the counselor can or will provide assistance in obtaining a goal and if the client feels the goal is worth pursuing, counseling proceeds. If either condition is absent, a recycling to subsystem two may be in order.

Subsystem seven, entitled *conduct task operations*, involves those counseling activities that directly help the client obtain the designated goals. Counseling strategies are selected and if the long-range goal is too complex, intermediate objectives are established. Counseling strategies and intermediate objectives may need to be modified, depending on client progress.

In subsystem eight the counselor must *evaluate* the *client's perfor-*

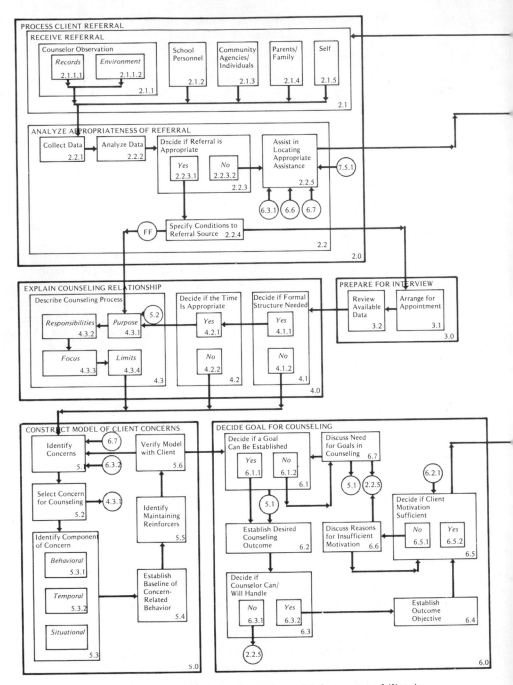

Source: B. B. Winborn, "Systemic counseling: A model for accountability in counseling and counselor education," *Impact* 2 (1973), pp. 15-22.

FIGURE 11.1. Flowchart for systematic counseling

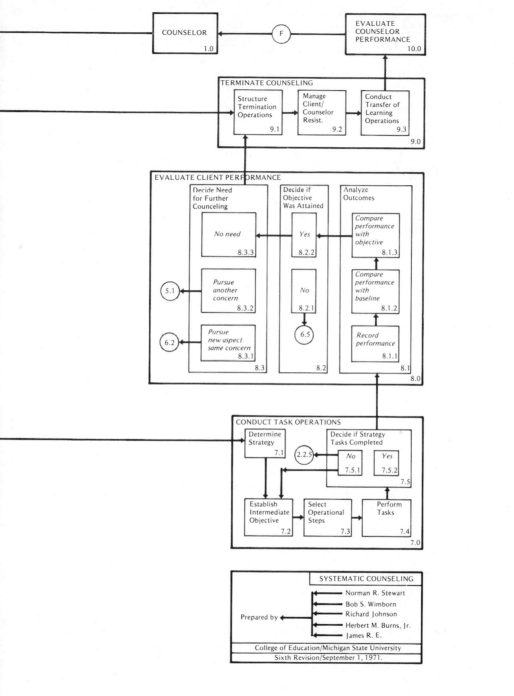

COUNSELOR

1.0

F

EVALUATE
COUNSELOR
PERFORMANCE

10.0

TERMINATE COUNSELING

Structure
Termination
Operations

9.1

Manage
Client/
Counselor
Resist.

9.2

Conduct
Transfer of
Learning
Operations

9.3

9.0

EVALUATE CLIENT PERFORMANCE

Decide Need
for Further
Counceling

No need

8.3.3

*Pursue
another
concern*

8.3.2

*Pursue
new aspect
same concern*

8.3.1

8.3

Decide if
Objective
Was Attained

Yes

8.2.2

No

8.2.1

8.2

Analyze
Outcomes

*Compare
performance
with
objective*

8.1.3

*Compare
performance
with
baseline*

8.1.2

*Record
performance*

8.1.1

8.1

8.0

5.1

6.2

6.5

CONDUCT TASK OPERATIONS

Determine
Strategy

7.1

2.2.5

Decide if Strategy
Tasks Completed

No

7.5.1

Yes

7.5.2

7.5

Establish
Intermediate
Objective

7.2

Select
Operational
Steps

7.3

Perform
Tasks

7.4

7.0

SYSTEMATIC COUNSELING

Prepared by

Norman R. Stewart
Bob S. Wimborn
Richard Johnson
Herbert M. Burns, Jr.
James R. E.

College of Education/Michigan State University

Sixth Revision/September 1, 1971.

mance. If the client is functioning beyond baseline at a level commensurate with the objective, then the counselor and client may pursue additional concerns or new aspects of the same concern. If improved performance is not apparent, a recycling to another subsystem may again be in order.

During subsystem nine the counselor must *terminate counseling* once its goals have been realized. This involves letting the client know that regularly scheduled meetings will be ended, dealing with any resulting client resistance, and teaching the client that many of the learned skills may be relevant to other difficulties he or she may experience in life.

Finally, in subsystem ten the counselor and supervisor *evaluate* the *counselor's performance*. Feedback that the counselor receives on his or her work should result in improved effectiveness with subsequent clients.

Thoresen and Associates

Concurrent with the development of systematic counseling at Michigan State University, Thoresen (1969, 1971) and his associates at Stanford University (Hendricks, Ferguson, & Thoresen, 1973; Krumboltz, Thoresen, & Zifferblatt, 1971) also incorporated features of systems thinking into their conceptualizations of counseling and counselor education. Thoresen (1971) initially proposed a six-function model of counseling, the elegant simplicity of which was lost in a later seventeen-step version (Hendricks et al., 1973). Figures 11.2 and 11.3 depict these two flowcharts; the subsystems are self-explanatory. The 1971 version offers the advantage of being an easily stored, cognitive road map for counseling depicting the major stopping points. The 1973 elaboration is a more complete travel guide but may not be as easily committed to memory.

Gottman and Leiblum

The flowchart of psychotherapy Gottman and Leiblum (1974) developed can be roughly divided into five parts, each containing a number of components (see figure 11.4). During part one, *problem assessment*, the tasks of the counselor are to decide who to see in counseling, discuss with the client the reasons for and expectations of counseling, and clearly define and quantify the problem behavior. In part two the counselor negotiates a therapeutic *contract* with the client to work on the problem in a specified manner. This could also involve, for example, termination,

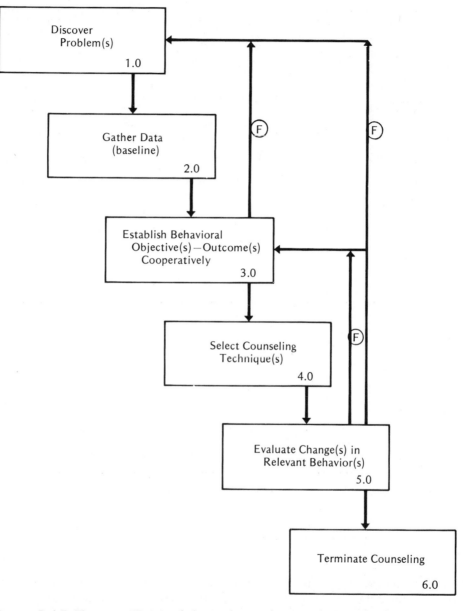

Source: Carl E. Thoresen, "Training behavioral counselors," in G. Hamerlynck, D. Evans, and F. Clark, eds., *Implementing behavioral programs in educational and clinical settings* (Calgary: University of Calgary Press, 1971).

FIGURE 11.2.   Behavioral counseling model

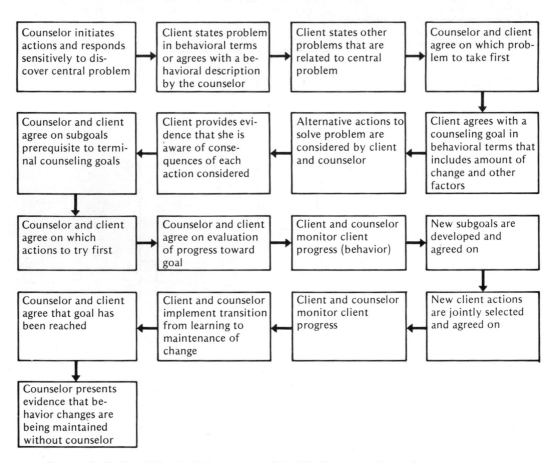

Source: C. G. Hendricks, J. G. Ferguson, and Carl E. Thoresen, "Toward counseling competence: The Stanford programs," *Personnel and Guidance Journal* 51, (Washington, D.C.: APGA, 1973), pp. 418-24. Copyright 1973 American Personnel and Guidance Association. Reprinted with permission.

FIGURE 11.3. Steps in counseling

referral elsewhere, or discussion of fees. In part three the counselor begins the *initial therapy efforts*. Here the counseling objectives are set and counseling strategies to achieve these objectives are implemented. Part four concerns how the counselor might deal with *resistance* arising from a variety of sources, such as client skill deficiency. Counseling strategies exist for each form of resistance, but a recycling back to part two is mandatory. Finally, part five of the flowchart involves *continuous monitoring of change and eventual follow-up*.

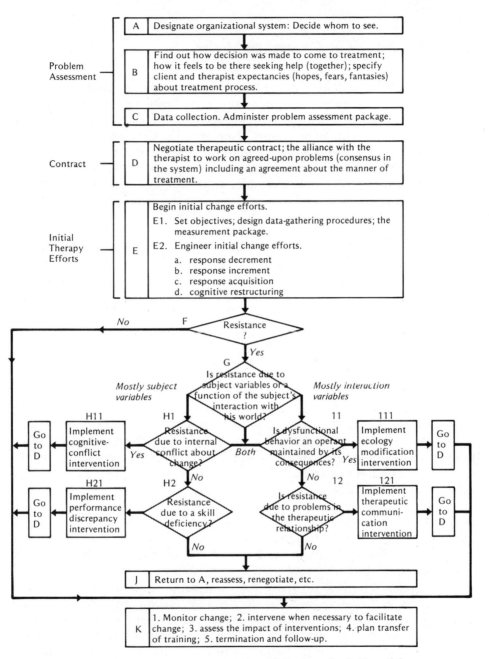

Source: From *How To Do Psychotherapy and How To Evaluate It: A Manual for Beginners* by John Mordechai Gottman and Sandra Risa Leiblum. Copyright © 1974 reprinted by permission of Holt, Rinehart and Winston.

FIGURE 11.4. Flowchart of psychotherapy

General Summary of Counseling Models

The reader has probably noted that the models of counseling just described bear a fairly close operational resemblance to each other. Counselor trainees following any of these road maps will cover roughly the same ground with their clients. Not only do they provide an excellent framework for the conduct of behavioral counseling, but with very minor modification even psychoanalytic and existential counselors can feel at home using them. For example, subsystems six and seven in systematic counseling deal with goal setting and the conduct of task operations. A Freudian counselor using the systematic counseling flowchart might work toward improved ego strength with a particular client via task operations such as free association, dream analysis, and symptom interpretation. A Rogerian counselor using the Thoresen (1971) model might try to improve the client's level of self-acceptance (in function three) via the counseling technique of reflective listening accompanied by the relationship qualities of empathy, congruence, and positive regard (in function four).

However ecumenical their products, the designers of these flowcharts were for the most part cognitive-behavioral in counseling orientation. Their models can be crudely condensed into three categories of counselor activity: assessment, intervention, and evaluation.

Assessment activities are primarily those concerned with identifying the client, helping the client define the counseling concerns, and determining what goals or objectives might ameliorate these concerns (Winborn et al., subsystems two through six; Thoresen, functions one to three; Hendricks et al., steps one to five, eight, twelve; Gottman & Leiblum, parts one to three).

Intervention activities are intended to enable the client to obtain his or her goals. A wide variety of counseling techniques may be employed either singly or in combination (Winborn et al., subsystem seven; Thoresen, function four; Hendricks et al., steps six, seven, nine, thirteen, and fifteen; Gottman & Leiblum, parts three and four).

Evaluation activities are those that determine if the client has in fact reached the goals of counseling. If so, termination and follow-up are included here; if not, a recycling to assessment or intervention activities may be in order (Winborn et al., subsystems eight through ten; Thoresen, functions five and six; Hendricks et al., steps ten, eleven, fourteen, sixteen, seventeen; Gottman & Leiblum, part five).

Although these categories of counselor activity are often sequential, in counseling practice it would be somewhat mistaken to view them as stages. Stages suggest a lockstep progression. Assessment, intervention, and evaluation activities, on the other hand, may recycle in the case of multiple goals or backstep when the goals have not been met.

Each of these categories of counselor activity in a particular kind of counseling, decision making, will be elaborated upon in chapters 12, 13, and 14 respectively. Now let us turn to the major stage theories of problem solving and decision making, many of which were conceptualized far apart from the context of counseling. After a brief review of these theories we shall look at the interface between our overview of counseling and the stages of problem solving and decision making.

Stages in Problem Solving

Formalized stage theories of problem solving span five decades. In this section I will briefly cover models proposed by Wallas (1926), Dewey (1933), and Gagné (1959), which are essentially descriptions of how individuals go about or ought to go about solving problems. I will also mention the thinking of D'Zurilla and Goldfried (1971) and Urban and Ford (1971), whose stage theories place problem solving in the domain of counseling.

Wallas

In a metaphysical treatise entitled *The Art of Thought*, Wallas (1926) proposed what is now considered one of the earliest stage theories of problem solving. Wallas was strongly influenced by some after-dinner remarks made by the German physicist Helmholtz on the occasion of the latter's seventieth birthday in 1891. Helmholtz said that after previous investigation of the problem "in all directions . . . happy ideas come unexpectedly without effort, like an inspiration. So far as I am concerned, they have never come to me when my mind was fatigued, or when I was at my working table. They came particularly readily during the slow ascent of wooded hills on a sunny day" (cited in Wallas, 1926, p. 80).

Wallas constructed the first three stages of his four-stage model from these reminiscences of Helmholtz. In the first stage, called *preparation*, the problem is investigated "in all directions." Then follows the *incubation* stage during which the problem situation is picked apart by unconscious processes while the problem solver is engaged in other activities on a conscious level. Stage three is the *illumination* or the "Eureka, I've found it!" experience, which occurs suddenly. Wallas derived the fourth stage, *verification*, from the writings of the mathematician Poincaré, who emphasized the need to examine in real life the adequacy of "inspired" solutions.

By giving credence to the incubation stage, the Wallas model differs from other problem-solving models to be discussed below. By definition this stage is unconscious and unobservable, so most problem-solving theorists and researchers do not include it in their formulations. But as Davis (1973, p. 16) wryly points out, "The same psychologists who doubt the existence of incubation or illumination also keep a pad and pencil on the bedstand for just such happenings."

Actually, the incubation stage need not really trouble even the most empirically oriented problem-solving researcher. Recall the discussion in chapter 10 of the vertical and horizontal processes in problem solving posited by the Kendlers (1962). Helmholtz's walk through the woods may have triggered associations pertinent to advancing his laboratory work. Though Wallas uses the mystique-laden word "unconscious" to characterize this stage, the phenomenon may not be any more mystical than the salivation of Pavlov's dogs.

Dewey

Reflective thinking, according to Dewey (1933, p. 12), can be distinguished from other thought processes in that it involves "(1) a state of doubt, hesitation, perplexity, mental difficulty, in which thinking originates, and (2) an act of searching, hunting, inquiring, to find material that will resolve the doubt, settle and dispose of the perplexity."

Dewey proposed a five-phase model of reflective thought that is perhaps the most widely cited description of the problem-solving process. Phase one is called *suggestion*, a term meaning "the idea of what to do when we find ourselves 'in a hole.'" Dewey maintained that where there are two or more suggestions "they collide with one another, maintain the state of suspense, and produce further inquiry" (1933, pp. 107-108). Some inhibition of direct action is necessary prior to the second phase, *intellectualization*. Dewey noted that a question well put is half-answered. The problem solver needs to define clearly "the conditions that constitute the trouble and cause the stoppage of action" (1933, p. 109). The third phase is the *guiding idea or hypothesis*. Here suggestions of stage one become tentative suppositions that can be tested. In phase four *reasoning* determines what are the logical consequences of adopting the guiding idea. But so far the conclusion is hypothetical. During phase five, *testing*, "conditions are deliberately arranged in accord with the requirements of an idea or hypothesis to see whether the results theoretically indicated by the idea actually occur" (1933, p. 114).

Dewey pointed out that the order of these five phases of reflective thought is not fixed. Moreover, some phases may be greatly expanded; others hurriedly passed over. The influence of Dewey's thinking on subsequent writings has been quite pronounced; for example, Kingsley and Garry's (1957) stage theory bears a strong resemblance.

Gagné

Dewey's thinking also apparently influenced Gagné (1959), except that Gagné incorporates concepts of classical decision theory into his five-stage problem-solving model. During phase one, *reception of the stimulus situation*, the problem solver is motivated to achieve some definable goal but cannot reach that goal through behaviors based on reflexes or habits. This leads in phase two to the occurrence of *concept formation or concept invention*. Such processes are greatly influenced by the rules problem solvers adopt. These rules may not be clearly articulated but they still dictate which parts of the stimulus situation are deserving of attention. The third phase involves *determining courses of action*. Here the problem solver generates alternatives that may differ along a conservative-risky dimension. Gagné uses a somewhat restrictive meaning of *decision making* to characterize the fourth phase; that is, the individual ought to select the alternative with the highest expected utility. The final phase, *verification*, concerns how the problem-solving endeavor is affected by feedback such as discovery that the attempted solution was functional or inadequate.

D'Zurilla and Goldfried

In their attempt to wedge the problem-solving literature into a behavior modification framework, D'Zurilla and Goldfried (1971) define "problem solving" as "a behavioral process, whether overt or cognitive in nature, which (a) makes available a variety of potentially effective response alternatives for dealing with the problematic situation and (b) increases the probability of selecting the most effective response from among these various alternatives" (p. 108).

They view problem solving in general and problem solving in the context of counseling as consisting of five stages. The first stage, *general orientation*, concerns the development of a proper attitudinal set (including, for example, suppression of the urge to respond impulsively). In the second stage, *problem definition and formulation*, the problem solver needs to define operationally all aspects of the situation, separate relevant from irrelevant information, and identify the primary goals. Stage three involves the *generation of alternatives*—as many as possible through brainstorming and similar procedures. In stage four, *decision making*, the problem solver selects the alternative that yields the highest expected utility. The fifth and last stage is *verification*. Effective problem solving demands feedback on the actual outcomes of the chosen alternative. If the outcome is unsatisfactory, a recycling of the problem-solving process may be in order.

Urban and Ford

Counseling and psychotherapy are also viewed by Urban and Ford (1971) as a problem-solving enterprise consisting of five stages. In stage one, the *identification of the problem*, a crucial task is to find the best way to conceptualize what it is that has gone wrong. Stage two, *analysis of the problem*, involves determining what it is that makes the problem function as it does. This stage presupposes formal knowledge of personality and counseling theory. During stage three the problem solver is concerned with the *selection of goals*. "Effective pursuit of the problem-solving approach calls for an explicit specification of the outcomes that one should seek" (1971, p. 15). Stage four focuses on *implementation of the problem solution*. Here the problem solver (with the aid of a counselor) proceeds to arrange for the conditions under which change will occur. In the final stage, *subsequent evaluation*, information with respect to the impact of the solution is fed back into the system.

Stages in Decision Making

Though the study of decision making predates the problem-solving literature by a couple of centuries, most descriptions of the stages in decision making are of relatively recent vintage. In this section I will initially cover the stages mentioned by Bross (1953) and Krumboltz (1966). Stewart and Winborn (1973) credit Krumboltz for inspiring their work; however, their creative flowchart for decision making in systematic counseling is worthy of special mention. The influence of these writers can be seen in several early models of decision-making counseling my colleagues and I have proposed. Finally, I will summarize the stages in Janis and Mann's (1977) conflict model of decision making.

Bross

In his book entitled *Design for Decision* Bross (1953) closely follows the concepts of classical decision theory. During stage one the decision maker begins with a *list of actions* (alternatives). A decision problem is defined by the existence of two or more possible alternative courses of action, only one of which may be taken. In stage two the decision maker must generate a *list of outcomes* for each action. Stage three involves the *estimation of probabilities* for these outcomes. For example, what is the likelihood of my getting wet if I do not take an umbrella? In stage four the decision maker *determines the desirability* of each outcome. Getting momentarily caught in a light summer shower, for instance, may be less aversive than carrying around an unused umbrella on a sweltering day. In stage five a *decision criterion* that yields the recommended course of action is applied. Typically this would involve selecting the alternative with the highest expected utility.

Krumboltz

In chapter 9 we saw that an eight-stage model of decision-making counseling developed by Krumboltz and his students (Krumboltz & Baker, 1973; Krumboltz & Thoresen, 1964) stimulated much of the existing research on behavioral decision-making counseling. In 1966 Krumboltz published a slightly more explicit version of the stages (that is, behaviors or goals) in adaptive decision making. His revised model also involves eight stages.

Initially the decision maker ought to be *generating a list of all possible courses of action*. Stage two involves *gathering relevant information about each feasible alternative course of action*. Stage three focuses on *estimating the probability of success in each alternative on the basis of the experience of others and projections of current trends*. In stage four the decision maker should be concerned with *considering the personal values which may be enhanced or diminished under each course of action*. In the fifth stage *deliberating and weighing the facts, probable outcomes, and values for each course of action* are the appropriate activities. The sixth stage focuses on *eliminating from consideration the least favorable courses of action*. In stage seven the decision maker ought to be *formulating a tentative plan of action subject to new developments and opportunities*. Finally, stage eight involves *generalizing the decision-making process to future problems*.

Other stage theories, essentially similar in content but consisting of fewer stages, have been proposed by Magoon (1969), Evans and Cody (1969), and Bergland, Quatrano, and Lundquist (1975).

Stewart and Winborn

In the overview of systematic counseling presented earlier in this chapter we saw that subsystem seven, entitled "conduct task operations," dealt with the implementation of counseling strategies designed to help clients reach their goals. Depending on the goal in question, any one of a number of possible strategies might be selected. As a further refinement to subsystem seven of systematic counseling, Stewart and Winborn (1973) proposed a flowchart for the stages of career decision-making counseling (see figure 11.5).

Under the heading *generate alternatives* (subsubsystem 7.4.1) the alternatives to a choice problem are listed and a decision is made if more alternatives are needed. Additional alternatives can be acquired from structured experiences, reference material, and resource material. If a sufficient supply is at hand, the appropriate task is to gather information concerning each alternative.

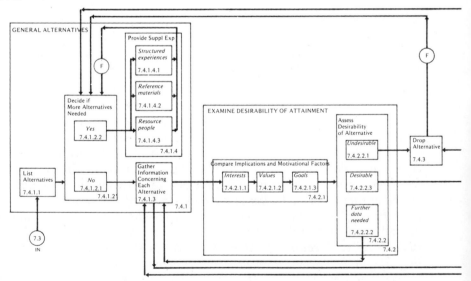

FIGURE 11.5.   Model for decision making

The search for information leads the client to *examine desirability of attainment* (subsubsystem 7.4.2). Essentially, the decision maker compares the consequences of an alternative with his or her interests, values, and goals and drops undesirable alternatives (subsubsystem 7.4.3). Further data on desirability may be needed on the remaining alternatives.

If the alternatives at hand are desirable, then the decision maker proceeds to *examine probability of attainment* (subsubsystem 7.4.4). (One can also arrive at this stage via the search for information.) Here the essential task is to compare one's personal and environmental factors with the requirements of the alternatives. Alternatives unlikely to be attained are then dropped. Further data on probability may be needed at this point.

Assuming a sufficient number of desirable and probable alternatives exist, the decision maker proceeds to *make final choice* (subsubsystem 7.4.5). This involves listing and ranking all surviving alternatives and selecting the leading one.

Baker, Herr, Horan, Hudson, and Wallace

Many of the foregoing descriptions of the stages in problem solving and decision making are relatively abstract. In contrast, Herr, Horan, and Baker (1973) proposed a relatively explicit description of sequential counselor behaviors in vocational counseling (see table 11.1). Their eighteen-step

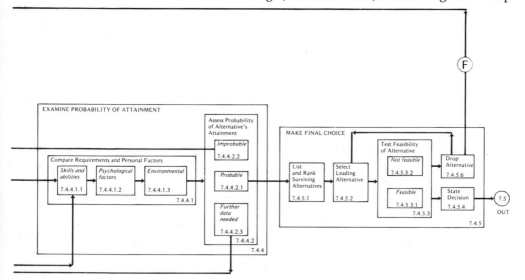

Source: N. R. Stewart and B. B. Winborn, "A model for decision-making in systemic counseling," *Educational Technology* 69 (1973), pp. 13-15.

Table 11.1. Model of vocational decision-making counseling

Sequential counselor behaviors in systematic vocational counseling

Counselor behavior	Necessary conditions	Criteria for successful performance
1. Counselor defines the purpose of counseling, and the roles of the counselor and student.	At the outset of the initial interview (unless the student discusses his concerns immediately, then before the end of the initial interview).	Definitions should correspond to a predetermined standard.
2. Counselor helps the client define the problem via specific counseling skills (see Ivey). *If the problem is one of vocational choice then the following counselor behaviors ought to ensue. Other kinds of student problems may require different types of counselor activity.*	During the initial interview and in as many subsequent interviews as are required.	The problem is defined when the student so indicates (e.g. "Yes, that's it," or "You really do understand me!")
3. Counselor determines if vocational choice is the primary concern (e.g., "It seems that although you have a lot of things on your mind, you're mainly interested in coming to some sort of vocational decision.")	After the student has expressed all he cares to concerning his problem or his reason for seeking counseling.	The student responds in an affirmative manner.

Counselor behavior	Necessary conditions	Criteria for successful performance
4. Counselor explains the decision-making paradigm. (e.g., "Arriving at a good vocational decision means that we have to look at all the alternatives, then weigh them in the light of information about you and the advantages and disadvantages of each course of action. I can't make the decision for you, but together we can arrive at and implement one.")	Immediately following Counselor Behavior No. 3.	The student indicates that he understands the process.
5. Counselor explains the preparatory behaviors needed to make a good decision (i.e., he provides an overview of the counselor behaviors depicted below).	Immediately following Counselor Behavior No. 4.	The student states that he understands the process.
6. Counselor determines if the student has sufficient motivation, (e.g., "How do you feel about proceeding along these lines?")	Usually after Counselor Behavior No. 5. May be repeated after subsequent Counselor Behaviors.	The student indicates willingness to proceed. (If the student hesitates, or is unwilling to proceed, then recycle to Counselor Behavior No. 2 or terminate.)
7. Counselor asks the student to identify all possible alternatives which come to mind.	The alternatives may be identified in the interview and/or as a between interviews assignment.	The student compiles a complete list of alternatives (oral or written).

Counselor behavior	Necessary conditions	Criteria for successful performance
8. Counselor identifies any additional alternatives which come to his mind and are ethically appropriate.	Counselor exhibits this behavior only if criterion for No. 7 is considered to be inadequate by either the counselor or the student.	A joint list of alternatives is compiled.
9. Counselor assembles all relevant information about the student (e.g., test scores, academic performance, vocational experience and interests) from records and/or from student inquiry.	This information may be gathered during the interview of, if not immediately available, between interviews.	All existing relevant information about the student is available for discussion.
10. Counselor assembles additional information about the student (e.g., schedules further testing)	Counselor exhibits this behavior only if the criterion for No. 9 is considered to be inadequate by the counselor.	All relevant information is compiled.
11. Counselor presents to the student any information about the student relevant to the potential vocational decision (e.g., predictive statements derived from expectancy tables).	Immediately following Counselor Behaviors No. 9 and/or 10.	The student indicates that he understands this information.
12. Counselor requests that the student identify the advantages and disadvantages of the alternatives which have been identified.	During the interview (in the context of counselor-student discussion) and/or as a between-interviews assignment.	The student provides a set of such statements.

Counselor behavior	Necessary conditions	Criteria for successful performance
13. Counselor identifies any additional advantages and disadvantages which come to his mind.	Counselor exhibits this behavior only if the criterion for No. 12 is considered to be inadequate by either the counselor or the student.	A joint list of such statements is compiled.
14. Counselor asks the student to evaluate the alternatives. (e.g., "In terms of what we know about you and the various alternatives, which alternatives seem most promising?")	Immediately following Counselor Behaviors No. 12 and/or 13.	The student rank orders the alternatives from most to least preferred.
15. Counselor helps the student obtain additional information about the most promising alternative(s). (e.g., He verbally reinforces the student for reading about the prospective profession(s) and talking to members of the prospective profession(s). He may also schedule modeling or simulation experiences for the student.)	The additional information is usually accumulated outside of the counseling interview.	The student gathers this information or participates in the scheduled experiences.
16. Counselor helps the student implement the most promising alternative.	Immediately following Counselor Behavior No. 15.	A tentative course of action is selected and tried out.
17. Counselor determines if the selected alternative is satisfactory.	Immediately following Counselor Behavior No. 16.	The student reports that he is happy with the decision. (If not, recycle to Counselor Behavior No. 16, "next most promising alternative.")

Counselor behavior	Necessary conditions	Criteria for successful performance
18. Counselor terminates the counseling relationship.	Immediately following Counselor Behavior No. 17.	The student has learned the decision-making paradigm and is able to engage in independent action.

Source: E. L. Herr, J. J. Horan, and S. B. Baker, "Performance goals in vocational guidance and counseling: Clarifying the counseling mystique," *American Vocational Journal* 48 (1973), pp. 66-72.

model shows the theoretical influence of Bross, Krumboltz, Mager, and systematic counseling. Its cumbersomeness and limited applicability led Horan (1972b) to offer a condensed version. Still another revision consisting of ten steps applicable to both vocational and nonvocational choice problems was later employed in a study by Wallace, Horan, Baker, and Hudson (1975) that examined the relative efficacy of several training modalities. Counseling students were rated on the presence or absence of these behaviors plus their ability to maintain neutrality concerning what the client ought to do. High interrater reliability and internal consistency (.89 and .85 respectively) on the rating scale suggest that these stages or behaviors are discrete and easily identifiable.

Janis and Mann

In the Janis and Mann (1977) conflict model personal decisions follow a five-stage sequence. The decision maker must respond to one or more key questions during each stage. In stage one, *appraising the challenge*, the decision maker asks "Are the risks serious if I don't change?" Stage two involves *surveying alternatives*. Here the decision maker needs to know if a particular alternative is an acceptable means for dealing with the challenge and if he or she has sufficiently surveyed the available alternatives. In stage three the decision maker is concerned with *weighing alternatives*. Key questions are "Which alternative is best?" and "Could the best alternative meet the essential requirements?" During stage four there is *deliberating about commitment*. The decision maker wonders whether to implement the best alternative and allow others to know. Finally, in stage five, there is *adhering despite negative feedback*. Here the decision maker must again ask "Are the risks serious if I *do* or *don't* change?"

Stages four and five in the Janis and Mann model emphasize points that most other decision theorists do not make. The activities Janis and Mann describe as "vigilant information processing" permeate stages two through four.

A Summary Model of the Stages in Problem Solving and Decision Making

By now it should be abundantly clear that most stage theories of problem solving and decision making are directly comparable. To be sure, there are differences in emphasis and minor variations, but most of these models can be readily synthesized into four sequential stages.

Initially, in stage one, the problem-solving or decision-making individual engages in *conceptualization*, that is, construction of a cognitive model of the troubling portions of the environment. The basic task here is to define the problem or decision clearly. Questions such as "What has gone wrong?" or "Why am I feeling uncomfortable?" occur during this stage.

After appraising the situation, the individual proceeds to stage two, *enlargement of the response repertoire*. Here the major activity is to generate as many potential alternative responses as possible. (Some authors speak of hypotheses, solutions, actions, plans, or simply alternatives.) The question "What can be done?" occurs repeatedly during this stage.

Stage three focuses on the *identification of stimuli discriminative of positive or aversive consequences for each response*. Probabilities of utilities accruing from the various possible responses are determined on the basis of past or newly acquired experiences or both. The question "What would happen if I did what could be done?" characterizes much of the information-gathering activity in this stage.

Finally, stage four deals with *response selection*. The possible responses are ranked and the most promising response is implemented. The choice may be tentative, however, subject to new developments and feedback. Essentially, the question "What will I do?" is answered.

Table 11.2 places this four-stage summary model in juxtaposition with the problem-solving and decision-making stage theories reviewed earlier in this and previous chapters. The summary model is depicted in the first column. Models offered by other authors are deployed in columns 2-25 in such a way as to allow cross-referencing of all stage theories. Several general observations can be made:

1. Problem-solving theorists tend to devote more print to initial conceptualization activities than do decision theorists. One might get the impression that decision theorists feel their work begins when the problem has already been defined as one of choice.
2. Although not necessarily reflected in table 11.2, chapter 10 would suggest that problem-solving theorists have also had more to say on how alternatives might be generated. Decision theorists often

TABLE 11.2. Summary model and cross-reference of stage theories in the problem-solving and decision-making literature

Summary model		Problem-solving and decision-making theorists		
	Wallas (1926)	Dewey (1933)	Kingsley & Gerry (1957)	Gagne (1959)
Conceptualization	1. Preparation	1. Suggestion 2. Intellectualization	1. Experience of difficulty 2. Problem definition 3. Search for clues	1. Reception of stimulus situation 2. Concept formation or invention
Enlargement of the response repertoire		3. Guiding idea or hypotheses	4. Appearance and trial of suggestions	3. Determination of courses of action
	2. Incubation			
Identification of stimuli discriminative of positive or aversive consequences for each response		4. Reasoning		
Response selection	3. Illumination 4. Verification	5. Testing	5. Acceptance of a suggestion 6. Testing of a solution	4. Decision making 5. Verification

Summary model	D'Zurilla & Goldfried (1971)	Urban & Ford (1971)	Carkhuff (1973b)	Parsons (1909)
Conceptualization	1. General orientation 2. Problem definition and formula-tion	1. Identification of the problem	1. Developing the problem	

	Bross (1953)	Gelatt (1962)	Katz (1966)	Krumboltz & Thoresen (1964) Krumboltz & Baker (1973)
Enlargement of the response repertoire	3. Generation of alternatives	2. Analysis of the problem	2. Breaking down the problem	1. Clear understanding of yourself . . . .
Identification of stimuli discriminative of positive or aversive consequences for each response		3. Selection of goals	3. Considering courses of action	2. Knowledge of . . . advantages . . . in different lines of work
Response selection	4. Decision making	4. Implementation of the problem solution	4. Developing courses of action	3. True reasoning on the relations between these two groups of facts
	5. Verification	5. Subsequent evaluation		

	Bross (1953)	Gelatt (1962)	Katz (1966)	Krumboltz & Thoresen (1964) Krumboltz & Baker (1973)
Conceptualization	1. List of actions	1. Purpose		1. Defining the problem and the counseling goals
				2. Agreeing mutually to achieve counseling goals
Enlargement of the response repertoire	2. List of outcomes	2. Prediction system	2. Identify options	3. Generating alternative problem solutions
	3. Estimation of probabilities			4. Collecting information about the alternatives
Identification of stimuli discriminative of positive or aversive consequences for each response	4. Estimation of desirabilities	3. Value system	1. Examine values	5. Examining the consequences of the alternatives

Response selection	5. Decision criteria	3. Determine greatest sum of value returns 4. Determine index of expected value	4. Criterion strategy 5. Terminal or investigatory decision	6. Revaluing goals alternatives and consequences 7. Making the decision or tentatively selecting an alternative contingent upon new developments and new opportunities 8. Generalizing the decision-making process to new problems

Synthesis	Krumboltz (1966)	McGoon (1969)	Bergland, Quatrano & Lundquist (1975)	Evans & Cody (1969)
Conceptualization		1. Define the problem		
Enlargement of the response repertoire	1. Generating a list of all possible courses of action		1. Generate alternatives	1. A consideration of alternative courses of action
Identification of stimuli discriminative of positive or aversive consequences for each response	2. Gathering relevant information about each feasible course of action 3. Estimating the probability of success of each alternative on the	2. Gather relevant information	2. Identify and obtain relevant information	2. A consideration of the consequences of each of the alternative courses of action 3. A consideration of past experiences appropriate to the problem

basis of the experience of others and projections of current trends

4. Considering the personal values that may be enhanced or diminished under each course of action

3. Weigh the evidence
4. Choose first and alternate plans
5. Take action on plans
6. Periodic reviewing

3. Organize and evaluate the information
4. Process the information to make tentative choices

4. A consideration of the desirability of the consequences accuring from alternate decisions

Response selection

5. Deliberating and weighing the facts, probable outcomes, and values for each course of action
6. Eliminating from consideration the least favorable courses of action
7. Formulating a tentative plan subject to new developments and opportunities
8. Generalizing in the decision-making process to future problems

5. The selection of a decision based on the considerations listed previously

Stewart & Winborn (1973)	Herr, Horan, & Baker (1973)	Horan (1972b)
Conceptualization	1. Counselor defines the purpose of counseling, and the role of the counselor and student	1. Define the problem as one of choice
	2. Counselor helps the client define the problem via specific counseling skills	
	3. Counselor determines if vocational choice is the primary concern	
	4. Counselor explains the decision-making paradigm	
	5. Counselor explains the preparatory behaviors needed to make a good decision	
	6. Counselor determines if student has sufficient motivation	
Enlargement of the response repertoire 1. Generate alternatives	7. Counselor asks the student to identify all possible alternatives that come to mind	2. Generate alternatives, first from the client's perspective, then from the counselor's perspective
	8. Counselor identifies any additional alternatives that come to mind and are ethically appropriate	

Identification of stimuli discriminative of positive or aversive consequences for each response

2. Examine desirability of attainment

3. Examine probability of attainment

Response selection

4. Make final choice

9. Counselor assembles all relevant information about the student

10. Counselor assembles additional information about the student

11. Counselor presents to the student any information about the student relevant to the potential vocational decision

12. Counselor requests that the student identify the advantages and disadvantages of the alternatives that have been identified

13. Counselor identifies any additional advantages and disadvantages that come to mind

14. Counselor asks the student to evaluate the alternatives

15. Counselor helps the student obtain additional information about the most promising alternative(s)

16. Counselor helps the student implement the most promising alternative

17. Counselor determines if the selected alternative is satisfactory

18. Counselor terminates the counseling relationship

3. Gather information about the client and the alternatives

4. Identify advantages and disadvantages for each alternative, first from the client's perspective, then from the counselor's perspective

5. Rank the alternatives and make a tentative selection

Wallace, Horan, Baker, & Hudson (1975)	Janis & Mann (1977) stages	Janis & Mann (1977) vigilance steps
Conceptualization	1. Appraising the challenge	
1. Define the problem as one of choice		
2. Explain the decision-making paradigm		
Enlargement of the response repertoire	2. Surveying the alternatives	1. Thoroughly canvasses a wide range of alternative courses of action
3. Identify possible alternatives		2. Surveys the full range of objectives to be fulfilled and the values implicated by the choice
Identification of stimuli discriminative of positive or aversive consequences for each response		4. Intensively searches for new information relevant to further evaluation of the alternatives
4. Gather relevant information from client		5. Correctly assimilates and takes account of any new information or expert judgment to which he is exposed, even when the information or judgment does not support the course of action he initially prefers
5. Present relevant information to client		
6. Request that the client identify advantages and disadvantages for each alternative		
7. Present any additional advantages and disadvantages for each alternative to the client		
9. Verbally cue and reinforce the client for gathering additional information about the most promising alternative		

Response selection

8. Request that the client select the most promising alternative

10. Help the client implement the alternative

3. Weighing the alternatives

4. Deliberating about commitment

5. Adhering despite negative feedback

3. Carefully weighs whatever he knows about the costs and risks of negative consequences, as well as the positive consequences, that could flow from each alternative

6. Reexamines the positive and negative consequences of all known alternatives, including those originally regarded as unacceptable, before making a final choice

7. Makes detailed provisions for implementing or executing the chosen course of action with special attention to contingency plans that might be required if various known risks were to materialize

write as if the list of alternatives is already at hand or easily acquired.

3. Decision-making theorists, however, have far outstripped their problem-solving counterparts in detailing the activities pertinent to determining the likelihood of various positive and aversive consequences of the alternatives. Problem-solving theorists are often rather vague about such data-gathering procedures.

4. Except when they have appropriated the work of decision theorists, authors in the problem-solving area have contributed relatively little to the matter of choosing among several viable responses. Much of the problem-solving literature seems to imply that a problem has a single, albeit hidden, solution. Moreover, although both groups emphasize the need for evaluation of any response selected, decision theorists may have the edge in the topic of response implementation.

These observations do not characterize all problem-solving or decision-making theorists. There is a good deal of variability within each camp, perhaps enough to wash out any differences between them. Thus these observations may in fact be crude stereotypes rather than apt descriptors. In any event, because the problem-solving literature seems to expand indefinitely and decision making implies those areas of problem solving where decision theorists have been less than explicit, from this point on I will refer to all the activities in table 11.2 as components of decision making.

Finally, although many authors use the words stage, step, or phase in referring to these components, this does not necessarily imply a rigid sequence of events. Such words are useful primarily for their "outlining" or expository capacity. As Davis (1973, p. 17) points out, "These simplifications are helpful if we keep some qualifications in mind. Whether solving an anagram or designing a generator, a person . . . will *overlap his steps*, as when he begins to think of solutions while defining the problem; he will *backtrack to earlier stages*, as when he finds it necessary to redefine or further clarify 'the givens'; and he may *skip some steps* entirely, especially the *incubation* one."

Decision Making in Counseling

We have just seen that decision making consists, or ought to consist, of four components: (1) conceptualization, (2) enlargement of the response repertoire, (3) identification of discriminative stimuli, and (4) response selection.

Most of our decisions are not made with the help of a professional counselor, though many of us do consult with others who *may* function as counselors whenever we face a difficult decision. For instance, the spouse who consults with a divorce attorney might attempt a reconciliation after carefully considering the consequences of various alternatives. Or a medical patient might decline elective surgery after thorough discussion with his or her physician.

Even though the majority of our decisions are made apart from the context of a formal counseling relationship, decision-making concerns are among the most common problems in living brought to the attention of counselors. Recall that counseling includes assessment, intervention, and evaluation. The four components of decision making can be merged into these counseling activities.

Assessment in decision-making counseling involves the identification of those skills presently lacking but required for the client to conceptualize the problem, to generate sufficient alternatives, to uncover pertinent discriminative stimuli, and to select an appropriate response. Once these skill deficits have been assessed, intervention in decision-making counseling deals with the application of specific counseling techniques in an attempt to foster the development of the necessary skills. Finally, evaluation in decision-making counseling focuses on the determination of whether or not the intervention activities have had any impact.

Summary

Three attempts to provide counselor trainees with a procedural road map for counseling are distinguished by their clarity and precision. Winborn and his associates developed a flowchart that depicts the ten essential ingredients of systematic counseling. Thoresen and his associates also incorporated features of systems thinking into their six- and later seventeen-step conceptualizations of counseling. Gottman and Leiblum's flowchart of psychotherapy consists of five major components. Each of these similar models can be condensed into three categories of counselor activity: assessment, intervention, and evaluation.

Wallas, Dewey, and Gagné have each offered a stage theory of problem solving; so have D'Zurilla and Goldfried, and Urban and Ford, whose stage theories place problem solving in the counseling domain. Similarly, Bross, Krumboltz, Stewart and Winborn, my colleagues and I, and Janis and Mann have described the stages of decision making. All of these formulations can be condensed into four stages: conceptualization, enlargement of the response repertoire, identification of discriminative stimuli, and response selection.

In decision-making counseling assessment refers to the identification of the skills implied by these stages that are needed to make an adaptive choice; intervention means the application of specific counseling techniques to foster the development of these skills; and evaluation involves determining the impact of intervention activities. The next three chapters focus on these categories of counselor activity in greater detail.

12

Assessment in Decision-Making Counseling

According to *Webster's Seventh New Collegiate Dictionary*, the word *assessment* has its origins in the Latin verb *assidere*, meaning "to sit beside, in the office of a judge." Today the word commonly refers to the determination or imposition of taxes; but in the counseling and psychotherapy literature assessment has a much different meaning, one very close to the concept of diagnosis in medicine. The analogy between assessment in counseling and diagnosis in medicine has a long historical precedent. About a hundred years ago Emil Kraepelin offered a system for classifying abnormal behavior, the tattered remnants of which are still displayed in textbooks, diagnostic manuals, and subscales of sundry psychological tests. Taking a cue from biological science and the practice of medicine, Kraepelin hoped that the classification of mental disorders into discrete categories would be followed by advances in treatment.

Unfortunately, Kraepelin's hopes have never been realized; diagnostic categories in use today have little relevance to or impact on counseling (Dailey, 1953). Meehl (1960), for example, reported that only 17 percent of a sample of therapists found psychological testing to be of any value in treating their patients. At least two reasons account for this lack of confidence in the utility of traditional assessment: In the first place many schools of counseling advocate the same treatment strategy regardless of the nature of the client's problems in living. Secondly, the diagnostic categories themselves are notoriously unreliable and invalid, as

187

might be expected from their presumption that disturbances emanate from *within* the individual apart from consideration of the environmental context (see Hersen, 1976; Kanfer & Phillips, 1970; Mischel, 1968).

This chapter begins with a discussion of the behavioral perspective on assessment, which can be applied to decision-making counseling. We shall then examine the individual client skills pertinent to making an adaptive decision. Should these skills be found deficient, they can be enhanced by a variety of cognitive-behavioral intervention strategies, which will be explored in chapter 13.

Behavioral Perspectives on Assessment

One of the hallmarks of exemplary behavioral counseling research is rigorous assessment of the problem behavior. Paul's (1966) classic study on insight versus desensitization in the treatment of public speaking anxiety, as one example, included ratings from therapists, impartial observers, the clients themselves, as well as physiological measures of speech anxiety. Moreover, obesity researchers not only look at pounds or percentage of body weight lost but through specialized techniques can examine dimunitions in fat tissue as well (see Mahoney, 1977). Finally, smoking behavior can be rather precisely assessed through the use of expired air carbon monoxide (see Horan, Hackett, & Linberg, 1978).

Although much attention has been paid to the issue of assessment in behavioral research, assessment in behavioral counseling practice is a sorely neglected area. The reasons for this relatively stunted development are obvious. The researcher often picks a problem behavior that easily lends itself to the generation of operational definitions; so after several projects involving the same problem behavior, the matter of assessment becomes almost routine. The practitioner, on the other hand, is confronted with a diverse array of complex client problems that often interact with the environment and are rarely, if ever, clearly defined at the outset of counseling. Determining the nature of the problem, let alone operationally defining it, is a tricky matter.

The literature on behavioral assessment in the practice of counseling can be roughly divided into two categories. The first category contains the writings of a number of authors who have suggested classification schemes for potential critical areas of client disfunction. Most kinds of client problems are presumed to emanate from these areas, a list of which can thus be used by the counselor on an a priori basis to ensure a general overview of client functioning. Wolpe's (1969) interview guide exemplifies this approach. Clients are asked a series of questions pertaining to (1) early family life, (2) educational and vocational experiences, (3) sexual history and current functioning, and (4) present social relationships.

Kanfer and his associates (Kanfer & Phillips, 1970; Kanfer & Saslow, 1969) posit a more elaborate assessment framework consisting of seven components: (1) analysis of the problem situation (including baseline construction of behavioral excesses and deficits), (2) clarification of the problem (especially determining people and circumstances that tend to maintain the problem), (3) motivational analysis (for example, identifying reinforcers in the client's life), (4) developmental analysis (questioning regarding the client's biological equipment, sociocultural experiences, and behavior patterns), (5) analysis of self-control, (6) analysis of social relationships, and (7) analysis of the social-cultural-physical environment. The work of Kanfer and his associates is frequently cited.

Lazarus (1973) uses the acronym BASIC ID to organize his seven-component assessment paradigm: *B*ehavior, *A*ffect, *S*ensation (for example, muscle tension), *I*magery, *C*ognition, *I*nterpersonal relationships, and *D*rugs. Difficulties in any of these modes of living suggest a number of treatment strategies to be applied concurrently—hence Lazarus's term "multimodal" behavior therapy.

Finally, Mischel (1973) identifies five "person" variables that might be included in behavioral assessment. These are (1) cognitive and behavioral construction competencies, (2) encoding strategies and personal constructs, (3) behavior-outcome and stimulus-outcome expectancies, (4) subjective stimulus values, and (5) self-regulation systems and plans.

In addition to offering classification schemes for potential critical areas of client disfunction, Wolpe, Kanfer, Lazarus, and Mischel all advocate precise specification of the problem behavior. This brings us to the second category of literature on behavioral assessment in counseling practice. If we take seriously Morganstern's (1976, p. 52) comment that the scope of assessment includes *"everything* that is relevant to the development of effective, efficient, and durable treatment interventions . . . and no more," then in certain instances counselors who employ any of the foregoing classification schemes might well be gathering superfluous data. Detailed counselor inquiry into a client's sexual history, for example, would probably have little bearing on the presenting problem of test anxiety. Our second and perhaps more pertinent category of assessment literature focuses on how client problems are specified.

A number of authors have independently but similarly addressed this topic (for example Cautela, 1968; Goldfried & Davison, 1976; Goldfried & Pomeranz, 1968; Peterson, 1968; Stuart, 1970). Their work has come to be known as the ABC approach to behavioral assessment, not to be confused with Ellis's (1962) ABC theory of neurosis.

The letter *B* in this assessment model refers to behavior. Both problematic and desirable behaviors need to be clearly defined. Any one or combination of three measurement modes may be employed: self-report, physiological recording, and observation of motor behavior. Once defined, the degree of the problem can be quantified in terms of a baseline prior to treatment in order to determine the impact of treatment. Baselines are usually expressed along the dimensions of frequency, intensity, and duration (for example, number of cigarettes smoked per day, pounds overweight, and length of tantrum, respectively, see Horan, 1974c).

Neither problematic nor desirable behaviors occur in a vacuum, however. The *A* in the model stands for antecedent conditions. Essentially, the behavioral assessor needs to know if there are certain discriminative stimuli in the environment that contribute to the problematic behavior. Of possibly greater importance is the question "Are there discriminative stimuli missing from the environment that could contribute to the development of desirable behavior?"

Finally, the letter *C* in this model means consequences. Are problematic behaviors being positively reinforced by the environment? Could they be suppressed by some form of punishment? Are desirable behaviors being extinguished by the environment? Could they be encouraged by some form of reinforcement? .

Assessment of Decision-Making Behaviors

The reader will have to personally come to terms with the appropriateness of the general assessment frameworks suggested by Wolpe, Kanfer, Lazarus, and Mischel applied to his or her own clinical practice. My own preference is to shy away from such checklists except in the case of relatively nonverbal clients or in certain situations where it is clear there is insufficient data for treatment. Most clients, especially those who are self-referred, seem able to articulate the general areas of concern if not the specific problems involved. Careful interviewing (to be discussed later) can usually delineate the specific problems. If more information is needed, it can be asked for on an ad hoc rather than a priori basis.

The specification of decision-making problems is somewhat more complex than the specification of other kinds of counseling concerns. For example, the problematic and desirable behaviors associated with maladaptive fear, overeating, and cigarette smoking lend themselves well to definition (if not modification). Decision making, on the other hand, consists of a broad *package* of behaviors. In adaptive decision making this package will be relatively complete; maladaptive decisions are characterized by missing items. Assessment in decision-making counseling essentially refers to the identification of those behaviors that would enhance the adaptiveness of a particular decision.

Our ABC assessment framework can be thought of as a guiding philosophy here that need not be applied obsessively. In decision-making assessment the Bs generally refer to the desirable behaviors, which if missing can be developed by As and Cs dispensed by the counselor. For ease in description I have organized these behaviors in terms of the four categories in our summary model of decision making.

Conceptualization

The conceptualization category includes three skills pertinent to decision-making assessment: (1) ability to maintain low level of affective arousal, (2) ability to define correctly the choice problem, and (3) ability to explain the decision-making paradigm.

A high level of affective arousal in the client almost certainly precludes the possibility of adaptive decision making. In fact it can be expected to prevent the client from even defining the choice problem. Rage at a spouse's infidelity, for example, can easily fog the client's perspective on possible alternatives to a quick divorce, or worse, assaultive behavior. Extreme anxiety can exert a similar obfuscating influence. For our purposes it should not be necessary to go into an elaborate behavioral definition of these emotions; most counselors in contact with reality have little trouble identifying and distinguishing high levels of client affect. There are counseling strategies for reducing such debilitating emotionality that I will discuss in the next chapter. As far as assessment is concerned, it is simply important to note the affective behavior and determine if there are any relevant antecedents and consequences for it.

The basic skill in the conceptualization category, however, is the ability to define the source of discomfort as a choice problem. Some clients have relatively little difficulty doing this, even when the stakes in the decision are high. Others seem baffled by the nature of their distress and have no idea that there may be alternative ways to resolve their dilemma. Sometimes this inability is not accompanied by high affect. It is simply a matter of "not having thought of it that way before."

Not infrequently the client will have defined the problem as one of choice but incorrectly defined the nature of the decision that needs to be made. For example, the student who reports indecision about staying in or dropping out of school or the woman debating about having another child perhaps ought to be looking at long-range options emanating from the question "What kind of career do I want to carve out for myself?" From this vantage point answers to the presenting choice problem become partial alternatives to a somewhat different decision.

In addition to noting whether the client can correctly define the problem as one of choice, the counselor needs to assess the client's ability to explain the decision-making paradigm verbally. (I use the word "explain" rather than "understand" because a client who cannot explain the decision-making paradigm probably does not understand it.) An open-ended question such as "Have you thought about what might be involved in coming to a good decision here?" may address the issue. Any explanation the client offers should include statements to the effect that there are alternatives and ways of finding out which alternatives are best. To the contrary, however, some clients have relatively fatalistic attitudes about their ability to have a positive impact on their lives. Others seem immobilized by guilt, as is occasionally the case with problem-pregnancy clients who feel that their present predicament is proper punishment for previous poor decisions. Still other clients expect the counselor to make the decision for them. Self-defeating thoughts and unrealistic expectations such as these must be confronted and replaced by an adaptive perspective on decision making.

Enlargement of the Response Repertoire

In the response repertoire category the counselor is concerned with noting whether the client has (1) avoided an impulsive response, (2) identified all alternatives known to the counselor, and (3) planned to search for additional alternatives.

A high level of affect cannot only obscure the client's view of a choice problem, but it can lead to impulsive, inefficient responding as well. In decision theory terminology the client is about to select (or has already implemented) an alternative without fully considering its consequences or identifying other, possibly better, alternatives. Impulsive choices can also be made for reasons other than a high level of affect. For example, our culture stereotypically applauds the executive who makes snap decisions, but in reality executives who habitually decide matters of consequence impulsively are likely to lose their jobs or bankrupt their companies in the long run. In any event some clients feel they must act in a hurry even when time considerations are not revelant. Thus, when assessing the client's response repertoire, it is crucial to ascertain if the client seems likely to make an impulsive response. Not infrequently, clients will have already implemented an impulsive response, a situation that calls for a different set of intervention procedures.

The second and third items of interest in this assessment category concern the number of alternatives generated. Quality is a separate issue; quantity is now of paramount importance. The counselor needs to know if the client has independently conjured up as many alternatives as are known to the counselor. Moreover, because the counselor's response repertoire may be limited in so far as a given choice problem is concerned, it is essential to note if the client plans to take steps to discover if other alternatives exist. A married couple, for example, may have decided to forego having children, but the mode of contraception may still be an unresolved issue. They may well be aware of the one or two less-than-ideal alternatives known to the counselor but totally ignorant of other possibilities, which could easily be discovered from a wide variety of sources.

Identification of Discriminative Stimuli

Every alternative to a given choice problem will yield consequences of varying utility. Recall from chapter 4 that in risky decisions the probability of any consequence is less than "1." Moreover, the assignment of such probabilities is a subjective matter influenced by the amount of information at hand. We are not only uncertain about the probability of known consequences, but for any alternative there may be numerous unknown consequences as well.

In behavioral jargon informational units that tip us off to the existence or probability of consequences arising from a particular alternative are known as discriminative stimuli. Adaptive decision making calls for "searching" behaviors directed toward identifying stimuli discriminative of positive or aversive consequences for each alternative.

In this assessment category the counselor is concerned with observing whether the client has (1) identified all discriminative stimuli known to the counselor and (2) planned to search for additional discriminative stimuli. The quantity of such information-seeking behaviors is, again, of major importance. Consider, for example, the matter of elective surgery. Has the decision-making patient actively searched for information on the potential effects and side effects of a given operation? Has he or she investigated alternative forms of treatment and tapped data sources such as consulting physicians, reference materials, and other patients? Competent surgeons are not annoyed by this sort of behavior and in fact even encourage it. In spite of the obvious adaptiveness of medical information searching, however, relatively few individuals engage in it (for example, Bracken & Kasl, 1975; Cobb, Clark, Carson, & Howe, 1954; Janis, 1958; Weinstein & Kahn, 1955). Particularly incredible are the statistics on how many cancer patients die each year because they failed to obtain even an initial medical opinion until the disease had spread throughout their bodies.

Response Selection

In the response-selection category the counselor is concerned with assessing three general decision-making skills: (1) the reporting of adaptive utilities and probability estimates, (2) the ability to explain a response-selection paradigm, and (3) the ability to implement a selected response.

Classical decision theory is based on the assumption that a client's utilities are rational and need not be tampered with by a decision-making consultant. Counselors, however, are continually confronted with clients who report irrational or maladaptive utilities, which often lead to considerable distress in the client's life. If these irrational utilities are permitted to go unchallenged in the process of decision-making counseling, we can assume that any alternative selected will perpetuate this distress. Consider, for example, the matter of career choice. If an individual is pursuing a parentally favored option because of the long-range rational reinforcers it offers, there is no problem. Parental approval simply provides an extra measure of utility. On the other hand, if the career alternative is selected because of inordinately high (maladaptive) utilities placed on parental approval, the decision will likely prove unsatisfactory at a later date.

It would be impossible to catalog all "crazy" utilities; but Ellis's (1962) compendium of illogical thoughts is a good starting point, as are the cognitive ecology writings of Beck (1970), Lazarus (1971), and Mahoney (1973). Before dismissing a particular utility as irrational or maladaptive, however, a word of caution is in order. We as counselors may have *different* utilities but they are not necessarily *better*. The profession of counseling itself is laden with individuals possessing widely different utilities. In our pluralistic society we should be fully prepared to encounter vast numbers of clients who don't "think like us." From the standpoint of cultural survival, this diversity is desirable. Thus our assessment of a client's utilities as being maladaptive brings to mind the ethical issues raised in chapter 6. Unless there is widespread professional consensus to the contrary, counselors ought to assume that the client's utilities are adaptive.

Unlike the question of utility, the determination of the adaptiveness of a client's probability estimate is a fairly straightforward matter. Any estimate made by the client at a given point in time on the basis of his or her own past experience is defensible. Probability estimation is always

a subjective process. However, the adaptiveness of a client's final estimate depends upon the extent to which it corresponds to figures gar-
nered by the new information-seeking activities described in the last
assessment category. For example, a tubal pregnancy poses a serious
health risk to any woman. The likelihood of maternal death increases
with the length of the gestation period. Presumably most clients so
afflicted would have little basis to assign probability estimates for their
own survival or that of the fetus when initially confronted with the decision to seek an abortion or to let nature take its hazardous course. Following information gathering on the latter alternative, however, if the
client reports a high fetal-survival estimate and a low health-risk estimate, then such estimates must be considered maladaptive and worthy of
counselor intervention.

   After noting if the client's utilities and probability estimates are
adaptive, a counselor must assess the client's ability to explain a
response-selection paradigm. This explanation ought to pay homage to
the facts that human information-processing capacity is limited to the
famous 7 ± 2 pieces of data (Miller, 1956) and that consistently good random decisions (for example, by flipping a coin) are improbable. A wide
variety of response-selection paradigms are available, ranging from Ben
Franklin's list of pros and cons to some of the more esoteric grids mentioned in earlier chapters. All operate by arranging the complex utility
and probability information in such a way that the most promising alternative emerges in some systematic manner. Although in many cases it
would appear that these paradigms simply enable the client to achieve a
profound grasp of the obvious, the adaptiveness of this skill or procedure has been empirically established (Hoyt & Janis, 1975; Mann, 1972).

   Finally, the counselor needs to assess whether the client has the ability to implement the selected response. At this juncture decision-making
counseling begins to blur with more traditional programming procedures.
For example, a homosexual client may have decided to become heterosexual but needs at the very least a capacity for heterosexual arousal before
being able to begin implementing this alternative.

Interviewing as an Assessment Tool

The interview is the primary assessment device in decision-making counseling. It serves as virtually the only source of data on the presence or
absence of behaviors prerequisite to the making of an adaptive choice, at
least in the typical practice of decision-making counseling. The routine

use of interest inventories with career choice concerns does not constitute an exception as these "assessment devices" are not employed to check on the occurrence of decision-making behaviors, but rather their use constitutes adaptive information-seeking behavior. Of course, other behavioral assessment modes might be employed in certain circumstances. For example, a research project might employ questionnaires to tap the extent of the clients' response repertoires or career counselors might use observational methods to determine if their clients are examining certain resource materials. But in most instances the interview will generate the assessment data for decision-making counseling.

Fortunately there is relatively close agreement among the various schools of counseling as to how the early stages of the interview ought to proceed. In fact, if we look at two of the most seemingly disparate schools, client-centered and behavioral counseling, it would be virtually impossible to distinguish representatives from each on the basis of counselor-client dialogue occurring in the first half of the initial interview.

This striking similarity is perhaps best exemplified by the work of Ivey (1971), who concerned himself with the problem of how the seemingly complex interviewing skills of client-centered counselors could be efficiently taught to counselor trainees. Ivey's solution was to define behaviorally a number of individual interviewing skills that taken as a whole would reflect his perspective on the complex process of counseling. Instructional booklets and videotape models were prepared for each skill, which could then be sequentially taught to trainees in but a fraction of time normally allotted to "hit and miss" counselor education programs. "Microcounseling," as Ivey calls his system, consists of several skill categories. The *beginning skills* include attending behaviors (eye contact, postural position, and verbal following), open invitations to talk, summarization of feeling, and summarization of content. Once these have been mastered, the counselor trainees learn a variety of *specialized skills* and *skills of self-expression.*

Studies of the microcounseling package (for example, Haase & Di Mattia, 1970; Ivey, Normington, Miller, Morrill, & Haase, 1968), suggest that it is a fairly efficient means of teaching the relationship qualities and skills espoused by Carl Rogers. The clarity of the desirable interviewer "behaviors," moreover, increases its acceptability to behaviorally inclined counselors. Since publication of Ivey's work many interviewer training manuals, by authors of apparently differing theoretical persuasions who seem to be espousing similar skills, have appeared on the market.

All the interviewing skills these various authors suggest reflect a common underlying principle: *Pay attention to (that is, positively reinforce) any cognitive, affective, motor, and somatic behavior displayed by the client.* Regardless of counselors' theoretical biases, they all view an atmosphere of noncontingent reinforcement as a *sine qua non* for obtaining accurate assessment data. Extended coverage of the topic of interviewing would seriously blur the focus of this book; yet the importance of skilled interviewing behavior in decision making or in any other kind of counseling cannot be overstated.

Before moving on to the discussion of intervention procedures in decision-making counseling, I would like to add two qualifications. Although there is close agreement among the various schools of counseling as to how the early stages of the interview ought to proceed, behavioral counseling demands a shifting of gears as the interview progresses. Once it becomes clear that noncontingent reinforcement has run its course and is producing no new assessment data, the behavioral counselor begins to employ selective reinforcement on two fronts.

In the first place clients invariably describe themselves and their problems in abstract terms. For example, if a client says, "I guess I'm a pretty uptight person," a variety of interpretations are possible (for example, "I'm anxious, mad, or moralistic"). Behavioral counselors supplement their reflective listening skills with *relentless* listening skills and pursue not only a clear rendition of the abstract term in question but also illustrations of the situations surrounding it. Relentless listening here simply means the cuing and reinforcement of concrete examples in the client's verbal behavior.

Second, although an atmosphere of noncontingent reinforcement is essential for the assessment of client problems, once these problems are discovered, behavioral counselors avoid reinforcing them. For example, a certain degree of attention must be paid to a client's depressed affect; however, once the affect and the stimuli supporting it have been assessed, the behavioral counselor shifts attention to adaptive behaviors. Continued attending to "crazy talk" only gives it credibility.

Bridging the Gap Between Assessment and Intervention in Decision Making

The adaptive behaviors clients ought to display in the context of decision-making counseling can be arranged in terms of eleven assessment questions (see table 12.1). If the answer to any of these questions is "no," then the counselor may apply a variety of intervention strategies. These strategies will be discussed more fully in the next chapter.

TABLE 12.1. **Assessment questions and intervention strategies in decision-making counseling**

Summary model	Assessment question	Intervention strategies (when the answer is "no")
Conceptualization	1. Is affective arousal low?	Listening (extinction) Relaxation training Desensitization and variations Cognitive restructuring
	2. Can client correctly define problem as one of choice?	Paraphrasing Probe (cuing and reinforcing) Socratic dialoguing
	3. Can client explain the decision-making paradigm?	Cognitive restructuring Emotional role playing Cognitive modeling Verbal reinforcement
Enlargement of response repertoire	4. Has client avoided an impulsive response?	Thought stopping-substitution Covert sensitization Outcome psychodrama Emotional role playing Cognitive restructuring Skill-building interventions
	5. Has client identified all alternatives known to counselor?	Creative instructional set Originality training Brainstorming Metaphorical thinking Modeling
	6. Will client search for additional alternatives?	Verbal cuing and reinforcement Modeling
Identification of discriminative stimuli	7. Has client identified all discriminative stimuli known to counselor?	Outcome psychodrama Modeling
	8. Will client search for additional discriminative stimuli?	Verbal cuing and reinforcement Modeling Simulation strategies

Response selection	9. Does client report adaptive utilities and probability estimates?	Cognitive restructuring Emotional role playing Outcome psychodrama Induced cognitive dissonance Awareness of rationalizations Peer modeling
	10. Can client explain a response-selection paradigm?	Modeling variations
	11. Are client's skills sufficient to implement the selected response?	Comprehensive behavioral programming Stress inoculation Emotional inoculation

When applying this list of questions in decision-making assessment, the counselor must realize that the adaptive behaviors need not be performed in rigid sequence. The four-category summary model is merely a synthesis of twenty-two stage theories of problem solving and decision making that have appeared in the literature since the turn of the century. The eleven questions pertain to client behaviors that are my attempts to define operationally the essential features of each category. In the practice of decision-making counseling, however, the order of the behaviors within each assessment category or even the categories themselves may need to be shifted or addressed simultaneously. For example, it may become apparent to a counselor that a client is not only operating at a high level of affective arousal but is also likely to make an impulsive response. In this case the fourth question would take priority over the second and third.

The boundaries between assessment and intervention are not clearly drawn. Because of their reactive effects, certain assessment procedures like self-monitoring actually can be thought of as interventions. This blurring of the distinctions between assessment and intervention frequently occurs in the conduct of decision-making counseling. For example, the counselor's assessment activities involved in determining if the client has correctly defined the problem as one of choice may actually help clarify the client's problem, or determining the extent of the client's response repertoire may have the desirable effect of enlarging it.

The actual process of decision-making counseling is an interplay between assessment and intervention activities: The counselor determines which decision-making skills the client lacks and then attempts to foster them. Counselors occasionally encounter clients who already exhibit all the skills implied by the list of eleven assessment questions. (The act of seeing a counselor is suggested by questions six and eight).

In such cases the client is in fact making an adaptive decision; the counselor may serve as an informational resource or a provider of reassurance and reinforcement for making an adaptive choice. No other formal decision-making interventions are necessary and unless the client indicates other kinds of concerns, termination of the counseling relationship would be appropriate.

SUMMARY

In the counseling literature the word *assessment* resembles the concept of diagnosis in medicine, but traditional assessment categories have had little relevance to or impact on counseling practice. Although rigorous assessment of problem behavior is a hallmark of behavioral counseling research, assessment in behavioral counseling practice is a sorely neglected area. Most literature on behavioral counseling assessment fits into one of two categories: classification schemes for potential critical areas of client disfunction and procedures for specifying problem or desirable behavior.

Assessment in decision-making counseling refers to the identification of those behaviors that would enhance the adaptiveness of a client's decision. Eleven such behaviors (which can be expressed as assessment questions) operationally define the four components of our summary model of decision making.

The interview is the primary assessment tool in decision-making counseling. All schools of counseling recommend that during the early stages of the interview the counselor should pay attention to (positively reinforce) any cognitive, affective, motor, or somatic behavior displayed by the client. Once it becomes clear that noncontingent reinforcement is producing no new assessment data, behavioral counseling calls for selective reinforcement.

The boundaries between assessment and intervention are not always clear; the next chapter focuses on cognitive-behavioral interventions available for promoting adaptive decision making.

13

Intervention in Decision-Making Counseling

In chapter 12 we saw that the interview serves as the primary assessment tool in decision-making counseling, and that there is fairly close agreement among the various schools of counseling as to how the early stages of the interview ought to proceed. Paying attention to any cognitive, affective, motor, and somatic behavior the client displays is important not only for the gathering of accurate assessment data but also for establishing the counselor as a "personified" secondary reinforcer. Counselors who develop this "reinforcing relationship," as it is sometimes labeled, are more likely to have an impact on their clients' behavior. Verbal reinforcement or modeling interventions, for example, become more powerful.

We should realize that acknowledging these facets of the laws of reinforcement does not detract one iota from the sincerity of our counseling motives. The fact that we may pay close attention to our clients out of deep concern for them does not alter the parallel fact that such attention may improve the efficacy of our counseling interventions.

In this chapter we shall explore a wide variety of cognitive-behavioral interventions that are available for the conduct of decision-making counseling. The choice of which techniques to use depends first of all upon the particular skill deficits the counselor assesses. For any given skill deficit, however, several interventions may be applicable. Unfortunately, there are relatively few comparative studies in the counseling literature that clearly demonstrate the superiority of one technique over another. A good guideline would be to select the counseling intervention with the firmest research basis whenever possible.

The summary model and assessment questions depicted in table 12.1 provide a convenient outline for our discussion of interventions in decision-making counseling. Although I have attempted to illustrate most pertinent interventions, undoubtedly many others could also be applied. Still others await discovery.

How to Help Clients Conceptualize the Problem

Interventions for Reducing Affective Arousal

Perhaps the major strategy for reducing high affective arousal in clients is the simple act of listening. At first blush it might seem out of place for cognitive-behaviorists to claim listening as a counseling technique in view of the fact that Rogerian counselors have been soundly roasted for advocating it, but there are important distinctions between these two perspectives on the use of listening.

In the first place, behavioral counselors do not suggest listening as a cure for all client ills. Rather, they see it as a specific intervention, the efficacy of which on certain kind of client problem, namely high affective arousal, is open to empirical scrutiny. Moreover, the potential effects of listening when applied to such client problems are readily interpretable in the language of behaviorism: Listening permits an *extinction* process to occur. Let us take, for example, the case of a client who begins talking about a situation that presently produces high levels of guilt or maladaptive anxiety. In talking about this situation, the client is in fact exposing himself or herself to the problematic conditional stimulus (CS) or source of discomfort. If the "listening" counselor presents a nonjudgmental, positively-reinforcing demeanor (that is, if the counselor does not introduce or reintroduce a noxious unconditional stimulus [UCS]), the client's learned guilt or anxiety can be expected to extinguish. This is why many clients report feeling better after a confession or a catharsis. "Nothing terrible happened after all!" It is also why the technique of systematic desensitization seems superfluous with some clients once the fear hierarchy has been constructed.

If listening alone does not reduce debilitating affective arousal to manageable levels, other intervention procedures may be employed. Relaxation training or any of the varieties of systematic desensitization, for example, are techniques for lowering anxiety and guilt. Cognitive restructuring is also apropos, particularly when the client seems immersed in self-defeating anger. Cognitive restructuring involves identification of the irrational self-statements that give rise to the negative emotion and counselor modeling of a more adaptive thought pattern.

Interventions for Defining the Problem

The intervention strategies for helping the client define the problem as one of choice are really not different from the assessment procedures that lead the counselor to the same judgment. Few clients enter counseling with an opening statement such as "My problem seems to be one of choice; as I see it there are several options open to me and I'm not certain which will prove most advantageous." Quite the contrary. Most clients begin by talking about their concerns or sources of discomfort in rather general terms far removed from the language of decision theory. For example, an unhappy spouse may recite a litany of complaints about the marriage partner. A high school senior may report being "really down" (depressed) about an upcoming graduation. An unexpected pregnancy may lead another client to obsessive self-recriminations. Although these concerns may eventually boil down to decisions about divorce, career, and abortion, there is really no way of determining if such is the case at the outset of counseling. A first task of the counselor is to wade through the murky waters of human misery and clarify the problem.

Paraphrasing is perhaps the principal intervention strategy to be used at this point. Paraphrasing is simply an extention of the assessment dictum to pay attention to all cognitive, affective, motor, and somatic behavior displayed by the client. My definition of paraphrasing is broader than Ivey's (1971); it includes reflection of feeling as well as content. Paraphrasing means to repeat what was said in the way it was said but more concisely.

Paraphrasing, of course, demands that the counselor understand what the client is saying, which brings me to a brief digression. Because clients will rarely aid the counselor by using clear, unambiguous language, the counselor must reflexively probe for specific examples of terms used by the client. Probing means to cue and reinforce the client for using operational definitions. For instance, the counselor might respond to a client's cloudy terminology as follows: " 'Inconsiderate.' Would you give me a few examples of how your (husband/wife) is inconsiderate of you?" (Client responds.) "That's helpful to me; I see what you mean." Or perhaps, "When do you feel 'really down'? Can you tell me what it's like, what's going on in your head?" (Client responds.) "Uh, huh. That's a pretty good description. I think I understand what's happening with you, but can you tell me a little bit more about the 'hassling' you've been getting from your parents?" Counselors should only attempt paraphrasing when they have a fairly firm grasp on what the client is saying.

As an intervention strategy paraphrasing has the immediate effect of reinforcing the client's continued talking about a given problem area. In other words it supplies the counselor with further assessment data that will then indicate whether the client's concern is a problem of choice. At the counselor's discretion paraphrasing may be supplemented with other interventions, such as Socratic dialoguing, in an attempt to clarify the problem. However, the assessment of the client's problem as one of choice and the intervention that defines it as such is a final paraphrase that tentatively sifts through and fits the data at hand into a choice framework that the client in turn will accept, reject, or modify.

Interventions for Inculcating the Decision-Making Paradigm

If the client has not developed a perspective on the process of adaptive decision making, the counselor's next task is to help foster it. Dilley (1968) spoke to this issue a decade ago when he suggested that a primary counselor function is to reinforce an attitude of personal responsibility in clients. Unfortunately, a good many clients make few if any statements indicative of personal responsibility, thus leaving the counselor with little to reinforce.

Cognitive restructuring procedures are apropos when clients seem to have a fatalistic or other self-defeating outlook on their ability to have a positive impact on their lives. For example, Ellis (1962) addresses one facet of this topic with his observations on the irrationality of needing to find someone on whom to depend. Not infrequently, clients will continue this dependency-seeking behavior in counseling by asking the counselor what course of action to follow. Counselors should scrupulously avoid donning this decision-making yoke, as it reinforces the client's avoidance of responsibility and sets the counselor up as an inevitable scapegoat when the choice proves less than ideal.

Other clients may recognize their concern as a problem of choice but fail to realize that "not to decide is to decide." In other words, procrastination or avoiding deliberate decision making is in fact tantamount to selecting an alternative that may prove relatively disadvantageous. "Maybe I'll decide to quit smoking after the first of the year" or "If that lump in my breast doesn't go away by next month, I'll have to do something about it" illustrates the dangers of this approach. Interventions such as emotional role playing that sensitize the client to the long-range consequences of indecisiveness may be useful in such cases. Kravetz and Thomas (1974) offer a number of behaviorally based suggestions for working with indecisive clients.

Cognitive modeling is probably the most pertinent strategy for helping clients develop an adaptive perspective on the process of decision making. A cognitive model "thinks out loud" in an attempt to foster a similar thought pattern in the observer. By serving as a live cognitive model, the counselor can efficiently inculcate the decision-making paradigm in the client. Key components of the counselor's script (that is, verbalized thought pattern) are that there are ways of generating alternatives and procedures for discovering which alternative is likely to be best. The script should also pay homage to the fact that the responsibility for selecting an alternative rests with the client, but if need be the counselor can provide help with its implementation. Any of the client's verbal behavior that suggests the development of an adaptive decision-making perspective should, of course, be met with liberal reinforcement from the counselor.

How to Help Clients Enlarge their Response Repertoires

Interventions for Thwarting Impulsive Responding

There are a variety of intervention strategies available for helping clients avoid making an impulsive response. Thought stopping or thought substitution, for example, may rid the client of the urge to act. Covert sensitization, outcome psychodrama, emotional role playing, or some other hybrid version of these very similar procedures may be appropriate as well. Each of these techniques permits the client to experience vicariously the logical consequences of the impulsive response.

Although the foregoing techniques are intended to prevent rash behavior, the client will frequently have already responded impulsively before talking to the counselor. In such cases cognitive restructuring in conjunction with other skill-building interventions such as behavioral rehearsal or covert modeling may prove useful.

To illustrate these interventions, let us consider the case of a client who is unfairly passed over for a promotion. He or she obviously has a career decision to make. Ruminations on the supervisor's ancestry or repeated urges to quit on the spot can be interrupted by thought stopping. The act of resigning impulsively may also be averted if the client covertly experiences some of the perhaps unconsidered outcomes of that response (for example, negotiation for a new job from a position of need rather than security). In the event the client has already impulsively resigned, the counselor may consider interventions designed to "undo" the response. For instance, cognitive restructuring (along the lines of "your personal adequacy does not depend upon this supervisor's appraisal") combined with behavioral rehearsal (directed toward asking that the resignation request be ignored) can restore the possibility of an adaptive choice.

In this example and in any other, the impulsive response might well prove to be the best alternative. The point is not to prevent the response from being made but to prevent it from being made impulsively. It may certainly be in the client's best interest to change jobs (that is, the SEUs for leaving may be higher than for staying); but to respond without deliberation would be maladaptive.

Interventions for (Jointly) Generating Alternatives

Once the problem has been conceptualized as one of choice and the dangers of impulsive responding no longer loom overhead, the counselor's next task is to ask the client what alternatives come to mind. Procedurally, it is probably a good idea to "coax" as many alternatives out of the client as possible rather than to suggest what might be done. Permitting successful alternative-discovery experiences will in all likelihood enhance the client's self-confidence and facilitate the transfer of alternative-generating skills to other decision-making problems.

The problem-solving literature has supplied the counselor with a diverse array of interventions for helping the client generate alternatives. In the first place the counselor can foster a creative instructional set by suggesting to the client that he or she has the ability to find potential solutions. In this optimistic atmosphere the counselor may also wish to invoke originality training, brainstorming, or some form of metaphorical thinking in an attempt to help the client develop a larger response repertoire.

Despite these interventions, however, the client in many instances will simply not discover viable alternatives known to the counselor. Thus the counselor may wish to model these alternatives. It is important that the counselor preface any such modeling procedures with the disclaimer that the alternatives to be modeled need not be implemented unless the client freely chooses to do so later. In other words the counselor should make it clear that he or she is suggesting what *might* be done rather than what *ought* to be done.

Counselor-generated alternatives may or may not be better than those already in the client's response repertoire; the client will ultimately have to evaluate their worth. At the moment of introduction they are simply other options to consider. However, at the very least they may stimulate the client to generate still more alternatives.

To illustrate the use of some of these procedures, let us consider the case of a rather shy, twenty-two-year-old epileptic bookkeeper who lost her job when flood waters destroyed her place of employment. Although her disease has been in remission for two years, she believes her inability to find work is due to medical prejudice on the part of potential employers. At the outset of counseling she viewed her only alternatives as withholding or not withholding the fact of her illness on future job applications. Brainstorming procedures generated additional alternatives: become self-employed, go back to school, remain unemployed and apply for welfare, move to another city where employers might be less prejudicial, and deny the history of epilepsy until after being hired. During the course of their interaction the counselor suspected from her reticent demeanor that her job interviewing skills might be deficient. So the counselor then modeled how she might present herself and her medical history to a potential employment interviewer as another alternative for further consideration.

Interventions for Generating Additional Alternatives

The creative instructional set, originality training, brainstorming, and metaphorical thinking techniques are counseling interventions in which both client and counselor may jointly discover novel responses to decision-making problems. But unless the decision-problem area happens to be one in which a counselor could have exhaustive knowledge of the finite number of possible alternatives (the area of contraception, for example), there is no assurance that the options the client and counselor generate cannot be easily increased or improved. No two individuals, regardless of the quality of their problem-solving interaction, can be expected to discover an adequate number of viable alternatives for all of life's decisions.

Therefore adaptive decision making may call for input on possible alternatives from beyond the counselor-client dyad. For example, in doing group counseling I am frequently pleased to observe the high quantity and quality of alternatives generated by the group for an individual's decision; these alternatives are often more promising than those the client and I would have generated in a dyad. Groups of clients, however, are not readily available when an individual client presents a decision-making concern. Nor are some clients open to the prospect of discussing their lives in the context of a group. Therefore verbal cuing and reinforcement along with modeling procedures are possible interventions for helping the individually seen client search for additional alternatives outside the context of counseling.

The extensive research on these techniques has been covered in chapter 9, so two brief examples should suffice here. The unemployed epileptic client might be cued and praised for planning to ask an epilepsy foundation (or a personal friend with a similar problem) about additional options. Another client with no vocational plans might view a model tape depicting a similar individual visiting a career resource center to get some idea about job opportunities.

There is no set cutoff point for determining when a sufficient number of external sources have been tapped. Procedurally, one might ask the most likely sources for alternatives and then ask these same sources about other potential sources. Within a fairly short time growth of the expanding list of alternatives will plateau and the search can be curtailed.

How to Help Clients Identify Discriminative Stimuli

Interventions for (Jointly) Identifying Discriminative Stimuli

All of the alternatives generated in a decision-making problem will yield outcomes of varying utility. At this point in the process of deciding, however, the client may not even be aware of these various utilities, much less of their probability of occurrence. Adaptive decision making thus calls for identifying stimuli that discriminate positive or aversive consequences for each alternative.

Procedurally, the counselor begins by asking the client what are the pros and cons and the likelihood of occurrence for each alternative. Many of the same problem-solving interventions used for the generation of alternatives can be continued at this point. For instance, brainstorming can now focus on the identification of potential consequences. Outcome psychodrama is designed to produce a similar effect. This technique essentially involves cuing the client to think about and vividly imagine what might happen following, for example, a divorce or the selection of a particular career.

The counselor's own experience will often suggest positive or aversive consequences the client may not know in spite of the foregoing interventions. For example, a youth indicating an interest in one of the construction trades may report that the comparatively large wage and the chance to work outdoors offer high utility and strong probability; yet the youth may be unaware that the seasonal nature of the work may lead to frequent periods of unemployment.

The counselor may find modeling an effective way of exposing potential consequences and probabilities the client does not already know. Management of this technique, however, can be tricky. It is imperative that the counselor guard against the easily given impression of advocating or speaking against a particular alternative; such a mistaken impression would seriously jeopardize the counselor's credibility with the client. More important, though, if such an impression were true, it would signal unconscionable meddling. The counselor's principal task at this point is to supplement the client's limited perspective with as much information as possible on the likely outcomes of each course of action. Even though the counselor may occasionally have biases as to which alternative might be better (from the standpoint of the counselor's idiosyncratic utilities and probability estimates), the counselor is ethically obliged to give all credible alternatives a fair and thorough hearing. Therefore the counselor should preface his or her script with comments to the effect that the information presented is not intended to steer the client in any direction but rather to identify consequences that may not have been considered.

Interventions for Identifying Additional Discriminative Stimuli

Few if any individuals are well versed in most topics. Because of the counselor's relatively limited life experiences, it would be rather unfortunate if the client relied exclusively on their interaction for the production of sufficient discriminative stimuli. Verbal cuing and reinforcement for making plans to consult with external reference sources are the major counseling interventions for helping clients identify potential consequences and their probabilities for each alternative.

Such reference sources abound in the field of occupational choice. For example, exhaustive information on various lines of work is attractively packaged and readily available in most career resource centers. This information can be supplemented by vocational interest and aptitude tests that identify in general terms the likelihood of a client's success in a given career.

Although verbal cuing and reinforcement are the principal intervention strategies for encouraging information seeking, audio or video modeling procedures are also promising if the frequency of a particular kind of decision is sufficiently high to make their development cost effective. For example, a film depicting a youth talking with individuals already employed in a prospective profession could be used extensively in a high school or college counseling setting. For less typical concerns, on the other hand, counselors may use themselves as live models illustrating how more information might be obtained. A client considering elective surgery, for example, could be shown what to ask the recommending and consulting physicians.

Simulation is another promising intervention for identifying additional discriminative stimuli. Essentially, this strategy allows the client to try out a given alternative without risk or commitment. Job simulation kits, discussed in chapter 9, have been used in the counseling field for the past decade. This same principle can be extended to nonvocational choices as well. For example, a childless couple ambivalent about the prospect of having children might acquire invaluable discriminative stimuli from weekend babysitting experiences or the temporary placement of a foster child in their home. Prior to divorce, a couple might likewise profit from experiencing the different life-style on a trial basis.

As with the generation of alternatives, there is no set cutoff point for determining when a sufficient number of discriminative stimuli have been identified. Eventually, however, a point of diminishing returns will set in and the costs (negative utility) for continuing the search will outweigh the perceived benefits of supplemental information. In establishing the market value of a common antique, for example, an exhaustive search of all sales records is not likely to add much information beyond what can be obtained from a representative sample of auction catalogs and dealer price lists.

How to Help Clients Select a Response

Interventions for Changing Maladaptive Utilities and Probability Estimates

Maladaptive utilities are self-defeating conditional reinforcers. Maladaptive probability estimates are those that do not conform to new information according to Bayes's theorum. Either or both of these influences become problematic in decision-making counseling when they dictate choice by loading heavily on a particular alternative. Perceived approval from others is an especially common maladaptive utility. For example, many individuals choose careers or even marriage partners in an attempt to please their parents. Others delve into drugs—including tobacco and alcohol—because of anticipated positive consequences from the peer group.

Maladaptive utilities are often accompanied by maladaptive probability estimates. Clients, for example, might report that if they change majors or temporarily drop out of school, their parents will disown them. A more adaptive perspective would be that in the long run, unpleasant as the prospect of being disowned may be, it really doesn't matter; moreover, the probability of actually being disowned is far less than a certainty. Although maladaptive utilities and probability estimates often occur together, in some instances the utilities may be adaptive but the probability estimates are out of kilter. Such might be the case with clients who over or underestimate their chances of being accepted at a particular university.

Cognitive restructuring is a very relevant intervention strategy should either of these client problems prevail. Essentially, this technique involves isolating and examining the irrationality of the utility or the probability estimate in question, followed by the counselor's modeling of a more adaptive point of view.

Emotional role playing and outcome psychodrama may be particularly helpful in exploring the logical consequences of a maladaptive utility. A young woman choosing marriage in order to experience the utility of "being taken care of" might be encouraged to think about what might happen if the marriage were to end in twenty years through death or divorce. Other more specific forms of cognitive restructuring that are also apropos for confronting maladaptive utilities include the induced-cognitive-dissonance and awareness-of-rationalization techniques described in chapter 5, both of which involve bringing competing adaptive utilities to the fore. It might be pointed out, for example, that a proclivity for academic perfectionism such as setting the curve in all course work, despite its real and rationalized benefits, may be detracting from the experience of utilities derived from other competencies. Or the social strokes gained from cigarette smoking may pale in comparison to the reinforcement that might be expected from a normal life span.

Although cognitive restructuring is perhaps the most applicable technique for confronting maladaptive probability estimates, other interventions may also be employed. Thoresen and Mehrens (1967), for example, suggest that peer models who verbally explore the discrepancies between their own previous subjective probability estimates and new data might reduce similar discrepancies in the client.

Finally, it should be clear to counselors that if clients report utilities and probability estimates that differ from their own, this does not constitute grounds for judging them maladaptive. Utilities are possibly maladaptive when there is general professional consensus that such is the case. If a client is planning to select a car, house, or university on the basis of prestige, for example, counselors have no right to impose their own utility for economy. Probability estimates are possibly maladaptive when they do not correspond to convincing new data. For example, a client may legitimately reject an expectancy table showing that high school math grades caution against selection of an engineering curriculum in college on the grounds of standard error of measurement, being an academic late bloomer, or a newfound interest in solving the problems encountered in that field. The evidence is against another client, however, who estimates recovery from the lung cancer caused by cigarette smoking to be higher than 10 percent. The major point here is that counselors need to be extremely judicious in their designation of a utility or probability estimate as being maladaptive.

Interventions for Inculcating a Response-Selection Paradigm

In view of the limited information-processing capacity of the human psyche (Miller, 1956) and the reams of alternatives, utilities, and probabilities that may need to be considered in a decision-making problem, clients could profit from learning how to use a response-selection paradigm, several of which have been illustrated in earlier chapters. Perhaps the simplest paradigm is Benjamin Franklin's "moral algebra," which consists of two columns labeled "pros" and "cons" under each alternative. The decision maker "cancels" instances of offsetting pros and cons and then selects the alternative with the greatest number of pros remaining.

Janis and Mann's (1977) balance sheet and Carkhuff's (1973b) decision-making grid (figures 5.2 and 7.1) are variations on Franklin's wisdom of the ages. All three response-selection paradigms condense and graphically depict the utilities assumed to be inherent in each alternative, allowing the decision maker to see clearly the alternative with the greatest utility. No experimental comparisons of these fairly similar paradigms have been attempted; however, Janis and Mann do present evidence that their own balance sheet results in reduction of postdecisional regret and increased adherence to the decision (Hoyt & Janis, 1975; Mann, 1972).

All the foregoing response-selection paradigms assume the probabilities for each identified utility are certain (that is, equal to "1"). There is no provision for dealing with the concept of differential expected utility (for example, two alternatives with the same possible utility but one offering a higher likelihood of the utility actually being realized). The decision-making grid designed by Katz (1966) and depicted in figure 8.2, on the other hand, does include this concept.

Katz's grid is apropos for vocational decision making but without modification it might be a bit imposing and unwieldy for nonvocational concerns. Any of the paradigms proposed by Franklin, Carkhuff, or Janis and Mann could be improved by simply including probability estimates to correct the utility data. Then, using the SEU model, one's choice would be dictated by the maximization of expected utility rule, that is, selection of the alternative with the highest utility-probability product.

Modeling variations are the primary counseling interventions for inculcating a response-selection paradigm. Typically, the counselor will serve as a live model, illustrating how the paradigm works. Elements of cognitive modeling, that is, teaching a client how to think through the system, would certainly be apparent. Other forms of modeling, ranging, for example, from programmed instructional booklets to videotapes illustrating individuals employing a response-selection paradigm in resolving a decision-making concern, might also be employed.

Interventions for Response Implementation

Once the client has selected a course of action, the process of deciding, per se, has been completed. Decision-making counseling, however, requires that the counselor help the client implement the response if the client is unable to do so alone.

Comprehensive behavioral programming is the appropriate intervention option for clients with seriously deficient skill levels. Chapter 3 illustrated comprehensive programs that may be helpful to individuals who have decided to lose weight or to stop smoking. The rationale behind a comprehensive treatment program is that although any individual technique might produce a statistically significant difference in promoting a given behavior, a practical difference is more likely to occur if the counseling concern is addressed on several fronts by a variety of interventions. The decision-making counseling model described in this chapter is actually a comprehensive counseling program wherein different interventions are brought to bear on various skill deficiencies.

With the implementation of a comprehensive program for helping a client implement a response the conduct of decision making becomes indistinguishable from other kinds of counseling. For example, the counselor no longer needs to be concerned about pushing a particular alternative; the client has already made the choice and the counselor is now free to dispense liberal social reinforcement for client progress in that direction. The focus of counseling shifts from deciding to doing what has been decided.

Many clients do not need comprehensive behavioral programming because their skill levels are sufficiently high to implement a selected response. If there is some question, however, as to the adequacy of these skills, either stress-inoculation or emotional-inoculation training, which prepare the client for potential difficulties arising during implementation, may be helpful. Such preparation includes education about what might happen, training in a variety of pertinent coping skills, and possibly practice in applying the coping skills to simulated stressful situations.

SUMMARY

In decision-making counseling the counselor's choice of intervention depends upon the client's particular skill deficits and the research status of possible interventions.

To help clients conceptualize the problem, counselors must focus on three skills. First, simple listening, relaxation training, systematic desensitization, or cognitive restructuring can reduce debilitating affective arousal. Second, paraphrasing, probing (cuing and reinforcing specificity), and Socratic dialoguing can help define the problem correctly. Third, cognitive restructuring, emotional role playing, and cognitive modeling along with verbal reinforcement are possible ways to inculcate the decision-making paradigm.

To help clients enlarge their response repertoires, counselors must intervene in three other skill areas. First, thought stopping, thought substitution, covert sensitization, outcome psychodrama, or emotional role playing may prevent clients from making an impulsive response. If a client has already responded impulsively, cognitive restructuring along with behavioral rehearsal or covert modeling may be employed. Second, a creative instructional set in conjunction with originality training, brainstorming, or metaphorical thinking can facilitate the generation of alternatives. Should the client not discover viable alternatives known to the counselor, modeling procedures may be apropos. Third, verbal reinforcement and modeling can be used to promote the generation of additional alternatives outside the counselor-client dyad.

To help clients identify discriminative stimuli, counselors must concentrate on two pertinent skill areas. First, many of the interventions used for alternative generation, along with outcome psychodrama or the judicious use of counselor modeling, may expose the client to previously unknown utilities and probabilities. Second, verbal reinforcement for consulting with other reference sources is a pertinent procedure for promoting a search for additional discriminative stimuli; modeling and simulation strategies may also be relevant.

To help clients select a response, counselors must direct their efforts on three final skill areas. First, cognitive restructuring, emotional role playing, outcome psychodrama, or peer modeling can be used to develop adaptive utilities and probability estimates. Second, modeling variations are the primary interventions for teaching clients how to employ a response-selection paradigm. Third, comprehensive behavioral programming with stress inoculation or emotional inoculation can facilitate response implementation.

Having discussed the assessment of decision-making skills and illustrated a variety of pertinent cognitive-behavioral counseling interventions, I focus in the next chapter on the topic of evaluation in decision-making counseling.

14

Evaluation in Decision-Making Counseling

In the field of counseling the terms "research" and "evaluation" are often used interchangeably; however, there are subtle differences. Research, it is traditionally argued, pertains to the testing of hypotheses, which, if verified, are used to construct scientific theories. Evaluation, on the other hand, usually refers to ascertaining the practical impact of a particular program or endeavor; related activities such as cost-benefit analysis are often included.

As might be expected, there is a good deal of overlap between these two terms. For example, one might hypothesize that the application of a certain intervention program, which has its origins in a scientific theory, will have a significant effect on a particular problem in an applied setting. If we accept the traditional distinctions between research and evaluation, we would be hard pressed to categorize such a project as either. Clearly it contains elements of both.

In this chapter I will restrict myself to the academic turf *commonly* occupied by researchers and evaluators of decision-making counseling. I hope to avoid wandering into fields that might be classified as either pure research or pure evaluation. All concepts to be discussed relate to the basic question "How do I know if my decision-making counseling procedures are having a positive impact on my clients' decision making?" To answer this question we shall explore the immediate and the long-range outcomes of decision-making counseling and several modes of evaluation.

The Immediate Outcomes of Decision-Making Counseling

The purpose of decision-making counseling is to promote certain client skills that are assumed to be essential to making a good decision. If decision-making counseling is to be judged successful, the counselor should be able to say "yes" to the eleven assessment questions that flow from the components of the summary model of decision-making depicted in table 12.1. Let us now take a closer look at some general and specific criteria for each component.

Outcomes Reflecting Adequate Conceptualization Skills

A wide variety of paper and pencil measures relate to this component. Two of the more frequently used measures are the Vocational Decision-Making Checklist (Harren, 1964) and the Career Maturity Inventory (Crites, 1973). (See Super, 1974, for excellent discussions of career maturity theory and measurement.) The Decision Dilemma Questionnaire (Branca, D'Augelli, & Evans, undated) and the Career Decision-Making Questionnaire (Egner & Jackson, 1978) are more recently developed inventories that attempt to tap the same sorts of attitudes and skills. Finally, a number of the projects reviewed in chapter 9 employed experimenter-made ad hoc measures to assess familiarity with the vocabulary of decision making and interest in pursuing decision-making activities.

The principal difficulty with vocabulary tests is that improved scores might reflect the acquisition of jargon rather than qualitative improvements in conceptualization. Learning the definition of "negative utility," for example, might not add anything to one's pretreatment understanding of "costs" or "disadvantages." Similarly, measures of interest in pursuing decision-making activities could be confounded, for example, by the client's correct realization that such activities may offer little promise of incremental utility. It is also not clear if paper and pencil measures such as those described above in fact at least partly reflect IQ, reading proficiency, social desirability, experimenter demands, and a host of other possible correlates.

In addition to these general paper and pencil measures, there are a number of specific criteria that might reflect adequate conceptualization. Recall that in our summary model of decision making the conceptualization component included three basic skills: (1) ability to maintain a low level of affective arousal, (2) ability to define correctly the choice problem, and (3) ability to explain the decision-making paradigm. We can judge the efficacy of our interventions for improving conceptualization by looking at these skills directly:

1. Anxiety and anger are perhaps the most common forms of affective arousal that impede the making of an adaptive choice. Both emotions can be quantified physiologically, psychometrically, and behaviorally. Affectively aroused people, for example, can be expected to exhibit elevated heart rates, palmar sweating, and muscle tension. Moreover, a large number of psychometric devices exist that purport to measure an individual's affective state (for example, see Levitt, 1967). Finally, affectively aroused individuals behave atypically; for instance, they might pace or sway or show hand tremors and speech disfluencies. Rigorous attention to the quantification of affective arousal would probably not be cost effective in the routine practice of decision-making counseling. Counselors can be trained to detect debilitating levels fairly easily (see Winborn, Hinds, & Stewart, 1971).

2. Determining whether the client can correctly define the problem as one of choice is a fairly straightforward task. Clients who have this ability can
   a. Describe their source of distress in operational terms (for example, not "This is a lousy place to work" but rather "My supervisor has publicly ridiculed me four times this week"; not "My marriage isn't working" but rather "My spouse has lost two jobs this year because of frequent intoxication").
   b. Implicitly or explicitly label their concern as a decision they must make (for example, not "That SOB is unfair to me" but rather "I've got to decide what I want to do about this undesirable situation").

   Although it might be possible to devise some sort of rating scale for the quantification of this ability on a continuum, for any given decision the appropriate criterion is really a matter of "can do" or "can't do." A high degree of proficiency here is a *sine qua non* for many of the decision-making skills to follow.

3. Verbal report is the only viable means of ascertaining the client's ability to explain the decision-making paradigm. We can quantify this ability by asking the client to provide such an explanation and then comparing the client's response with a preexisting standard explanation. The resulting "difference" score can be used as an index of proficiency. To illustrate, let us assume that the eleven skills emerging from our summary model of decision making constitute the basis of our standard explanation. If the

client's response implies only two of these activities, we can posit that his or her knowledge of adaptive decision making is relatively weak. Maximal effectiveness of an intervention such as cognitive modeling would be suggested by a client's response that contains all eleven skills.

Outcomes Reflecting an Adequate Response Repertoire

Most measures that address this decision-making component focus on the number of alternatives generated. For example, Russell and Thoresen (1976) played audiotaped stories about finding a lost wallet, stealing flowers, concealing a friend's toy, and igniting firecrackers. Then they tallied the number of alternative solutions to these problems students generated before and after treatment programming. The Preschool Interpersonal Problem-Solving (PIPS) Test (Shure & Spivack, 1974) described in chapter 10 employs a similar rationale. Moreover, Jones (1976) has developed an interesting set of evaluation materials that tap not only the number of alternatives but also the amount of time spent considering the alternatives and their adequacy.

All of the foregoing measures are "canned" in the sense that they use hypothetical decision-making concerns. Thus though highly appropriate for evaluating the skills of large audiences, they may be slightly off the point in terms of gauging the progress of an individual client receiving decision-making counseling. In our summary model the response repertoire component consists of (1) avoiding an impulsive response, (2) identifying all alternatives known to the counselor, and (3) searching for additional alternatives. Each of these decision-making behaviors can be directly examined:

1. The premature implementation of an alternative can be easily verified by direct observation. The acts of quitting a job, dropping out of school, or filing for divorce, for example, leave indelible imprints on our environment. Steps taken to "undo" impulsive responses are likewise easily observable. If the impulsive response has not yet been made, the counselor can determine the impact of a given intervention by noting, for example, if there is a diminution in the frequency and intensity of the client's reported "urges to act." The major index of success here, however, would appear to be a form of response latency. That is, has the client delayed the implementation of an alternative until after displaying all other adaptive decision-making behaviors? (See Messer, 1976, for a critical review of related evaluation procedures.)

2. Determining if the client has identified all the alternatives known to the counselor is a simple matter. Essentially, the counselor asks the client what alternatives come to mind. The number of alternatives the client does not know can be considered an indicator of the work to be done at this point. Mastery, of course, would be suggested by a difference score of zero.

3. There are two basic criteria for judging the client's progress in generating additional alternatives. The first is a frequency count; the more alternatives generated, the better. At this point we should not be concerned with the quantity versus quality issue. In problem-solving literature there is evidence that as quantity increases so does quality (see Davis, 1973). Logically, because clients will in all likelihood implement only one alternative (the best), they are more likely to find this kernel of wheat in a bucket full than in a thimble full of chaff. The second criterion focuses on the number of alternative-generating behaviors the client engages in. For example, how many sources has the client consulted for possible courses of action? Ten alternatives "drained" from a single source may be redundant and inferior to ten alternatives "creamed" from five different sources. Thus the number of alternative-generating behaviors the client displays may be even more important than the absolute quantity of alternatives generated.

Outcomes Reflecting the Adequate Identification of Discriminative Stimuli

Knowledge of the probability of experiencing various utilities following the selection of a given alternative can be directly determined from specially constructed achievement tests. Career education materials, for example, at the very least should foster increasing amounts of information about the world of work (see Westbrook and Mastie's 1974 Cognitive Vocational Maturity Test). This component of decision making, however, has traditionally been evaluated by noting the frequency and variety of information-seeking behaviors the client makes outside the counseling relationship. Krumboltz and his associates developed and validated questionnaires that yield numerical scores on each dimension. For example, talking with three similarly employed source persons and reading two articles pertinent to a decision would yield a frequency score of five and a variety score of two. Questionnaires of this sort were used in the majority of research projects reviewed in chapter 9.

Permutations of this approach have also been suggested. Stewart

(1969), for example, posited six modes of inquiry that can be used to gather information. LaFleur and Johnson (1972) provided their subjects with the opportunity to solicit information from several sources. Tallying which inquiry modes were in fact employed or what sources were actually contacted will yield a score very much akin to Krumboltz's concept of variety. Finally, Jones's (1976) evaluation materials produce not only a behavior frequency index but also a measure of the time spent considering the potential outcomes of each alternative.

In our summary model of decision making the discriminative stimuli component is addressed by noting if the client has (1) identified all the discriminative stimuli known to the counselor and (2) planned to search for additional discriminative stimuli. Both of these points can be examined directly:

1. The counselor is a resource individual who by dint of his or her own life experiences will be able to identify utilities and probabilities for many of the alternatives the client is considering. By asking the client to estimate the likelihood of all consequences that come to mind, the counselor can easily gauge how much, if any, intervention activity will be needed at this point. Mastery would of course be implied by the client having a relevant informational base equal to or exceeding the counselor's.

2. There are two ways of quantifying the client's progress in searching for additional discriminative stimuli. The first would focus on informational increments alone. This can easily be determined from achievement tests, open-ended questionnaires, or simple counselor inquiries such as "What have you found out since we last talked?" Obviously, the more discriminative stimuli the client uncovers the better. The second method for quantifying the client's progress here derives from the information-seeking behaviors themselves. Such activity should be frequent and directed toward a wide variety of sources. Any of the aforementioned Krumboltz-inspired evaluation instruments can be applied at this point.

Outcomes Reflecting Adequate Response-Selection Skills

There are several self-report inventories that are slightly related to this component of decision making, including Ross's (1977) and Jones's (1968) irrational personality measures and Rotter's (1966) Locus of Control Scale. Perhaps more relevant are questionnaires devised by Mausner (1973) and Carr (1974), which yield specific information on the utilities and subjective probabilities held by individuals facing a particular decision. Finally, Brim, Glass, Lavin, and Goodman (1962) and Dilley (1965) developed instruments that essentially tap the individual's understanding that the alternative selected should be the one with the highest subjectively expected utility (SEU). (Recall that SEU equals the product of utility and subjective probability.)

Against this general backdrop let us look at some specific criteria. In the summary model of decision making, the response-selection component consists of the client being able to (1) report adaptive utilities and probability estimates, (2) explain a response-selection paradigm, and (3) implement a selected response. Each of these points can be directly examined:

1. Maladaptive utilities can be quantified in terms of both frequency and severity. For example, following information-searching activities a client might be asked to list all the advantages that might accrue from selection of a given alternative. The number of maladaptive utilities listed or ratios of maladaptive utilities divided by the total number of utilities identified could provide a frequency score. Severity scores could be obtained by having independent judges rate the client's reported utilities on some sort of degree-of-maladaptiveness scale.

   Maladaptive probability estimates are those that do not correspond to convincing new data. This lack of correspondence might be determined through difference scores obtained by subtracting the client's probability estimates from those of independent judges exposed to the same informational materials.

2. The client's ability to explain a response-selection paradigm is rather easily quantified by comparing the client's explanation with a preexisting "standard" explanation (for example, Ben Franklin's definition of moral algebra in chapter 1). This skill might be more easily evaluated, however, through criterion referenced achievement tests or through normative instruments such as Dilley's (1965).

3. Procedures for determining if the client has the ability to implement the selected response are highly diverse and in fact do not differ from procedures used to determine a client's progress in resolving any other counseling concern. Let us assume, for example, that a timid client has decided to refuse someone's unreasonable request. Some form of assertion training would be the likely intervention, the effects of which can be determined from a wide variety of self-report, behavioral, and physiological measures (see Rich & Shroeder, 1976).

The Long-Range Outcomes of Decision-Making Counseling

All the immediate outcomes of decision-making counseling just discussed might be thought of as counseling-process objectives. They may or may not be worthy of pursuit in their own right. In the context of decision-making counseling, however, the attainment of these objectives is assumed to increase the probability that the client will select the most advantageous course of action. Whether in fact the client does select the best course of action as a result of decision-making counseling is an evaluation question that is difficult to answer.

One possible answer might be to have "experts" rank the alternatives in terms of the client's best interests. The success of decision-making counseling then would depend on whether the client selected an alternative from the top or the bottom of the list. Of course, the major difficulty with this approach is that it assumes the expert's utilities and probability estimates are "better" than the client's. Not too many years ago we would have been hard pressed to find an expert who would concede the possibility of rationality in a decision to drop out of school, to get a divorce, or to end one's own life in the face of incurable illness. Even now the lack of consensus on issues of this sort underscores the futility of this approach.

One variation on the use of expert opinion in evaluating decision-making counseling is to construct a hypothetical decision situation in which pertinent information is well known or at least controlled by the evaluator. Subjects are asked to imagine themselves to be a particularly described person who can do one of several things and to pick the best course of action for that person. Because the alternatives in hypothetical examples can be objectively ranked on the basis of available information, the relative stature of each subject's selection is considered a good indicator of decision-making ability. Although tests of this sort do perhaps reflect the degree to which respondents can manipulate the concepts of decision theory, they do not address long-range criteria of decision-making counseling. We still do not know if our decision-making interventions with real clients will result in any meaningful improvement in their lives.

The literature on vocational choice suggests another possible answer to this question. Because interest tests reflect the degree of similarity between our client and other individuals employed in a given occupation and because these other individuals are probably happier in their present occupation than they would be in another, the success of vocational decision-making counseling might hinge upon whether our client selects an occupation compatible with his or her measured interest profile. There are difficulties inherent in this answer as well. In the first place the principle of parsimony would demand that counselors abandon all features of decision-making counseling and redirect their efforts toward cuing and reinforcing the alternatives dictated by interest tests. Second, the appropriate practice of vocational decision-making counseling will likely involve using interest tests; hence the treatment may confound the evaluation criterion. Finally, interest inventories are self-report devices, the validities of which depend on vocational choice behaviors displayed by respondents. Thus a client's selection of an alternative not suggested by the interest test could represent nothing more than an artifact of the test's less-than-perfect validity.

The most appropriate answer to the long-range evaluation question comes from carefully following up individuals who have been previously exposed to decision-making counseling. As a result of counseling they should show greater satisfaction with, for example, their college, their curriculum, or their career and less postdecisional regret and concern than individuals who did not receive counseling. Depending upon the nature of the decision, any one of a wide variety of attitude scales or satisfaction-with-life type questionnaires can be employed (see, for example, Mann, 1972).

Self-report devices of this sort can often be fortified with behavioral data. For example, following decision-making counseling uncommitted students who decide to stay in school might show fewer changes in academic majors, unemployed adults who choose to obtain a job might evidence less absenteeism and turnover, unmarried individuals who opt for a change might file for fewer divorces, and so forth. In one interesting study Hoyt and Janis (1975) noted that a single decision-making counseling procedure (balance sheeting) resulted in a greater attendance among those who had signed up for an early-morning health class.

A word of caution is in order on the subject of long-range evaluation of decision-making counseling. Any criterion selected must be considered crude and hardly definitive for an individual case. Recall that adaptive decisions are based on all the information that can be reasonably acquired. The act of implementing an alternative and actually experiencing the utilities of that alternative may provide new information that was simply unavailable beforehand. Though decision-making counseling attempts to ward off the possibility of selecting an unfavorable alternative, unhappy surprises can occasionally occur. Presumably, such occurrences will be relatively infrequent in any long-range evaluation of decision-making counseling.

Evaluation Modes

When doing decision-making counseling, practitioners are usually more concerned with promoting their clients' display of the various decision-making skills than with adding to the body of experimental evidence in support of a given technique. They seem less interested, for example, in showing that covert modeling can produce information-seeking behavior than they are in simply getting as much of this behavior going as possible. Certainly, covert modeling might be applied, but so might verbal reinforcement, cognitive restructuring, and whatever placebo influence the counselor can muster. Apart from the matter of technique evaluation, counseling practitioners have been relatively unconcerned with presenting evidence that their efforts—whatever they may be—have resulted in improved decision making in their clients.

There are a variety of reasons for this state of affairs. In the first place counseling practitioners are not usually reinforced for gathering this sort of data. Second, although doctoral programs may involve extensive course work on the topic of evaluation, most counseling practitioners have only a masters degree; and it is a rare masters program that equips the counselor trainee with more than rudimentary evaluation skills. Counseling practitioners are simply not trained or encouraged to evaluate their work empirically.

At the other end of the spectrum, counseling researchers have conspicuously avoided the task of evaluating interventions for promoting decision-making skills. Most of the experimental work in this area has evolved from Krumboltz's notion that verbal reinforcement and modeling procedures can promote information seeking. Interventions for other decision-making skills have not received much attention.

Perhaps the principal reason for this lack of activity is that researchers quickly learn the road to academic success is paved with easily manipulated independent variables and easily quantified dependent variables. Few aspiring researchers want to run the risk of an unfavorable tenure review for failing to emerge from the decision-making quagmire with a handful of clean experiments. And after being awarded tenure, most are committed to the lines of research that have already proved reinforcing.

In the last few pages of this book I would like to suggest ways to facilitate a slight change in priority. There are several evaluation modes for decision-making counseling that are well suited to the interests and skills of counseling practitioners. Still other evaluation modes are particularly appropriate for counseling researchers.

Evaluation Modes for the Practitioner

Perhaps the simplest method by which the counseling practitioner can determine if he or she has had any impact on the client's decision-making behavior is by using pretest-posttest change scores. For example, at the outset of counseling the client might be able to identify only one or two alternatives. If after a particular intervention the client is able to identify eight or ten alternatives, the counselor can report that this dimension of the client's decision making has been improved. Changes in other decision-making skills can be similarly documented.

With individual clients, change scores such as the foregoing, however, are somewhat limited in their usefulness. They suggest only that the client changed; they do not establish the efficacy of a given intervention. For example, similar changes might result from a few minutes of solitary meditation. In applied settings criticisms of this sort should be taken with a grain of salt. The major task is to gauge quickly the client's progress in a particular direction, not to replicate classic, tightly controlled research ad infinitum. Change scores do indicate that progress has been made even if they do not clearly delineate why.

Goal Attainment Scaling (GAS) is another method for evaluating client progress. The GAS technique was originally devised by Kiresuk and Sherman (1968) as a human services accountability procedure (see also Goodyear & Bitter, 1974), but recent investigations (for example, Clark, 1978) have also demonstrated the incremental therapeutic usefulness of GAS.

Essentially, the technique involves construction of a grid called the "Goal Attainment Follow-up Guide." The columns on the grid represent the client's idiosyncratic problem areas. In decision-making counseling these would be the specific decision-making skills judged to be deficient during the assessment phase of counseling. Provision is also made for weighting the problem areas according to their degree of importance. The rows on the grid specify five levels of outcome for each problem area. The middle level (scored "0") represents the most realistic prediction of the outcome the client will have reached on the date of the follow-up interview. The top two levels (scored +1 and +2) indicate "somewhat more" and "much more" than the expected level of outcome; the bottom two levels (scored −1 and −2) suggest "somewhat less" and "much less" than the expected level of outcome. Each level is anchored by specific behavioral criteria. For example, level "3" of a deficient response repertoire problem might involve engaging in three alternative-generating activities and identifying six possible alternatives.

Data from the grid can be used in the following formula, which yields a summary goal attainment score:

$$T = 50 + \frac{10 \, \Sigma w_i x_i}{\sqrt{(1 - \rho)\Sigma w_i^2 + \rho(\Sigma w_i)^2}}$$

where x_i is the score on the i th scale, w_i is the relative weight assigned to x_i, and ρ is an arbitrary but intuitive average correlation among the x_i computed to be .29.

The statistic that emerges from this formula is essentially an average of all scales corrected for the weights of the scales and the scale intercorrelations. Goal attainment scores reportedly form a normal distribution with a range of 15 to 85, a mean of 50, and a standard deviation of 10. A score of 50 indicates that the client has on the average met the expected level of success.

Unless considerable attention is paid to the matter of experimental control, GAS cannot appropriately be used to compare client progress, counselor competence, or treatment efficacy. For the practitioner its main use would appear to be a means of gauging counseling progress with an individual client. A summary score of 50 indicates the counseling goals have been satisfactorily met. Change scores calculated by subtracting an intake interview score from the summary follow-up score reflect the amount of improvement or deterioration.

Evaluation Modes for the Practitioner-Researcher

Single-subject experimental designs not only allow the counselor to document client progress on a given dimension but also allow the gradual accumulation of evidence that supports or fails to support the efficacy of a particular counseling procedure. Two of these designs are particularly applicable to certain portions of decision-making counseling.

The AB design involves gathering baseline data on a target behavior during the A phase, then intervening with the counseling technique in question, and finally, observing subsequent behavior changes during the B phase. For example, in a decision-making problem a client might report being "obsessed" with the urge to respond impulsively. After having the client graph the frequency of these urges and noticing that they seem to be occurring at a fairly steady high rate, the counselor might wish to explore the effects of the thought-stopping technique. If this technique is successful, the client's continuing records should indicate a dramatic decrease in the frequency of this problem behavior.

Although the AB design clearly documents changes in client behavior, it does not rule out the possibility that something occurring outside the counseling relationship was in fact responsible for the changes. The multiple-baseline design offers more control over this possibility. There are three common variations on this design: The first involves sequentially changing several of an individual's behaviors. The second focuses on the individual's behavior in several situations. The third deals with the behavior of several individuals.

To illustrate this latter variation, for example, the counselor would first gather baseline data on several clients all deficient in the same decision-making skill. Then the counselor would continue to collect baseline data on all but one client, who would now receive the decision-making counseling intervention in question. If positive changes occurred, the counselor would deploy the intervention on a second client while continuing to monitor the skills of the other clients. Then a third client would receive the intervention, and so forth. If the pattern of results shows that baselines were stable with all clients and that positive changes occurred with each successive client following application of the counseling strategy, the counselor can reasonably conclude not only that improvements were made in all clients' decision making but also that these improvements were due to the technique under investigation.

There are a variety of other single-subject experimental designs that may have relevance to certain portions of decision-making counseling. Readers are invited to consult Hersen and Barlow (1976), Kazdin (1973c), and Thoresen (1972a) for more complete coverage.

Evaluation Modes for the Researcher

Systematic desensitization is perhaps the most thoroughly researched and empirically validated counseling strategy. Yet of the hundreds of published studies on this technique only a handful used adequate control procedures (Kazdin & Wilcoxon, 1976). If such is the state of affairs with desensitization, the need to evaluate other counseling strategies for promoting decision-making skills should be obvious.

There are a variety of ways for the researcher to evaluate the impact of decision-making counseling interventions, all of which require large numbers of clients (more than thirty) and the opportunity to assign these clients randomly to two or more experimental conditions. First the researcher must determine whether to focus on immediate or long-range outcomes or both. Examining the long-range outcomes requires at the very least an extensive time commitment; clients must be followed up (long) after they receive counseling. Moreover, we cannot really expect measures of long-range outcomes to be particularly sensitive to subtle manipulations in our decision-making counseling procedures. On the other hand, when changes do register on long-range criteria, they provide dramatic evidence for the efficacy of our interventions. Perhaps a good rule of thumb would be that inclusion of long-range outcome measures is mandatory if we intend to demonstrate the practical utility of a package of decision-making counseling interventions. Immediate outcome measures alone, however, provide an adequate test of isolated counseling techniques.

In its simplest form the experimental evaluation of a given counseling technique consists of comparing the outcomes of two groups of clients following treatment. One of the groups receives the counseling technique under investigation; the other does not. This latter group, labeled "control," must receive instead an equally credible "placebo" treatment that fosters the same counselor demands and client expectations for improvement.

Relatively few counseling technique evaluations employ adequate controls; no-treatment or delayed-treatment control groups are often used. These "weak" control procedures render differences in favor of the experimental treatment difficult to interpret. The evaluator knows something happened but does not know why. For example, was it the counselor's physical presence, empathy, advice, or verbal reinforcement that fostered greater information gathering? The experimental group received all of these "treatments"; the control group received none. If such control conditions are to be used at all, they should only be included as adjuncts to more adequate control treatments or for illustrative purposes in very preliminary investigations of new counseling procedures.

There are several variations on this basic mode of evaluation, one of which involves comparing the experimental counseling technique with the "best" traditional counseling procedure. Is cognitive restructuring, for example, better than the old standby, systematic desensitization, in terms of reducing affective arousal? With slight elaborations in the evaluation project's design, it is also possible to determine if certain types of clients are differentially affected by the treatments under investigation. This kind of evaluation project directly addresses the issue of improving the practice of counseling.

Another variation focuses on comparisons between two new or well-established counseling techniques. With the latter, control groups are superfluous; the basic experimental question is not do they work but which works better? One might ask, for example, "Is brainstorming or metaphorical thinking more effective in terms of generating alternatives?"

Still another variation examines possible permutations of new or established counseling techniques. Many of the studies reviewed in chapter 9, for example, compared the effects of different modeling treatments on clients' information seeking.

A final variation explores the incremental effectiveness of techniques that can easily be combined. Will originality training, for example, produce more alternatives than simply providing the client with a creative instructional set? Are verbal-reinforcement and model-reinforcement techniques more powerful when employed in combination than in isolation?

Most experimental research projects in the field of counseling employ the various evaluation strategies described above. Such strategies are highly relevant to the building of a technology for decision-making counseling in spite of their relative disuse in this particular area. Perhaps counseling researchers have been discouraged by the mistaken notion that a given decision-making counseling technique should be expected to produce profound changes on long-range criteria. Although such would be desirable, the positive evaluation of a given technique requires only that improvements be made on the targeted decision-making skill(s). As the armamentarium of validated counseling techniques increases for myriad decision-making skills, the assemblage of these techniques into an intervention package and the incorporation of long-range evaluation criteria become more and more a research priority.

It would be far beyond the scope of this chapter to provide detailed coverage of nuances in experimental design, control, and analysis procedures; other sources (for example, Campbell & Stanley, 1967; Horan, 1973b) explore such topics in greater detail. The question of how to evaluate comprehensive programming, however, has not received much attention.

The maxim "First show an effect, then isolate its cause" echoed by Mahoney (1973, p. 2) reflects the sympathies of a number of researchers who are growing weary of the flood of studies showing that a particular technique produces a trivial but statistically significant change on a given criterion. For example, an average weight loss of five pounds or an average decrease in tobacco consumption of a few cigarettes per day is of little practical consequence. Comprehensive programs involving numerous techniques that effect permanent weight losses of fifty pounds or complete abstinence from tobacco are worthy of note even if they are not tightly controlled. (Actually, the historical failure of most approaches to such problems provides a meaningful backdrop for comparison.)

Another mode for the evaluation of decision-making counseling then would be to look at the practical effects of a comprehensive program on both immediate and long-range outcomes. For example, given the fact that 40 percent of today's marriages end in divorce, a premarital decision-making counseling program that resulted in ninety-five out of one hundred couples still married after ten years would be deserving of considerable attention even if no control groups were employed.

Once a pronounced effect has been demonstrated, there are a variety of ways to isolate the cause(s). Dismantling strategies, for example, systematically drop features of the comprehensive program and note if there are consequent decreases in the success level. Component analyses, on the other hand, directly explore the effects of the various treatment ingredients alone and in combination.

Summary

Evaluation in decision-making counseling pertains to the question, "How do I know if my decision-making counseling procedures are having a positive impact on my client's decision making?"

The immediate outcomes of decision-making counseling (that is, the display of the eleven skills implied by the summary model) are essentially counseling process objectives. They may or may not be worthy of pursuit in their own right, but their attainment is assumed to increase the likelihood of a favorable outcome. There are many general and specific criteria for gauging client skill development.

The long-range outcomes of decision-making counseling reflect whether the client has in fact selected the most advantageous course of action. Long-range evaluation, however, is a difficult task; some deficient methods include the use of expert opinion, hypothetical decision situations, and choice compatibility scores derived from interest profiles. The most appropriate method involves self-reported and behavioral measures of postdecisional satisfaction or regret.

Evaluation modes for the practitioner include pretest-posttest change scores and Goal Attainment Scaling, which are useful for gauging client progress even though they cannot pinpoint the reason for the change. Single-subject experimental designs are ideal evaluation modes for the practitioner-researcher because they permit the gradual accumulation of evidence that supports or fails to support the efficacy of a particular intervention. Evaluation modes for the researcher all require large numbers of clients and the opportunity to assign clients randomly to experimental and control conditions. It is then possible to show on either immediate or long-range outcomes whether a given intervention is effective at all or better than another intervention or whether permutations or combinations of interventions are more effective than a particular intervention applied in a traditional manner.

Epilogue

I was recently amused by Protinski and Popp's (1978) study, which detected the presence of irrational philosophies in 82 percent of a sample of several hundred popular songs. It would appear that the entertainment industry and the media are dousing the young and old in this culture with a deluge of irrational drivel. One cannot flick on the radio, for example, and escape from being tainted by psychologically polluting lyrics like those found in "Touch Your Woman": "Woman needs a helpin' hand, needs someone to understand. Needs the man she loves to help her stand."* Although many of us simply like to hum along with a pleasant melody, undoubtedly a significant percentage of our population actually buys into the attitudes and belief systems expressed by such songs.

In any event, I subsequently began ruminating on the relationship between decision making as presented in this book and decision making as reflected in the popular politics and literature of our culture. It appears that the degree of fit is frequently strained or mismatched. Let me cite two examples.

In a speech endorsing Dwight D. Eisenhower for the 1952 Republican presidential nomination, Senator Everett Dirksen reportedly strummed the fear chords of party members with some particularly potent polemics: "On the battlefields of indecision lie the bleached bones of thousands who in a moment of indecision waited and in waiting died." The gravel-throated senator's message was clear. The Republican party was doomed unless it immediately leaped into action in support of his candidate. Recall, however, that adaptive decision making demands at least temporary suppression of an impulsive response. How do we reconcile our version of decision making with Dirksen's strident quote?

First of all it might be illuminating if we substitute two words in the senator's message: "On the battlefields of indecision lie the bleached bones of thousands who in a moment of indecision *leaped* and in *leaping* died." Every proverb has its antithesis. "He who hesitates is lost" conveys a meaning opposite to that of "out of the frying pan into the fire." Dirksen's plea and my own modification of his words are both faulty generalizations that at most describe only individual cases. Certainly if a live grenade falls into one's foxhole, doing just about anything is better than doing nothing. To hesitate, in fact, is to select an alternative with absolutely certain mortal

---

consequences. On the other hand if one were in a foxhole and under enemy rifle fire, it might be wiser to remain there temporarily and survey one's alternatives before springing to an ill-considered course of action. The best alternative in fact might be to stay put, that is, to hesitate, until help arrives.

Another illustration of faulty fit comes from the gentle poetry of Robert Frost. In "The Road Not Taken" Frost (1960, p. 223) reminisces about coming to a point in the woods where two roads diverged: "I took the one less traveled by, And that has made all the difference." Although there is some debate as to Frost's meaning, a common interpretation is that when he was faced with the matter of career choice, Frost took the road that seemed less traveled—that of a poet—and this alternative has proved to be immensely satisfying.

Frost's self-disclosure amounts to pleasant reading, though it is an incomplete description of his decision-making process. Undoubtedly, he perceived other utilities in the life of a poet. As a decision-making prescription, however, such advice is abysmally bad. There may be very good reasons why a particular road is not well traveled! Certainly there is a measure of adaptive utility in opting for an uncommonly selected alternative. A Sunday afternoon meander down a country lane, for example, may be viewed as infinitely more enjoyable than the prospect of contending with our car-clogged interstate highway system, especially when the arrival time is not important. On the other hand, in matters of consequence to choose an alternative simply because it is unpopular can hardly be construed as adaptive.

In closing I would like to reiterate the fact that although decision-making counseling may reduce the burden of choice for our clients, they cannot escape it entirely. Fitz-James Stephen expressed this point eloquently in 1874:

In all important transactions of life we have to take a leap in the dark. . . . If we decide to leave the riddles unanswered, that is a choice; if we waver in our answer, that, too, is a choice: but whatever choice we make, we make it at our peril. . . . Each must act as he thinks best; and if he is wrong, so much the worse for him. We stand on a mountain pass in the midst of whirling snow and blinding mist, through which we get glimpses now and then of paths which may be deceptive. If we stand still we shall be frozen to death. If we take the wrong road we shall be dashed to pieces. We do not certainly know whether there is any right one. What must we do? "Be strong and of a good courage." Act for the best, hope for the best, and take what comes. . . . If death ends all, we cannot meet death better (cited by James, 1912, p. 31).

References

Abelson, R. P. Computer simulation of "hot" cognition. In S. Tomkins & S. Messick (Eds.), *Computer simulation of personality*. New York: Wiley, 1963.

Adams, H. E., & Sturgis, E. T. Status of behavioral reorientation techniques in the modification of homosexuality: A review. *Psychological Bulletin*, 1977, *84*, 1171-1188.

Addis, J. W., & Horan, J. J. A note on the use and interpretation of electric shock therapy in "A comparison of four behavioral treatments of alcoholism." *Journal of Behavioral Therapy and Experimental Psychiatry*, 1975, *6*, 363-364.

Alberti, R., & Emmons, M. *Your perfect right: A guide to assertive behavior*. San Luis Obispo, Cal.: Impact, 1970.

Allport, G. W. *Pattern and growth in personality*. New York: Holt, Rinehart and Winston, 1961.

American Personnel and Guidance Association. *Ethical standards*. Washington, D.C.: APGA, undated.

American Psychological Association. *Casebook on ethical standards of psychologists*. Washington, D.C.: APA, 1967.

American Psychological Association. *Ethical standards of psychologists*. Washington, D.C.: APA, 1972.

Asch, S. E. *Social psychology*. Englewood Cliffs, N.J.: Prentice-Hall, 1952.

Atkinson, D. R. Effect of selected behavior modification techniques on student-initiated action. *Journal of Counseling Psychology*, 1971, *18*, 395-400.

Atkinson, J. W. Motivational determinants of risk-taking behavior. *Psychological Review*, 1957, *64*, 359-372.

Ayllon, T. Intensive treatment of psychotic behavior by stimulus satiation and food reinforcement. *Behavior Research and Therapy*, 1963, *1*, 53-61.

Ayllon, T., Haughton, E., & Hughes, H. B. Interpretation of symptoms: Fact or fiction. *Behavior Research and Therapy*, 1965, *3*, 1-7.

Azrin, N. H., & Fox, R. M. *Toilet training in less than a day*. New York: Simon and Schuster, 1974.

Azrin, N. H., & Holz, W. C. Punishment. In W. K. Hoening (Ed.), *Operant behavior: Areas of research and application*. New York: Appleton-Century-Crofts, 1966. Pp. 380-447.

Bandura, A. *Principles of behavior modification*. New York: Holt, 1969.

Bandura, A. (Ed.). *Psychological modeling: Conflicting theories*. New York: Aldine/Atherton, 1971.

Barlow, D. H., & Agras, W. S. Fading to increase heterosexual responsiveness in homosexuals. *Journal of Applied Behavior Analysis*, 1973, *6*, 355-366.

Bayless, O. L. An alternative pattern for problem-solving discussion. *Journal of Communication*, 1967, *17*, 188-197.

Beck, A. T. Cognitive therapy: Nature and relation to behavior therapy. *Behavior therapy*, 1970, *1*, 184-200.

Becker, G. M., & McClintock, C. G. Value: Behavioral decision theory. *Annual Review of Psychology*, 1967, *18*, 239-286.

Berenson, B. G., & Carkhuff, R. R. *Sources of gain in counseling and psychotherapy.* New York: Holt, Rinehart and Winston, 1967.

Bergland, B. W., & Krumboltz, J. D. An optimal grade level for career exploration. *Vocational Guidance Quarterly,* 1969, *18,* 29-33.

Bergland, B. W., Quatrano, L. A., & Lundquist, G. W. Group social models and structured interaction in teaching decision-making. *Vocational Guidance Quarterly,* 1975, *24,* 28-36.

Blocher, D. *Developmental counseling.* New York: Ronald Press, 1974.

Bloom, B. S., & Broder, L. J. *Problem-solving processes of college students.* Chicago: University of Chicago Press, 1950.

Boocock, S. S. The life career game. *Personnel and Guidance Journal,* 1967, *46,* 328-334.

Boocock, S. S. *Life Career Instructor's Manual.* New York: Western Publishing Company, Inc., 1968.

Bordin, E. S., Nachman, B., & Segal, S. J. An articulated framework for vocational development. *Journal of Counseling Psychology,* 1963, *10,* 107-116.

Borow, H. *Career guidance for a new age.* Boston: Houghton Mifflin, 1973.

Bracken, M. B., & Kasl, S. V. Delay in seeking induced abortion: A review and theoretical analysis. *American Journal of Obstetrics and Gynecology,* 1975, *121,* 1008-1019.

Branca, M. C., D'Augelli, J. F., & Evans, K. L. Development of a decision-making skills education program: Study I. Addictions Prevention Laboratory Report, The Pennsylvania State University, undated.

Brehm, J. W. Attitude change from threat to attitudinal freedom. In A. G. Greenwald, T. C. Brock, & T. M. Ostrom (Eds.), *Psychological foundations of attitudes.* New York: Academic Press, 1968.

Brill, A. A. *Basic principles of psychoanalysis.* Garden City, N.Y.: Doubleday, 1949.

Brim, O., Glass, D., Lavin, D., & Goodman, N. *Personality and decision processes.* Stanford, Cal.: Stanford University Press, 1962.

Brinkers, H. S. (Ed.). *Decision-making: Creativity, judgment, and systems.* Columbus: Ohio State University Press, 1972.

Broadbent, D. E. *Decision and stress.* London: Academic Press, 1971.

Broadhurst, A. Applications of the psychology of decisions. In M. P. Feldman & A. Broadhurst (Eds.), *Theoretical and experimental bases of the behavior therapies.* London: Wiley, 1976. Pp. 269-287.

Brosin, H. W. The psychology of overeating. *New England Journal of Medicine,* 1953, *248,* 974-975.

Bross, I. D. J. *Design for decision: An introduction to statistical decision-making.* New York: Macmillan, 1953.

Burck, H. D., Cottingham, H. F., & Reardon, R. C. *Counseling and accountability: Methods and critique.* New York: Pergamon, 1973.

Byrne, R. H. *Guidance: A behavioral approach.* Englewood Cliffs, N.J.: Prentice-Hall, 1977.

Campbell, D. T. Blind variation and selective retention in creative thought and in other knowledge processes. *Psychological Review,* 1960, *67,* 380-400.

Campbell, D. T., & Stanley, J. C. *Experimental and quasi-experimental designs for research.* Chicago: Rand McNally, 1967.

Carkhuff, R. R. *Helping and human relations: A primer for lay and professional helpers. Vol. I, selection and training.* New York: Holt, Rinehart and Winston, 1969. (a)

Carkhuff, R. R. *Helping and human relations: A primer for lay and professional helpers. Vol. II, practice and research.* New York: Holt, Rinehart and Winston, 1969. (b)

Carkhuff, R. R. *The development of human resources.* New York: Holt, Rinehart and Winston, 1971.

Carkhuff, R. R. People, programs, and organizations: The effective ingredients of human resource development. Paper presented at the American Educational Research Association, New Orleans, February 1973. (a)

Carkhuff, R. R. *The art of problem solving.* Amherst, Mass.: Human Resource Development Press, 1973. (b)

Carkhuff, R. R., & Berenson, B. G. *Beyond counseling and psychotherapy.* New York: Holt, Rinehart and Winston, 1967.

Caron, A. J., Unger, S. M., & Parloff, M. B. A test of Maltzman's theory of originality training. *Journal of Verbal Learning and Verbal Behavior,* 1963, *1,* 436-442.

Carr, A. T. Compulsive neurosis: A review of the literature. *Psychological Bulletin,* 1974, *81,* 311-318.

Cattell, R. B. *The scientific analysis of personality.* Baltimore: Penguin Books, 1965.

Cautela, J. R. Behavior therapy and the need for behavioral assessment. *Psychotherapy: Theory, Research and Practice,* 1968, *5,* 175-179.

Cautela, J. R. Behavior therapy and the need for behavorial assessment. *Psychotherapy: Theory, Research and Practice,* 1968, *5,* 175-179.

Cautela, J. R. Covert reinforcement. *Behavior Therapy,* 1970, *1,* 33-50. (a)

Cautela, J. R. Covert negative reinforcement. *Journal of Behavior Therapy and Experimental Psychiatry,* 1970, *1,* 273-278. (b)

Cautela, J. R. Covert extinction. *Behavior Therapy,* 1971, *2,* 192-200. (a)

Cautela, J. R. Covert modeling. Paper presented to the Association for the Advancement of Behavior Therapy, Washington, D.C., 1971. (b)

Cautela, J. R. Rationale and procedures for covert conditioning. In R. D. Rubin, H. Fensterheim, J. D. Henderson, & L. P. Ullman (Eds.), *Advances in behavior therapy.* New York: Academic Press, 1972. Pp. 85-96.

Cautela, J. R. Covert processes and behavior modification. *Journal of Nervous and Mental Disease,* 1973, *157,* 27-36.

Cautela, J. R. The present status of covert modeling. *Journal of Behavior Therapy and Experimental Psychiatry,* 1976, *6,* 323-326.

Cautela, J. R., Flannery, R. B., & Hanley, S. Covert modeling: An experimental test. *Behavior Therapy,* 1974, *5,* 494-502.

Chernoff, H., & Moses, L. E. *Elementary decision theory.* New York: John Wiley, 1959.

Chomsky, N. Review of *Verbal Behavior* by B. F. Skinner. *Language,* 1959, *35,* 26-58.

Christensen, P. R., Guilford, J. P., & Wilson, R. C. Relation of creative responses to working time and instructions. *Journal of Experimental Psychology,* 1957, *53,* 82-88.

Clark, C. H. *Brainstorming.* New York: Doubleday, 1958.

Clark, D. P. A study in the therapeutic and differential applications of goal attainment scaling as an adjunct in work adjustment counseling. Unpublished doctoral dissertation, Pennsylvania State University, 1978.

Clarke, R., Gelatt, H. B., & Levine, L. A decision-making paradigm for local guidance research. *Personnel and Guidance Journal*, 1965, *44*, 40-51.

Cobb, B., Clark, R., Carson, M., & Howe, C. D. Patient-responsible delay of treatment in cancer. *Cancer*, 1954, *7*, 920-926.

Cohen, J. Uncertainty and risk-taking in crime. *Bulletin of the British Psychological Society*, 1970, *23*, 293-296.

Cohen, J., & Hansel, C. E. M. Subjective probability, gambling, and intelligence. *Nature*, 1958, *181*, 1160-1161.

Colgrove, M. A. Stimulating creative problem solving: Innovative set. *Psychological Reports*, 1968, *22*, 1205-1211.

Cotter, L. H. Operant conditioning in a Vietnamese mental hospital. *American Journal of Psychiatry*, 1967, *124*, 23-28.

Covington, M. V., Crutchfield, R. S., & Davies, L. B. *The productive thinking program.* Berkeley, Cal.: Brazelton, 1966.

Crites, J. O. *Career maturity inventory.* Monterey, Cal.: CBT/McGraw-Hill, 1973.

Cronbach, L., & Gleser, G. C. *Psychological tests and personnel decisions.* Urbana: University of Illinois Press, 1957.

Dailey, C. A. The practical utility of the clinical report. *Journal of Consulting and Clinical Psychology*, 1953, *17*, 297-302.

Danaher, B. G. The theoretical foundations and clinical applications of the Premack Principle: A review and critique. *Behavior Therapy*, 1974, *5*, 307-324.

Davidson, D., Supes, P., & Siegel, S. *Decision-making: An experimental approach.* Stanford, Cal.: Stanford University Press, 1957.

Davis, G. A. Current status of research and theory in human problem solving. *Psychological Bulletin*, 1966, *66*, 36-54.

Davis, G. A. *Psychology of problem solving: Theory and practice.* New York: Basic Books, 1973.

Davis, G. A., & Manske, M. E. An instructional method of increasing originality. *Psychonomic Science*, 1966, *6*, 73-74.

Davis, G. A., & Manske, M. E. Effects of prior serial learning of solution words upon anagram problem solving: II. A serial position effect. *Journal of Experimental Psychology*, 1968, *77*, 101-104.

Davis, G. A., & Roweton, W. E. Using idea checklists with college students: Overcoming resistance. *Journal of Psychology*, 1968, *70*, 221-226.

Dewey, J. *How we think.* Boston: Heath, 1933.

Dewey, J. *Logic: The theory of inquiry.* New York: Holt, 1938.

Dilley, J. S. Decision-making ability and vocational maturity. *Personnel and Guidance Journal*, 1965, *44*, 423-427.

Dilley, J. S. Counselor actions that facilitate decision making. *The School Counselor*, 1968, *15*, 247-252.

Dixon, D. N. A problem solving/relationship (PS/R) model for counseling. Paper presented at the annual meeting of the American Educational Research Association. San Francisco, April 1976.

Dollard, J., & Miller, N. *Personality and psychotherapy: An analysis in terms of learning, thinking, and culture.* New York: McGraw-Hill, 1950.

Duncan, C. P. Recent research on human problem solving. *Psychological Bulletin*, 1959, *56*, 397-429.

D'Zurilla, T. J., & Goldfried, M. R. Problem solving and behavior modification. *Journal of Abnormal Psychology*, 1971, *78*, 107-126.

Eastman, C. M. Toward a working theory of automated design. In H. S. Brinkers (Ed.), *Decision-making: Creativity, judgment, and systems.* Columbus: Ohio State University Press, 1972. Pp. 85-111.

Edwards, W. The theory of decision making. *Psychological Bulletin,* 1954, *51,* 380-417.

Edwards, W. Behavioral decision theory. *Annual Review of Psychology,* 1961, *12,* 473-498.

Edwards, W., & Tversky, A. *Decision-making.* Baltimore: Penguin Books, 1967.

Egner, J. R., & Jackson, D. J. Effectiveness of a counseling intervention program for teaching career decision-making skills. *Journal of Counseling Psychology,* 1978, *25,* 45-52.

Ellis, A. *Reason and emotion in psychotherapy.* New York: Lyle Stuart, 1962.

Ellis, A. *Sex and the single man.* New York: Lyle Stuart & Dell, 1965.

Ellis, A. *The intelligent woman's guide to manhunting.* New York: Lyle Stuart & Dell, 1966.

Ellis, A. *The civilized couple's guide to extra-marital adventure.* New York: Pinnacle Books, 1973.

Emery, R. E., & Marholin, D. An applied behavioral analysis of delinquency: The irrelevancy of relevant behavior. *American Psychologist,* 1977, *32,* 860-873.

Emmelkamp, P. M. G., & Kwee, K. G. Obsessional ruminations: A comparison between thought-stopping and prolonged exposure in imagination. *Behavior Research and Therapy,* 1977, *15,* 441-444.

Estes, W. K. An experimental study of punishment. *Psychological Monographs,* 1944, *57* (3, Whole No. 263).

Evans, I. M. The logical requirements for explanations of systematic desensitization. *Behavior Therapy,* 1973, *4,* 506-514.

Evans, J. R., & Cody, J. J. Transfer of decision-making skills learned in a counseling-like setting to similar and dissimilar situations. *Journal of Counseling Psychology,* 1969, *16,* 427-432.

Evans, R. I., Rozelle, R. M., Lasater, T. M., Dembroski, T. M., & Allen, B. P. Fear arousal, persuasion, and actual versus implied behavioral change. *Journal of Personality and Social Psychology,* 1970, *16,* 220-227.

Eysenck, H. J. *Handbook of abnormal psychology: An experimental approach.* New York: Basic Books, 1961.

Farr, J., & Tucker, D. Extension of the covert sensitization paradigm with sexual deviance. Unpublished manuscript. Pennsylvania State University, 1974.

Feather, N. T. Subjective probability and decision under uncertainty. *Psychological Review,* 1959, *66,* 150-164.

Feldman, B. A. An investigation of a decision-based counseling paradigm for use with alcoholics. Unpublished masters thesis, Pennsylvania State University, 1976.

Fenichel, O. *The psychoanalytic theory of neurosis.* New York: Norton, 1945.

Ferster, C. B., & Perrott, M. C. *Behavior principles.* New York: Appleton-Century-Crofts, 1968.

Ferster, C. B., & Skinner, B. F. *Schedules of reinforcement.* New York: Appleton-Century-Crofts, 1957.

Festinger, L. *A theory of cognitive dissonance.* Evanston, Ill.: Row, Peterson, 1957.

Fishburn, P. C. Decision under uncertainty: An introductory exposition. *Journal of Industrial Engineering,* 1966, *17,* 341-353.

Fishburn, P. C. Methods of estimating additive utilities. *Management Science*, 1967, *13*, 435-453.

Fishburn, P. C. Personalistic decision theory: Exposition and critique. In H. S. Brinkers (Ed.), *Decision-Making: Creativity, judgment, and systems*. Columbus: Ohio State University Press, 1972. Pp. 19-41.

Fisher, T. J., Reardon, R. C., & Burck, H. D. Increasing information-seeking behavior with a model reinforced videotape. *Journal of Counseling Psychology*, 1976, *23*, 234-238.

Fletcher, I. *Situation ethics: The new morality*. Philadelphia: Westminster Press, 1966.

Forer, B. R. Personality factors in occupational choice. *Educational & Psychological Measurement*, 1953, *13*, 361-366.

Foreyt, J. P., & Hagen, R. L. Covert sensitization: Conditioning or suggestion? *Journal of Abnormal Psychology*, 1973, *82*, 17-23.

Franzini, L. R., & Tilker, H. A. On the terminological confusion between behavior therapy and behavior modification. *Behavior Therapy*, 1972, *3*, 279-282.

Freedman, J. L. Increasing creativity by free-association training. *Journal of Experimental Psychology*, 1965, *69*, 89-91.

Freud, S. [*The collected papers of Sigmund Freud (10 volumes)*]. (P. Rieff, Ed.). New York: Collier, 1963. (Originally published, various dates 1888-1937.)

Freud, S. [*A general introduction to psychoanalysis*]. (Riviere, Trans.). New York: Washington Square Press, 1967. (Originally published, 1924.)

Frost, R. *Robert Frost's poems*. New York: Washington Square Press, 1960.

Fuller, G. D. Current status of biofeedback in clinical practice. *American Psychologist*, 1978, *33*, 39-48.

Gagné, R. M. Problem solving and thinking. *Annual Review of Psychology*, 1959, *10*, 147-172.

Gagné, R. M. Problem solving. In A. W. Melton (Ed.), *Categories of human learning*. New York: Academic Press, 1964. Pp. 293-317.

Gagné, R. M. *The conditions of learning*. New York: Holt, Rinehart and Winston, 1970.

Gardner, J. W. *Self-renewal*. New York: Harper & Row, 1965.

Gelatt, H. B. Decision-Making: A conceptual frame of reference for counseling. *Journal of Counseling Psychology*, 1962, *9*, 240-245.

Gellhorn, R. *Principles of autonomic-somatic integration: Physiological basis and psychological and clinical implications*. Minneapolis: University of Minnesota Press, 1967.

Gershman, L., & Stedman, J. M. Oriental defense exercises as reciprocal inhibitors of anxiety. *Journal of Behavior Therapy and Experimental Psychiatry*, 1971, *2*, 117-119.

Goldfried, M. R., & Davison, G. C. *Clinical behavior therapy*. New York: Holt, Rinehart and Winston, 1976.

Goldfried, M. R., & Pomeranz, D. M. Role of assessment in behavior modification. *Psychological Reports*, 1968, *23*, 75-87.

Goldstein, A., Serber, M., & Piaget, G. Induced anger as a reciprocal inhibitor of fear. *Journal of Behavior Therapy and Experimental Psychiatry*, 1970, *1*, 67-70.

Goodyear, D., & Bitter, J. Goal attainment scaling as a program evaluation measure in rehabilitation. *Journal of Applied Rehabilitation Counseling*, 1974, *24*, 19-25.

Gordon, W. J. J. *Synectics*. New York: Harper & Row, 1961.

Gottman, J. M., & Leiblum, S. R. *How to do psychotherapy and how to evaluate it: A manual for beginners*. New York: Holt, Rinehart and Winston, 1974.

Greenspoon, J. The reinforcing effect of two spoken sounds on the frequency of two responses. *American Journal of Psychology*, 1955, *68*, 409-416.

Greenwald, H. *Direct decision therapy*. San Diego, Cal.: Edits, 1973.

Guilford, J. P. Creativity. *American Psychologist*, 1950, *5*, 444-454.

Guilford, J. P. *Personality*. New York: McGraw-Hill, 1959.

Haase, R. F., & DiMattia, D. J. The application of the microcounseling paradigm to the training of support personnel in counseling. *Counselor Education and Supervision*, 1970, *10*, 16-22.

Hackett, G., & Horan, J. J. Behavioral control of cigarette smoking: A comprehensive program. *Journal of Drug Education*, 1977, *7*, 71-79.

Hackett, G., & Horan, J. J. Focused smoking: An unequivocally safe alternative to the rapid smoking procedure. *Journal of Drug Education*, 1978, in press.

Hackett, G., Horan, J. J., Buchanan, J., Zumoff, P. Improving the exposure component and generalization potential of stress inoculation. Paper presented at the annual meeting of the American Educational Research Association, Toronto, March 1978.

Hackett, G., Horan, J. J., Stone, C. I., Linberg, S. E., Nicholas, W. C., & Lukaski, H. C. Further outcomes and tentative predictor variables from an evolving comprehensive program for the behavioral control of smoking. *Journal of Drug Education*, 1977, *7*, 225-229.

Hamilton, J. A., & Bergland, B. W. A strategy for creating peer social models. *Vocational Guidance Quarterly*, 1972, *20*, 271-278.

Hamilton, J. A., & Krumboltz, J. D. Simulated work experience: How realistic should it be? *Personnel and Guidance Journal*, 1969, *48*, 39-44.

Harper, R. A. *Psychoanalysis and psychotherapy: 36 systems*. Englewood Cliffs, N.J.: Prentice-Hall, 1959.

Harren, V. A. A study of the vocational decision-making process among college males. Unpublished doctoral dissertation, University of Texas, 1964.

Hayes, S. C., & Cavior, N. Multiple tracking and the reactivity of self-monitoring. I. Negative behaviors. *Behavior Therapy*, 1977, *8*, 819-831.

Hedberg, A. G., & Campbell, L. A comparison of four behavioral treatments of alcoholism. *Journal of Behavior Therapy and Experimental Psychiatry*, 1974, *5*, 251-256.

Hendrick, I. Work and the pleasure principle. *Psychoanalytic Quarterly*, 1943, *12*, 311-329.

Hendricks, C. G., Ferguson, J. G., & Thoresen, C. E. Toward counseling competence: The Stanford program. *Personnel and Guidance Journal*, 1973, *51*, 418-424.

Heppner, P. P. Problem solving and the relationship to the counseling process. Paper presented at the annual meeting of the American Educational Research Association, San Francisco, April 1976.

Herr, E. L. Unifying an entire system of education around a career development theme. Paper presented at the National Conference on Exemplary Projects and Programs of the 1969 Vocational Education Amendment, Atlanta, March 1969.

Herr, E. L. *Decision-making and vocational development*. Boston: Houghton Mifflin, 1970.

Herr, E. L. (Ed.). *Vocational guidance and human development.* Boston: Houghton Mifflin, 1974.

Herr, E. L., & Cramer, S. H. *Vocational guidance and career development in the schools: Toward a systems approach.* Boston: Houghton Mifflin, 1972.

Herr, E. L., & Horan, J. J. An inservice training model for Bureau of Employment Security Personnel. *Journal of Employment Counseling,* 1973, *10,* 31-35.

Herr, E. L., Horan, J. J., & Baker, S. B. Performance goals in vocational guidance and counseling: Clarifying the counseling mistique. *American Vocational Journal,* 1973, *48,* 66-72.

Hersen, M. Historical perspectives in behavioral assessment. In M. Hersen & A. S. Bellack (Eds.), *Behavioral assessment.* Elmsford, N. Y.: Pergamon, 1976. Pp. 3-22.

Hersen, M., & Barlow, D. H. *Single case experimental designs: Strategies for studying behavior change.* New York: Pergamon Press, 1976.

Heubusch, N. J., & Horan, J. J. Some effects of profanity in counseling. *Journal of Counseling Psychology,* 1977, *24,* 456-458.

Hills, J. R. Decision theory and college choice. *Personnel and Guidance Journal,* 1964, *43,* 17-22.

Hoffman, F. R. Conditions for creative problem solving. *Journal of Psychology,* 1961, *52,* 429-444.

Holmes, D. P., & Horan, J. J. Anger induction in assertion training. *Journal of Counseling Psychology,* 1976, *22,* 570-572.

Homme, L. E. Perspectives in psychology: XXIV Control of coverants, the operants of the mind. *Psychological Record,* 1965, *15,* 501-511.

Homme, L. E., & Tosti, D. T. Contingency management and motivation. *Journal of the National Society for Programmed Instruction,* 1965, *4,* 14-16.

Horan, J. J. Behavioral goals in systematic counselor education. *Counselor Education and Supervision,* 1972, *11,* 162-170. (a)

Horan, J. J. Decision-making counseling. Unpublished course materials, 1972. (b)

Horan, J. J. On MacDonald on Behavioral Humanism. *Educational Researcher,* 1973, *2* (4), Inside front cover. (a)

Horan, J. J. Basic experimental designs. In L. A. Abrams, E. Garfield, & J. D. Swisher (Eds.), *Accountability in drug education: A model for evaluation.* Washington, D.C.: Drug Abuse Council, 1973. Pp. 29-35. (b)

Horan, J. J. Obesity: Toward a behavioral perspective. *Rehabilitation Counseling Bulletin,* 1973, *17,* 6-14. (c)

Horan, J. J. "In vivo" emotive imagery: A technique for reducing childbirth anxiety and discomfort. *Psychological Reports,* 1973, *32,* 1328. (d)

Horan, J. J. Preventing drug abuse through behavior change technology. *Journal of SPATE,* 1973, *11,* 145-152. (e)

Horan, J. J. Counselor behavior in behavioral counseling. *Pennsylvania Personnel and Guidance Association Journal,* 1973, *1,* 1-4. (f)

Horan, J. J. Outcome difficulties in drug education. *Review of Educational Research,* 1974, *44,* 201-211. (a)

Horan, J. J. Negative coverant probability: An analogue study. *Behavior Research and Therapy,* 1974, *12,* 265-266. (b)

Horan, J. J. An efficient system for improving observer reliability. *Behavioral Engineering,* 1974, *1,* 1-3. (c)

Horan, J. J. On playing God in psychotherapy and being ethical about it. *Pennsylvania Personnel and Guidance Association Journal*, 1974, 2, 19-23. (d)

Horan, J. J. What life was like before the revolution. Review of D. H. Blocher, *Developmental counseling*. *Contemporary Psychology*, 1975, 20, 802-803.

Horan, J. J. Coping with inescapable discomfort through "in vivo" emotive imagery. In J. D. Krumboltz & C. E. Thoresen (Eds.), *Counseling Methods*. New York: Holt, 1976. Pp. 316-320.

Horan, J. J. Guidance, Quo Vadis? Review of Richard H. Byrne, Guidance: A behavioral approach. *Contemporary Psychology*, in press.

Horan, J. J., Baker, S. B., Hoffman, A. M., & Shute, R. E. Weight loss through variations in the coverant control paradigm. *Journal of Consulting and Clinical Psychology*, 1975, 43, 68-72.

Horan, J. J., D'Amico, M. M., & Williams, J. M. Assertiveness and patterns of drug use: A pilot study. *Journal of Drug Education*, 1975, 5, 217-221.

Horan, J. J., DeGirolomo, M. A., Hill, R. L., & Shute, R. E. The effect of older peer participant models on deficient academic performance. *Psychology in the Schools*, 1974, 11, 207-212.

Horan, J. J., & Dellinger, J. K. In vivo emotive imagery: A preliminary test. *Perceptual and Motor Skills*, 1974, 39, 359-362.

Horan, J. J., & Hackett, G. Partial component analysis of a comprehensive smoking treatment program. Unpublished manuscript. Pennsylvania State University, 1978.

Horan, J. J., Hackett, G., Buchanan, J. D., Stone, C. I., & Demchik-Stone, D. Coping with pain: A component analysis of stress-inoculation. *Cognitive Therapy and Research*, 1977, 1, 211-221.

Horan, J. J., Hackett, G., & Linberg, S. Factors to consider when using expired air carbon monoxide in smoking assessment. *Addictive Behaviors*, 1978, 3, 25-28.

Horan, J. J., Hackett, G., Nicholas, W. C., Linberg, S. E., Stone, C. I., & Lukaski, H. C. Rapid smoking: A cautionary note. *Journal of Consulting and Clinical Psychology*, 1977, 45, 341-343.

Horan, J. J., Herr, E. L., & Warner, R. W., Jr. Effects of video and audio monitoring on interviewer discomfort. *Journal of Employment Counseling*, 1973, 10, 40-43.

Horan, J. J., Hoffman, A. M., & Macri, M. Self-control of chronic fingernail biting. *Journal of Behavior Therapy and Experimental Psychiatry*, 1974, 5, 307-309.

Horan, J. J., & Johnson, R. G. Coverant conditioning through a self-management application of the Premack principle: Its effect on weight reduction. *Journal of Behavior Therapy and Experimental Psychiatry*, 1971, 2, 243-249.

Horan, J. J., Layng, F. C., & Pursell, C. Preliminary study of the effect of "in vivo" emotive imagery on dental discomfort. *Perceptual and Motor Skills*, 1976, 42, 105-106.

Horan, J. J., Linberg, S. E., & Hackett, G. Nicotine poisoning and rapid smoking. *Journal of Consulting and Clinical Psychology*, 1977, 45, 344-347.

Horan, J. J., Robb, N. S., & Hudson, G. R. Behavior therapy for chubby behavior therapists. *Journal of Counseling Psychology*, 1975, 22, 456-457.

Horan, J. J., Shute, R. E., Swisher, J. D., & Westcott, T. B. A training model for drug abuse prevention: Content and evaluation. *Journal of Drug Education*, 1973, 3, 121-126.

Horan, J. J., Smyers, R., Dorfman, D., & Jenkins, W. W. Two analogue attempts to harness the negative coverant effect. *Behavior Research and Therapy*, 1975, *13*, 183-184.

Horan, J. J., Stone, C., & Herold, P. Systematic desensitization as an instructional module. *Counselor Education and Supervision*, 1976, *15*, 286-291.

Horan, J. J., Westcott, T. B., Vetovich, C., & Swisher, J. D. Drug usage: An experimental comparison of three assessment conditions. *Psychological Reports*, 1974, *35*, 211-215.

Horan, J. J., & Williams, J. M. The tentative drug use scale: A quick and relatively problem-free outcome measure for drug abuse prevention projects. *Journal of Drug Education*, 1975, *5*, 91-94.

Hosford, R. E. Behaviorism is humanism. In G. F. Farwell, N. R. Gamsky, & P. Mathieu-Coughlan (Eds.), *The counselor's handbook*. New York: In text, 1974. Pp. 295-312.

Hoyt, M. F., & Janis, I. L. Increasing adherence to a stressful decision via a motivational balance-sheet procedure: A field experiment. *Journal of Personality and Social Psychology*, 1975, *31*, 833-839.

Hull, C. L. *A behavior system*. New Haven, Conn.: Yale University Press, 1952.

Ivey, A. E. *Microcounseling*. Springfield, Ill.: Thomas, 1971.

Ivey, A. E., Normington, C. J., Miller, C. D., Morrill, W. H., & Haase, R. F. Microcounseling and attending behavior: An approach to prepracticum counselor training. *Journal of Counseling Psychology*, 1968, *15*, 1-12.

Jacobson, N. S. Problem solving and contingency contracting in the treatment of marital discord. *Journal of Consulting and Clinical Psychology*, 1977, *45*, 92-100.

Jacobson, N. S., & Baucom, D. H. Design and assessment of nonspecific control groups in behavior modification research. *Behavior Therapy*, 1977, *8*, 709-719.

Jacobson, N. S., & Martin, B. Behavioral marriage therapy: Current status. *Psychological Bulletin*, 1976, *83*, 540-556.

James, W. *The principles of psychology*. New York: Holt, 1890.

James, W. *The will to believe*. New York: 1912. (Originally published, 1896.)

Janis, I. L. *Psychological stress: Psychoanalytic and behavioral studies of surgical patients*. New York: Wiley, 1958.

Janis, I. L. *Stress and frustration*. New York: Harcourt Brace Jovanovich, 1971.

Janis, I. L., & Mann, L. A conflict-theory approach to attitude change and decision making. In A. G. Greenwald, T. C. Brock, & T. M. Ostrom (Eds.), *Psychological foundations of attitudes*. New York: Academic Press, 1968.

Janis, I. L., & Mann, L. *Decision making: A psychological analysis of conflict, choice, and commitment*. New York: The Free Press, 1977.

Job Experience Kits, Chicago: Science Research Associates, 1970.

Johnson, R. H., & Euler, D. E. Effect of the Life Career Game on the learning and retention of educational-occupational information. *The School Counselor*, 1972, *19*, 155-159.

Jones, E. The significance of the sublimating process for education and reeducation. *Psychoanalysis*. New York: Wood, 1923.

Jones, G. B. Evaluation of problem-solving competence. In J. D. Krumboltz & C. E. Thoresen (Eds.), *Counseling methods*. New York: Holt, Rinehart and Winston, 1976. Pp. 405-414.

Jones, G. B., & Krumboltz, J. D. Stimulating vocational exploration through film-mediated problems. *Journal of Counseling Psychology*, 1970, *17*, 107-114.

Jones, M. C. A laboratory study of fear: The case of Peter. *Pedagogical Seminary,* 1924, *31,* 308-315.

Jones, R. G. A factored measure of Ellis' irrational belief systems. Wichita, Kan.: Test Systems Inc., 1968.

Kaldor, D. R., & Zytowski, D. G. A maximizing model of occupational decision making. *Personnel and Guidance Journal,* 1969, *47,* 781-788.

Kanfer, F. H., & Phillips, J. S. *Learning foundations of behavior therapy.* New York: Wiley, 1970.

Kanfer, F. H., & Saslow, G. Behavioral diagnosis. In C. M. Franks (Ed.), *Behavior therapy: Appraisal and status.* New York: McGraw-Hill, 1969.

Karlins, M., & Schroder, H. M. Discovery learning, creativity, and the inductive teaching program. *Psychological Reports,* 1967, *20,* 867-876.

Katz, D., Sarnoff, I., & McClintock, C. G. Ego-defense and attitude change. *Human Relations,* 1956, *9,* 27-46.

Katz, M. A model of guidance for career decision-making. *Vocational Guidance Quarterly,* 1966, *15,* 2-10.

Katzell, R. Personal values, job satisfaction, and job behavior. In H. Borow (Ed.), *Man in a world of work.* Boston: Houghton Mifflin, 1964.

Kazdin, A. E. Covert modeling and the reduction of avoidance behavior. *Journal of Abnormal Psychology,* 1973, *81,* 87-95. (a)

Kazdin, A. E. Effects of covert modeling and reinforcement on assertive behavior. *Proceedings of the 81st Annual Convention of the American Psychological Association,* 1973, *8,* 537-538. (b)

Kazdin, A. E. Methodological and assessment considerations in evaluating reinforcement programs in applied settings. *Journal of Applied Behavioral Analysis,* 1973, *6,* 517-531. (c)

Kazdin, A. E. Self-monitoring and behavior change. In M. J. Mahoney & C. E. Thoresen (Eds.), *Self-control: Power to the person.* Monterey, Cal.: Brooks/Cole Publishing Company, 1974. Pp. 218-246. (a)

Kazdin, A. E. Covert modeling, model similarity, and reduction of avoidance behavior. *Behavior Therapy,* 1974, *5,* 325-340. (b)

Kazdin, A. E. Covert modeling, imagery assessment, and assertive behavior. *Journal of Consulting and Clinical Psychology,* 1975, *43,* 716-724.

Kazdin, A. E. Effects of covert modeling, multiple models, and model reinforcement on assertive behavior. *Behavior Therapy,* 1976, *7,* 211-222.

Kazdin, A. E., & Bootzin, R. R. The token economy: An evaluative review. *Journal of Applied Behavior Analysis,* 1972, *5,* 343-372.

Kazdin, A. E., & Wilcoxon, L. A. Systematic desensitization and nonspecific treatment effects: A methodological evaluation. *Psychological Bulletin,* 1976, *83,* 729-758.

Kendler, H. H., & Kendler, T. S. Vertical and horizontal processes in problem solving. *Psychological Review,* 1962, *69,* 1-16.

Kierkegaard, S. *Fear and trembling and the sickness unto death.* New York: Doubleday, 1954. (Originally published, 1843 and 1849.)

Kiesler, C. A. (Ed.). *The psychology of commitment.* New York: Academic Press, 1971.

Kingsley, H. L., & Garry, R. *The nature and conditions of learning.* Englewood Cliffs, N.J.: Prentice-Hall, 1957.

Kiresuk, T., & Sherman, R. Goal attainment scaling: A general method for evaluating comprehensive community mental health programs. *Community Mental Health Journal,* 1968, *4,* 443-453.

Köhler, W. *The mentality of apes.* New York: Harcourt Brace, 1925.

Krasner, L. Studies of the conditioning of verbal behavior. *Psychological Bulletin,* 1958, *55,* 148-170.

Krasner, L. The operant approach in behavior therapy. In A. E. Bergin & S. L. Garfield (Eds.), *Handbook of psychotherapy and behavior change.* New York: Wiley, 1971. Pp. 612-652.

Kravetz, S. P., & Thomas, K. R. A learning theory approach to indecisive clients. *Rehabilitation Counseling Bulletin,* 1974, *18,* 198-208.

Krop, H., Calhoon, B., & Verrier, R. Modification of the "self-concept" of emotionally disturbed children by covert self-reinforcement. *Behavior Therapy,* 1971, *2,* 201-204.

Krop, H., Perez, F., & Beaudoin, C. Modification of "self-concept" of psychiatric patients by covert reinforcement. In R. D. Rubin, J. P. Brady, & J. D. Henderson (Eds.), *Advances in behavior therapy* (Vol. 4). New York: Academic Press, 1973. Pp. 139-144.

Krumboltz, J. D. *Stating the goals of counseling.* California Counseling and Guidance Association Monograph No. 1., 1966.

Krumboltz, J. D. An accountability model for counselors. *The Personnel and Guidance Journal,* 1974, *52,* 639-646.

Krumboltz, J. D., & Baker, R. D. Behavioral counseling for vocational decisions. In H. Borow (Ed.), *Career guidance for a new age.* Boston: Houghton Mifflin, 1973. Pp. 235-284.

Krumboltz, J. D., Baker, R. D., & Johnson, R. G. Vocational problem-solving experiences for stimulating career exploration and interest Phase II. Final Report, Office of Education Grant 4-7-070111-2890. School of Education, Stanford University, 1968.

Krumbotz, J. D., & Bergland, B. W. Experiencing work almost like it is. *Educational Technology,* 1969, *9* (3), 47-49.

Krumboltz, J. D., & Schroeder, W. W. Promoting career exploration through reinforcement. *Personnel and Guidance Journal,* 1965, *44,* 19-26.

Krumboltz, J. D., & Sheppard, L. E. Vocational problem-solving experiences. In J. D. Krumboltz & C. E. Thoresen (Eds.), *Behavioral counseling: Cases and techniques.* New York: Holt, Rinehart and Winston, 1969.

Krumboltz, J. D., Sheppard, L. E., Jones, G. B., Johnson, R. G., & Baker, R. D. Vocational problem-solving experiences for stimulating career exploration and interest. Final Report, Office of Education Grant 5-8-5059. School of Education, Stanford University, 1967.

Krumboltz, J. D., & Thoresen, C. E. The effect of behavioral counseling in group and individual settings on information seeking behavior. *Journal of Counseling Psychology,* 1964, *11,* 324-333.

Krumboltz, J. D., & Thoresen, C. E. *Behavioral counseling: Cases & techniques.* New York: Holt, Rinehart and Winston, 1969.

Krumboltz, J. D., & Thoresen, C. E. *Counseling methods.* New York: Holt, 1976.

Krumboltz, J. D., Thoresen, C. E., Zifferblatt, S. M. Behavioral systems training program: Processes and products. Paper presented at the annual meeting of the American Educational Research Association, New York City, February 1971.

Krumboltz, J. D., & Varenhorst, B. Molders of pupil attitudes. *Personnel and Guidance Journal,* 1965, *43,* 443-446.

Krumboltz, J. D., Varenhorst, B., & Thoresen, C. E. Non-verbal factors in effectiveness of models in counseling. *Journal of Counseling Psychology,* 1967, *14,* 412-418.

Kwiterovich, D. K., & Horan, J. J. Solomon evaluation of a commercial assertiveness training program for women. *Behavior Therapy,* 1977, *8,* 501-502.

LaFleur, N. K., & Johnson, R. G. Separate effects of social modeling and reinforcement in counseling adolescents. *Journal of Counseling Psychology,* 1972, *19,* 292-295.

Langer, E. J., Janis, I. L., & Wolfer, J. A. Reduction of psychological stress in surgical patients. *Journal of Experimental Social Psychology,* 1975, *11,* 155-165.

Lazarus, A. A. *Behavior therapy and beyond.* New York: McGraw-Hill, 1971.

Lazarus, A. A. Multimodal behavior therapy: Treating the "Basic Id." *Journal of Nervous and Mental Disease,* 1973, *156,* 404-411.

Lazarus, A. A. *Multi-modal behavior therapy.* New York: Springer, 1976.

Lazarus, A. A., & Abramovitz, A. The use of "emotive imagery" in the treatment of children's phobias. *Journal of Mental Science,* 1962, *108,* 191-195.

Lea, S. E. G. The psychology and economics of demand. *Psychological Bulletin,* 1978, *85,* 441-466.

Lent, R. W., & Russell, R. K. Treatment of test anxiety by cue-controlled desensitization and study-skills training. *Journal of Counseling Psychology,* 1978, *25,* 217-224.

Levis, D. J. Implosive therapy: A critical analysis of Morganstern's review. *Psychological Bulletin,* 1974, *81,* 155-158.

Levitt, E. E. *The psychology of anxiety.* New York: Bobbs-Merrill, 1967.

Lewin, K. Deferring the "field" at a given time. *Psychological Review,* 1943, *50,* 292-310.

Lewin, K., Dembo, T., Festinger, L., & Sears, P. S. Level of aspiration. In J. McV. Hunt (Ed.), *Personality and the behavior disorders.* New York: Ronald Press, 1944. Pp. 333-378.

Liberman, R. P. Michael Serber: In memorium. *Behavior therapy,* 1974, *5,* 605.

Lichtenstein, E., & Danaher, B. G. Modification of smoking behavior: A critical analysis. In M. Hersen, R. M. Eisler, & P. M. Miller (Eds.), *Progress in behavior modification* (Vol. 3). New York: Academic Press, 1977.

Lichtenstein, E., Harris, D. E., Birchler, G. R., Wahl, J. M., & Schmahl, D. P. Comparison of rapid smoking, warm smoky air, and attention placebo in the modification of smoking behavior. *Journal of Consulting and Clinical Psychology,* 1973, *40,* 92-98.

Lindley, D. V. *Making decisions.* London: Wiley, 1971.

Little, L. M., & Curran, J. P. Covert sensitization: A clinical procedure in need of some explanations. *Psychological Bulletin,* 1978, *85,* 513-531.

Lofquist, L. H., & Dawis, R. V. *Adjustment to work: A psychological view of man's problems in a work-oriented society.* New York: Appleton-Century-Crofts, 1969.

London, P. *The modes and morals of psychotherapy.* New York: Holt, 1967.

Lovaas, O. I. A behavior therapy approach to the treatment of childhood schizophrenia. In J. P. Hill (Ed.), *Minnesota symposia on child psychology* (Vol. 1). Minneapolis: University of Minnesota Press, 1967. Pp. 108-159.

Luce, R. D. Psychological studies of risky decision making. In W. Edwards & A. Tversky (Eds.), *Decision-making*. Baltimore: Penguin Books, 1967. Pp. 334-353.

Luchins, A. S. Mechanization in problem solving—the effect of Einstellung. *Psychological Monographs*, 1942, *54* (6, Whole No. 248).

MacCorquodale, K. Chomsky's review of Skinner's *Verbal Behavior*. *Journal of the Experimental Analysis of Behavior*, 1970, *13*, 83-99.

MacCrimmon, K. R. An overview of multiple objective decision making. In J. L. Cochrane and M. Zeleny (Eds.), *Multiple criteria decision making*. Columbia: University of South Carolina Press, 1973.

Mager, R. F. *Preparing instructional objectives*. Belmont, Cal.: Fearon, 1962.

Magoon, T. M. Developing skills for solving educational and vocational problems. In J. D. Krumboltz & C. E. Thoresen (Eds.), *Behavioral counseling: Cases and techniques*. New York: Holt, Rinehart and Winston, 1969. Pp. 343-396.

Mahoney, K. Adipose cellularity as a predictor of responsiveness to treatment of obesity. Unpublished doctoral dissertation, Pennsylvania State University, 1977.

Mahoney, M. J. Toward an experimental analysis of coverant control. *Behavior Therapy*, 1970, *1*, 510-521.

Mahoney, M. J. The self-management of covert behavior: A case study. *Behavior Therapy*, 1971, *2*, 575-578.

Mahoney, M. J. Clinical issues in self-control training. Paper presented at the American Psychological Association, Montreal, August 1973.

Mahoney, M. J. *Cognition and behavior modification*. Cambridge, Mass.: Ballinger, 1974.

Mahoney, M. J., & Mahoney, K. *Permanent weight control*. New York: Norton, 1976.

Mahoney, M. J., & Thoresen, C. E. *Self-control: Power to the person*. Monterey, Cal.: Brooks/Cole Publishing Company, 1974.

Maier, N. R. F. Reasoning in humans: III. The mechanisms of equivalent stimuli and of reasoning. *Journal of Experimental Psychology*, 1945, *35*, 349-360.

Maier, N. R. F., & Burke, R. J. Response availability as a factor in the problem solving performance of males and females. *Journal of Personality and Social Psychology*, 1967, *5*, 304-310.

Maltzman, I. Thinking: From a behavioristic point of view. *Psychological Review*, 1955, *62*, 275-286.

Maltzman, I. On the training of originality. *Psychological Review*, 1960, *67*, 229-242.

Maltzman, I., Bogartz, W., & Breger, L. A procedure for increasing word association originality and its transfer effects. *Journal of Experimental Psychology*, 1958, *56*, 392-398.

Maltzman, I., Simon, S., Raskin, D., & Licht, L. Experimental studies in the training of originality. *Psychological Monographs*, 1960, *74* (6, Whole No. 493).

Mann, L. The effects of emotional role playing on smoking attitudes and behavior. *Journal of Experimental Social Psychology*, 1967, *3*, 334-348.

Mann, L. Use of a "balance-sheet" procedure to improve the quality of personal decision making: A field experiment with college applicants. *Journal of Vocational Behavior*, 1972, *2*, 291-300.

Mann, L., & Janis, I. L. A follow-up study on the long-term effects of emotional role playing. *Journal of Personality and Social Psychology*, 1968, *8*, 339-342.

Marquis, J. N. Orgasmic reconditioning: Changing sexual object choice through controlling masturbation fantasies. *Journal of Behavior Therapy and Experimental Psychiatry*, 1970, *1*, 263-271.

Marquis, J. N. An expedient model for behavior therapy. In A. Lazarus (Ed.), *Clinical behavior therapy*. New York: Brunner/Mazel, 1972. Pp. 41-72.

Mason, J. G. *How to be a more creative executive*. New York: McGraw-Hill, 1960.

Mausner, B. An ecological view of cigarette smoking. *Journal of Abnormal Psychology*, 1973, *81*, 115-126.

Mausner, B., & Platt, E. S. *Smoking: A behavioral analysis*. New York: Pergamon, 1971.

May, K. O. Transitivity, utility, & aggregation in performance patterns. *Econometrica*, 1954, *22*, 1-13.

McFall, R. M., & Hammen, C. L. Motivation, structure, and self-monitoring: Role of nonspecific factors in smoking reduction. *Journal of Consulting and Clinical Psychology*, 1971, *37*, 80-86.

McGuire, W. J. Cognitive consistency and attitude change. *Journal of Abnormal and Social Psychology*, 1960, *60*, 345-353.

McGuire, W. J. The nature of attitudes and attitude change. In G. Lindzey & E. Aronson (Eds.), *The handbook of social psychology* (Vol. 3). Reading, Mass.: Addison-Wesley, 1969.

Mednick, S. A. The associative basis of the creative process. *Psychological Review*, 1962, *69*, 220-232.

Meehl, P. E. The cognitive activity of the clinician. *American Psychologist*, 1960, *15*, 19-27.

Meichenbaum, D. Examination of model characteristics in reducing avoidance behavior. *Journal of Personality and Social Psychology*, 1971, *17*, 298-307.

Meichenbaum, D. Cognitive modification of test anxious college students. *Journal of Consulting and Clinical Psychology*, 1972, *39*, 370-380.

Meichenbaum, D. Cognitive factors in behavior modification: Modifying what clients say to themselves. In C. M. Franks & G. T. Wilson (Eds.), *Annual review of behavior therapy theory and practice* (Vol. 1). New York: Brunner/Mazel, 1973. Pp. 416-431.

Meichenbaum, D. Enhancing creativity by modifying what subjects say to themselves. *American Educational Research Journal*, 1975, *12*, 129-145.

Meichenbaum, D., & Cameron, R. Training schizophrenics to talk to themselves. A means of developing attentional controls. *Behavior Therapy*, 1973, *4*, 515-534.

Meichenbaum, D., & Cameron, R. The clinical potential of modifying what clients say to themselves. *Psychotherapy: Theory, Research, & Practice*, 1974, *11*, 103-117.

Meichenbaum, D., & Goodman, J. Training impulsive children to talk to themselves: A means of developing self-control. *Journal of Abnormal Psychology*, 1971, *77*, 115-126.

Meichenbaum, D., & Turk, D. The cognitive-behavioral management of anxiety, anger, and pain. In P. O. Davidson (Ed.), *The behavioral management of anxiety, depression, and pain*. New York: Brunner/Mazel, 1976. Pp. 1-34.

Mendonca, J. D., & Siess, T. F. Counseling for indecisiveness: Problem-solving and anxiety-management training. *Journal of Counseling Psychology*, 1976, *23*, 339-347.

Messer, S. B. Reflection-Impulsivity: A review. *Psychological Bulletin*, 1976, *83*, 1026-1052.

Meyer, J. B., Strowig, W., & Hosford, R. E. Behavioral-reinforcement counseling with rural high school youth. *Journal of Counseling Psychology*, 1970, *17*, 127-132.

Miller, D. W., & Starr, M. K. *The structure of human decisions.* Englewood Cliffs, N.J.: Prentice-Hall, 1967.

Miller, G. A. The magical number seven, plus or minus two. *Psychological Review*, 1956, *63*, 81-97.

Mischel, W. *Personality and assessment.* New York: Wiley, 1968.

Mischel, W. Toward a cognitive social learning reconceptualization of personality. *Psychological Review*, 1973, *80*, 252-283.

Morganstern, K. P. Implosive therapy and flooding procedures: A critical review. *Psychological Bulletin*, 1973, *79*, 318-334.

Morganstern, K. P. Issues in implosive therapy: Reply to Levis. *Psychological Bulletin*, 1974, *81*, 380-382.

Morganstern, K. P. Behavioral interviewing: The initial stages of assessment. In M. Hersen & A. S. Bellack (Eds.), *Behavioral assessment.* Elmsford, N.Y.: Pergamon, 1976. Pp. 51-76.

Mosteller, F., & Nogee, P. An experimental measure of utility. *Journal of Political Economy*, 1951, *59*, 371-404.

Mowrer, O. H. Learning theory and the neurotic paradox. *American Journal of Orthopsychiatry*, 1948, *18*, 571-610.

Munson, W. W., Horan, J. J., Miano, L., & Stone, C. I. Another look at the Life Career Game. *Pennsylvania Personnel and Guidance Association Journal*, 1976, *4*, 36-38.

Nawas, N. M. Wherefore cognitive therapy: A critical scrutiny of three papers by Beck, Bergin, & Ullman. *Behavior Therapy*, 1970, *1*, 359-370.

Nelson, D. E., & Krumboltz, J. D. Encouraging career exploration through "simulated work" and "vocational detective" experiences. *Journal of Employment Counseling*, 1970, *7*, 58-65.

Novaco, R. W. *Anger control.* Lexington, Mass.: Lexington Books, 1975.

O'Leary, K. D., & Wilson, G. T. *Behavior therapy: Application and outcome.* Englewood Cliffs, N.J.: Prentice-Hall, 1975.

Olson, R. P., & Greenberg, D. J. Effects of contingency-contracting and decision-making groups with chronic mental patients. *Journal of Consulting and Clinical Psychology*, 1972, *38*, 376-383.

Olton, R. M., & Crutchfield, R. S. Developing the skills of productive thinking. In P. Mussen, J. Langer, & M. V. Covington (Eds.), *Trends and issues in developmental psychology.* New York: Holt, Rinehart and Winston, 1969. Pp. 68-91.

Osborn, A. F. *Applied imagination: Principles and procedures of creative problem solving.* New York: Scribner's, 1963.

Osipow, S. H. *Theories of career development.* New York: Appleton-Century-Crofts, 1968.

Papanek, V. J. Tree of life: Bionics. *Journal of Creative Behavior*, 1969, *3*, 5-15.

Parloff, M. B., & Handlon, J. H. The influence of criticalness on creative problem solving in dyads. *Psychiatry*, 1964, *27*, 17-27.

Parnes, S. J. *Creative behavior guidebook*. New York: Scribner's, 1967.

Parsons, F. *Choosing a vocation*. Boston: Houghton Mifflin, 1909.

Paul, G. L. *Insight vs. desensitization in psychotherapy: An experiment in anxiety reduction*. Stanford, Cal.: Stanford University Press, 1966.

Penney, R. K., & McCann, B. Application of originality training to the mentally retarded. *Psychological Reports*, 1962, *11*, 347-351.

Perls, F. S. *Gestalt therapy verbatim*. Lafayette, Cal.: Real People Press, 1969.

Peterson, D. R. *The clinical study of social behavior*. New York: Appleton-Century-Crofts, 1968.

Poitras-Martin, D., & Stone, G. L. Psychological education: A skill-oriented approach. *Journal of Counseling Psychology*, 1977, *24*, 153-157.

Premack, D. Reinforcement theory. In D. Levine (Ed.), *Nebraska Symposium on Motivation: 1965*. Lincoln: University of Nebraska Press, 1965.

Preston, M. G., & Baratta, P. An experimental study of the auction-value of an uncertain outcome. *American Journal of Psychology*, 1948, *61*, 183-193.

Prince, G. The operational mechanism of synectics. *Journal of Creative Behavior*, 1968, *2*, 1-13.

Protinski, H., & Popp, R. Irrational philosophies in popular music. *Cognitive Therapy and Research*, 1978, *2*, 71-74.

Rachlin, H. *Introduction to modern behaviorism*. San Francisco: W. H. Freeman & Co., 1970.

Rachman, S., & Teasdale, J. *Aversion therapy and the behavior disorders*. Coral Gables, Fla.: University of Miami Press, 1969.

Raimy, V. C. *Training in clinical psychology*. New York: Prentice-Hall, 1950.

Rapoport, A., & Wallsten, T. S. Individual decision behavior. *Annual Review of Psychology*, 1972, *23*, 131-176.

Reed, H. D., & Janis, I. L. Effects of the new type of psychological treatment on smokers' resistance to warnings about health hazards. *Journal of Consulting and Clinical Psychology*, 1974, *42*, 748.

Rich, A. R., & Shroeder, H. E. Research issues in assertiveness training. *Psychological Bulletin*, 1976, *83*, 1081-1096.

Rimm, D. C., & Litvak, S. B. Self-verbalization and emotional arousal. *Journal of Abnormal Psychology*, 1969, *74*, 181-187.

Robinson, M. N. *The power of sexual surrender*. New York: Signet, 1959.

Rogers, C. R. A theory of therapy, personality, and interpersonal relationships as developed in the client-centered framework. In S. Koch (Ed.), *Psychology a study of science* (Vol. I, II), *Formations of the person and the social context*. New York: McGraw-Hill, 1959. Pp. 184-258.

Rogers, C. R. *On becoming a person*. Boston: Houghton Mifflin, 1961.

Rogers, C. R. *Three approaches to psychotherapy: Film No. 1–Dr. Carl Rogers*. Psychological Films, 1968.

Rokeach, M. Long range experimental modification of values, attitudes, and behaviors. *American Psychologist*, 1971, *26*, 453-459.

Rosenbaum, M. E., Arenson, S. J., & Panman, R. A. Training and instructions in the facilitation of originality. *Journal of Verbal Learning and Verbal Behavior*, 1964, *3*, 50-56.

Ross, G. R. Reducing irrational personality traits, trait anxiety, and intra-interpersonal needs in high school students. Paper presented at the annual meeting of the Florida Educational Research Association, St. Petersburg Beach, Florida, January 1977.

Rotter, J. B. *Social learning and clinical psychology*. New York: Prentice-Hall, 1954.

Rotter, J. B. Generalized expectancies for internal versus external control of reinforcement. *Psychological Monographs*, 1966, *80* (1, Whole No. 609).

Russell, M. L. A program of clinical research development: Developing decision-making skills in children. Paper presented at the annual meeting of the American Education Research Association, New York, April 1977.

Russell, M. L., & Thoresen, C. E. Teaching decision-making skills to children. In J. D. Krumboltz & C. E. Thoresen (Eds.), *Counseling methods*. New York: Holt, Rinehart and Winston, 1976. Pp. 377-383.

Russell, R. K., & Sipich, J. F. Treatment of test anxiety by cue-controlled relaxation. *Behavior Therapy*, 1974, *5*, 673-676.

Ryan, T. A., & Krumboltz, J. D. Effect of planned reinforcement counseling on client decision-making behavior. *Journal of Counseling Psychology*, 1964, *11*, 315-323.

Samaan, M. K., & Parker, C. A. Effects of behavioral (reinforcement) and advice-giving counseling on information-seeking behavior. *Journal of Counseling Psychology*, 1973, *20*, 193-201.

Sarason, I. G. Test anxiety and cognitive modeling. *Journal of Personality and Social Psychology*, 1973, *28*, 58-61.

Sarason, I. G., & Ganzer, V. J. Developing appropriate social behaviors in juvenile delinquents. In J. D. Krumboltz & C. E. Thoresen (Eds.), *Behavioral counseling: Cases & techniques*. New York: Holt, Rinehart and Winston, 1969. Pp. 178-193.

Savage, L. J. *The foundations of statistics*. New York: John Wiley, 1954.

Schachter, S. Nesbitt's paradox. In W. L. Dunn (Ed.), *Smoking behavior: Motives and incentives*. Washington, D.C.: V. H. Winston & Sons, 1973.

Schlichter, J., & Horan, J. J. Some effects of stress inoculation training on aggressive delinquents. Unpublished manuscript. Pennsylvania State University, 1978.

Schmahl, D. P., Lichtenstein, E., & Harris, D. E. Successful treatment of habitual smokers with warm, smoky air and rapid smoking. *Journal of Consulting and Clinical Psychology*, 1972, *38*, 105-111.

Sheerer, M. Problem solving. *Scientific American*, 1963, *208*, 118-128.

Sherman, T. M., & Cormier, W. H. The use of subjective scales for measuring interpersonal reactions. *Journal of Behavior Therapy & Experimental Psychiatry*, 1972, *3*, 279-280.

Shoemacher, G. In Hints from Heloise, *The Center Daily Times*, June 29, 1976, p. 5.

Shure, M. B., & Spivack, G. *Preschool interpersonal problem-solving (PIPS) test: Manual*. Philadelphia: Department of Mental Health Sciences, Hahnemann Community Mental Health/Mental Retardation Center, 1974.

Sidman, M. *The tactics of scientific research: Evaluating experimental data in psychology*. New York: Basic Books, 1960.

Silverin, L. C. "Systems approach"—What is it? *Educational Technology*, 1968, *8*, 5-6.

Siminov, P. V. Studies of emotional behavior of humans and animals by Soviet physiologists. Paper presented at Conference on Experimental Approaches to the Study of Behavior, New York, 1967.

Simon, H. A. *The new science of management decisions.* New York: Harper & Row, 1960.

Skinner, B. F. *Science and human behavior.* New York: Macmillan, 1953.

Skinner, B. F. An operant analysis of problem solving. In B. Kleinmuntz (Ed.), *Problem Solving: Research, method, and theory.* New York: Wiley, 1966. Pp. 225-257.

Skinner, B. F. *Beyond freedom and dignity.* New York: Knopf, 1971.

Slovack, P., Fischhoff, B., & Lichtenstein, S. Behavioral decision theory. *Annual Review of Psychology,* 1977, *28,* 1-39.

Small, L. Personality determinants of vocational choice. *Psychological Monographs,* 1953, *67* (1, Whole No. 351).

Smith, R. D., & Evans, J. R. Comparison of experimental group guidance and individual counseling as facilitators of vocational development. *Journal of Counseling Psychology,* 1973, *20,* 202-208.

Sobell, M. B., & Sobell, L. C. Evidence of controlled drinking by former alcoholics: A second year evaluation of individualized behavior therapy. Paper presented at the 81st annual meeting of the American Psychological Association, Montreal, August 1973.

Solomon, R. L. Punishment. *American Psychologist,* 1964, *19,* 239-253.

Spivack, G., Platt, J. J., & Shure, M. B. *The problem-solving approach to adjustment.* San Francisco: Jossey-Bass, 1976.

Staats, A. W. An integrated-functional learning approach to complex human behavior. In B. Kleinmuntz (Ed.), *Problem solving: Research, method, and theory.* New York: Wiley, 1966. Pp. 259-339.

Stern, R. M., & Ray, W. J. *Biofeedback and the control of internal bodily activity.* Homewood, Ill.: Richard D. Irwin, 1975.

Stewart, N. R. Exploring and processing information about educational and vocational opportunities in groups. In J. D. Krumboltz & Carl E. Thoresen (Eds.), *Behavioral counseling: Cases and techniques.* New York: Holt, Rinehart and Winston, 1969. Pp. 213-234.

Stewart, N. R., & Winborn, B. B. A model for decision-making in systematic counseling. *Educational Technology,* 1973, *69,* 13-15.

Stilwell, W. E., & Thoresen, C. E. Social modeling and vocational behaviors of Mexican-American and Non-Mexican-American Adolescents. *Vocational Guidance Quarterly,* 1972, *20,* 279-286.

Stone, C. I., Demchik-Stone, D., & Horan, J. J. Coping with pain: A component analysis of Lamaze and cognitive-behavioral procedures. *Journal of Psychosomatic Research,* 1977, *21,* 451-456.

Stone, C. I., & Shute, R. E. Persuader sex differences and peer pressure effects on attitudes toward drug abuse. A paper presented at the annual meeting of the American Educational Research Association, San Francisco, April 1976.

Stuart, R. B. Behavioral control over eating. *Behavior Research and Therapy,* 1967, *5,* 357-365.

Stuart, R. B. *Trick or treatment: How and when psychotherapy fails.* Champaign, Ill.: Research Press, 1970.

Stuart, R. B., & Davis, B. *Slim chance in a fat world: Behavioral control of obesity.* Champaign, Ill.: Research Press, 1972.

Stunkard, A. J. The management of obesity. *New York State Journal of Medicine,* 1958, *58,* 79-87.

Stunkard, A. J. The results of a treatment for obesity. *Archives of Internal Medicine,* 1959, *103,* 79-85.

Stunkard, A. J., & Mahoney, M. J. Behavioral treatment of the eating disorders. In H. J. Leitenberg (Ed.), *Handbook of behavior modification and behavior therapy.* Englewood Cliffs, N.J.: Prentice-Hall, 1976. Pp. 45-73.

Super, D. E., Starishevsky, R., Matlin, N., & Jordaan, J. P. *Career development: Self-concept theory.* New York: College Entrance Examination Board, 1963.

Super, D. E. (Ed.). *Measuring vocational maturity for counseling and evaluation.* Washington, D.C.: American Personnel and Guidance Association, 1974.

Supes, P., & Walsh, K. A non-linear model for the experimental measurement of utility. *Behavioral Science,* 1959, *4,* 204-211.

Swails, R. G., & Herr, E. L. Vocational development groups for ninth-grade students. *Vocational Guidance Quarterly,* 1976, *24,* 256-260.

Swisher, J. D., & Horan, J. J. Effecting drug attitude change in college students via induced cognitive dissonance. *Journal of the Student Personnel Association for Teacher Education,* 1972, *11,* 26-31.

Tasto, D. L., & Chesney, M. A. The deconditioning of nausea and of crying by emotive imagery: A report of two cases. *Journal of Behavior Therapy and Experimental Psychiatry,* 1977, *8,* 139-142.

Taylor, D. W., & McNemar, O. W. Problem solving and thinking. *Annual Review of Psychology,* 1955, *6,* 455-482.

Thase, M. E., & Moss, M. K. The relative efficacy of covert modeling procedures and guided participant modeling on the reduction of avoidance behavior. *Journal of Behavior Therapy and Experimental Psychiatry,* 1976, *7,* 7-12.

Thoresen, C. E. The systems approach and counselor education: Basic features and implications. *Counselor Education and Supervision,* 1969, *9,* 3-18.

Thoresen, C. E. Training behavioral counselors. In G. Hamerlynck, D. Evans, & F. Clark (Eds.), *Implementing behavioral programs in educational and clinical settings.* Calgary: University of Calgary Press, 1971.

Thoresen, C. E. The intensive design: An intimate approach to counseling research. Paper presented at the annual meeting of the American Educational Research Association, Chicago, 1972. (a)

Thoresen, C. E. Behavioral humanism. Paper presented at a colloquium sponsored by the Department of Counselor Education, Pennsylvania State University, University Park, July 1972. (b)

Thoresen, C. E. *Behavioral Humanism.* Stanford, Cal.: Stanford Center for Research and Development in Teaching, 1972. (c)

Thoresen, C. E., & Hamilton, J. A. Peer social modeling in promoting career behaviors. *Vocational Guidance Quarterly,* 1972, *20,* 210-216.

Thoresen, C. E., Hosford, R. E., & Krumboltz, J. D. Determining effective models for counseling clients of varying competencies. *Journal of Counseling Psychology,* 1970, *17,* 369-375.

Thoresen, C. E., & Krumboltz, J. D. Relationship of counselor reinforcement of selected responses to external behavior. *Journal of Counseling Psychology,* 1967, *14,* 140-144.

Thoresen, C. E., & Krumboltz, J. D. Similarity of social models and clients in behavioral counseling. *Journal of Counseling Psychology,* 1968, *15,* 393-401.

Thoresen, C. E., Krumboltz, J. D., & Varenhorst, B. Sex of counselors and models:

Effect on client career exploration. *Journal of Counseling Psychology*, 1967, *14*, 503-508.

Thoresen, C. E., & Mahoney, M. J. *Behavioral self-control.* New York: Holt, Rinehart and Winston, 1974.

Thoresen, C. E., & Mehrens, W. A. Decision theory and vocational counseling: Important concepts and questions. *Personnel and Guidance Journal*, 1967, *96*, 165-172.

Thorndike, E. L. Animal intelligence: An experimental study of the associative process in animals. *Psychological Review Monograph Supplement*, 1898, *2* (4, Whole No. 8).

Thorndike, E. L. *Animal intelligence.* New York: Macmillan, 1911.

Thorpe, G. L., Amater, H. I., Blakely, R. S., & Burns, L. E. Contributions of overt instructional rehearsal and "specific insight" to the effectiveness of self-instructional training: A preliminary study. *Behavior Therapy*, 1976, *7*, 504-511.

Tiedeman, D. V., & O'Hara, R. P. *Career development: Choice & adjustment.* New York: College Entrance Examination Board, 1963.

Tolman, E. C. Principles of performance. *Psychological Review*, 1955, *62*, 315-326.

Toomey, M. Conflict theory approach to decision making applied to alcoholics. *Journal of Personality and Social Psychology*, 1972, *24*, 199-206.

Truax, C. B. Reinforcement and non-reinforcement in Rogerian psychotherapy. *Journal of Abnormal Psychology*, 1966, *71*, 1-9.

Truax, C. B., & Carkhuff, R. R. *Toward effective counseling and psychotherapy.* Chicago: Aldine, 1967.

Tyler, L. *The work of the counselor.* New York: Appleton-Century-Crofts, 1969.

Ullman, L. P., & Krasner, L. *Case studies in behavior modification.* New York: Holt, 1965.

Urban, H. B., & Ford, D. H. Some historical and conceptual perspectives on psychotherapy and behavior change. In A. E. Bergin & S. L. Garfield (Eds.), *Handbook of psychotherapy and behavior change: An empirical analysis.* New York: Wiley, 1971.

Varenhorst, B. Learning the consequences of life's decisions. In J. D. Krumboltz & C. E. Thoresen (Eds.), *Behavioral counseling: Cases and techniques.* New York: Holt, Rinehart and Winston, 1969.

Veltin, E. A laboratory task for the induction of mood states. *Behavior Research and Therapy*, 1968, *6*, 473-482.

Verplanck, W. S. The control of content of conversation: Reinforcement of statements of opinion. *Journal of Abnormal and Social Psychology*, 1955, *51*, 668-676.

Vinokur, A. Cognitive and affective processes influencing risk taking in groups: An expected utility approach. *Journal of Personality and Social Psychology*, 1971, *20*, 472-486.

VonNeumann, J & Morgenstern, O. *Theory of games and economic behavior.* Princeton, N.J.: Princeton University Press, 1947.

Wachowiak, D. G. Model-reinforcement counseling with college males. *Journal of Counseling Psychology*, 1972, *19*, 387-392.

Wallace, W. G., Horan, J. J., Baker, S. B., & Hudson, G. R. Incremental effects of modeling and performance feedback in teaching decision-making counseling. *Journal of Counseling Psychology*, 1975, *22*, 570-572.

Wallas, G. *The art of thought.* New York: Harcourt, Brace & Company, 1926.

Warner, R. W., Swisher, J. D., & Horan, J. J. Drug abuse prevention: A behavioral approach. *National Association of Secondary School Principals Bulletin,* 1973, *57,* 49-54.

Warren, T. F., & Davis, G. A. Techniques for creative thinking: An empirical comparison of three methods. *Psychological Reports,* 1969, *25,* 207-214.

Waters, W. F., McDonald, D. G., & Koresko, R. L. Psychophysiological responses during analogue systematic desensitization and nonrelaxation control procedures. *Behavior Research and Therapy,* 1972, *10,* 381-393.

Watson, D. L. & Tharp, R. G. *Self-directed behavior: Self-modification for personal adjustment.* Monterey, Cal.: Brooks/Cole, 1972.

Watson, J. B., & Reyner, R. Conditioned emotional reactions. *Journal of Experimental Psychology,* 1920, *3,* 1-14.

Weinstein, E., & Kahn, R. *Denial of illness.* Springfield, Ill.: Thomas, 1955.

Weitzel, W. B., Horan, J. J., & Addis, J. W. A new olfactory aversion apparatus. *Behavior Therapy,* 1977, *8,* 83-88.

Westbrook, B. W., & Mastie, M. M. The cognitive vocational maturity test. In D. E. Super (Ed.), *Measuring vocational maturity for counseling and evaluation.* Washington, D.C.: American Personnel and Guidance Association, 1974.

Westcott, T. B., & Horan, J. J. The effects of anger and relaxation forms of in vivo emotive imagery on pain tolerance. *Canadian Journal of Behavioral Science,* 1977, *9,* 216-223.

Whitehead, A. N. *Modes of thought.* New York: Macmillan, 1938.

Williams, R. L., & Long, J. D. *Toward a self-managed life style.* Boston: Houghton Mifflin, 1975.

Wilson, G. T., & Rosen, R. C. Training controlled drinking in an alcoholic through a multifaceted behavioral treatment program: A case study. In J. D. Krumboltz & C. E. Thoresen (Eds.), *Counseling methods.* New York: Holt, Rinehart and Winston, 1976. Pp. 144-150.

Winborn, B. B. Systematic counseling: A model for accountability in counseling and counselor education. *Impact,* 1973, *2,* 15-22.

Winborn, B. B., Hinds, W. C., & Stewart, N. R. Instructional objectives for the professional preparation of counselors. *Counselor Education and Supervision,* 1971, *10,* 133-137.

Winkler, R. C. What types of sex-role behavior should behavior modifiers promote? *Journal of Applied Behavioral Analysis,* 1977, *10,* 549-552.

Wolpe, J. *Psychotherapy by reciprocal inhibition.* Stanford, Cal.: Stanford University Press, 1958.

Wolpe, J. *The practice of behavior therapy.* New York: Pergamon, 1969.

Wolpe, J. Behavior therapy and its malcontents—I. Denial of its bases and psychodynamic fusionism. *Journal of Behavior Therapy and Experimental Psychiatry,* 1976, *7,* 1-5.

Wolpe, J., & Lazarus, A. A. *Behavior therapy techniques: A guide to the treatment of neuroses.* New York: Pergamon, 1966.

Zillboorg, G. The problem of constitution in psychopathology. *Psychoanalytic Quarterly,* 1934, *3,* 339-362.

Index